Phony Culture

Phony Culture:

CONFIDENCE AND MALAISE IN CONTEMPORARY AMERICA

James Combs

Bowling Green State University Popular Press
Bowling Green, OH 43403

Other books by James Combs

American Political Movies: A Filmography
Dimensions of Political Drama
Polpop: Politics and Popular Culture in America
The Reagan Range

Co-author
Film Propaganda and American Politics
Mediated Political Realities
The New Propaganda
Nightly Horrors: Crisis Coverage in Television Network News
The Political Pundits
A Primer of Politics
Subliminal Politics: Myths and Mythmakers in America

Editor
Movies and Politics

Co-editor
Drama in Life: The Uses of Communication in Society

*The Orwellian Movement: Hindsight and Foresight
in the Past-1984 World*

ISBN: 0-87972-667-9 Clothbound
       0-87972-668-7 Paperback

Library of Congress Catalogue No.: 94-72414

Cover design and type by Laura Darnell-Dumm

In fond memory of

Bubbles, Winsocki, Elizabeth Barrett, and Robert Browning

Worthy cat friends, all—

And not a phony amongst them!

PREFACE
AND
ACKNOWLEDGMENTS

This book is the product of the author's conviction that the American nation suffers from a fundamental confusion, caused by the inconclusive dialectic in our culture, and ourselves, between confidence and malaise. As we observe the dominating practices and changes occurring in our country and our lives, we are puzzled by these transformations, and wonder if this is what we really wanted after all. Our puzzlement occurs in the context of desiring to have confidence in our collective and individual futures on the one hand, and the uneasy feeling that something is amiss. Our wonder occurs in the context of witnessing processes underway that are beyond our capacity to understand or control, but which test our faith in the future of our country and our grasp of our own personal destiny. We like to feel that we are at home in our own land, and confident of who we are; but as this book will attempt to explain, there are forces at work which threaten to make us all strangers in a strange land. Books such as this one are written as a warning and as hope. In the former motive, the book attempts to point to what we are becoming and what might become of us as a consequence; in the latter, it is done in the hope that we enter the new century by recognizing and abandoning those cultural habits which threaten to make us all into phonies.

The author wishes to acknowledge his appreciation of Pat Browne and her able staff at the Popular Press, always a pleasure to work with. I would also like to express my admiration for the American vernacular language, which is much more expressive and insightful than more pretentious academic vocabularies, and I hope the reader also finds, as I did, that the vernacular is a "natural" product of popular experience, and gives us hope as a source of direct and honest speech and thought that expresses a healthy popular skepticism. Finally, thanks are also due to my last best wife, Sara, who understands, tolerates, and sympathizes so very well.

CONTENTS

INTRODUCTION

THE TRIUMPH OF PHONY CULTURE

✦　✦　✦

POPULAR MALAISE

As the United States approached the millennial turn into the twenty-first century, many of its citizens were troubled by the nagging feeling that something was terribly wrong. As the symbolic year 2001 approached, a great body of evidence existed that the public mood was fickle, dissatisfied, gloomy, and often despairing and hopeless. Both polls and casual observation found that Americans were typically not satisfied with things and wished things to be different, but were at the same time unsure as to what was wrong and what to do about it. Presidents and political agendas and ideological statements and policy innovations and political movements came and went without truly satisfying or calming our restless and unsettled spirits. We soared up with moments of hope, only to sink down again into distrust and cynicism. Despite all the rhetorical reassurances of manifest national destiny and a glorious future propounded by politicians and of continued divine blessing promised by eminent divines, we could not sustain belief in their official optimism. In our heart of hearts, we thought that *something was wrong.*

A disinterested observer from a distant land might find this pervasive sense of "wrongness" astonishing and curious. On face, the American sense of "dis-ease," the outside observer might contend, is misplaced. The United States, after all, successfully completed its historical mission in the twentieth century by leading the defeat of both fascism and communism. Both the values of liberal democracy and competitive capitalism now seemed so entrenched in the world that oracles confidently predicted the "end of history," despite the continued problems of China and Russia. Although such predictions are at the least premature, nevertheless one might think the United States, as the last superpower and actually in better economic shape than much of the rest of the world, could be justly proud of its achievement and confident of its future. Despite all this,

1

the uneasy feeling that something was wrong persisted. But what was wrong, and why were we in such a bad mood?

For many observers, the sudden and stunning historical victory of American power and values—the end of the Cold War, the collapse of the Soviet Union, the advent of peace and nuclear disarmament—was the source of the problem. All too quickly, the United States had no "Other" against whom to contest and compare ourselves favorably. History had done us the terrible turn of taking our enemy away. In the 1990s, we had to compare ourselves with other countries, Western Europe and Japan in particular, not always favorably to ourselves. The inward turn of our national search for identity made us look into the mirror of our domestic face, and we did not altogether like what we saw. We thought ourselves to be "decentered," as if the American center that had created a successful democracy, prosperous economy, and diverse culture no longer could hold. We waxed nostalgic for a prelapsarian past from which the centering came, but which now was slipping away in a "postlapsarian" world devoid of the charm and harmony attributed to that mythic previous time. Advocates of "family values," evangelical religion, democratic participation, the work ethic, schooling, and so on all pointed to the American past as a better time from which we have fallen but to which we cannot return. We were afraid that, as Yeats wrote, things were falling apart, that the center could not hold, and that mere anarchy was indeed being loosed on the American world. Fundamental and puzzling questions haunted us: why was there no longer a social and political center that seemed substantial and permanent? Why did we now feel that we were part of an insubstantial pageant, the stuff that nightmarish historical dreams are made of? What had we lost, and when did we lose it? *What was wrong?*

The prevalent sense of "wrongness"—we were headed in the wrong direction, or in no direction at all—was complemented by a sense of "lateness," that somehow we were late in the American story, that history had passed us by, that our historical function and greatness was now receding in the wake of new centers of power and initiative. In a dramatic sense, the current time seemed anticlimactic: the great competition of the second half of the twentieth century was over, and now we were somehow drifting nowhere, close to the end, without the moorings that gave us direction and meaning as a political culture. Was it possible that we were going nowhere fast? We heard challenges to many of the venerable myths that had inspired us—the stories of the expansion of benevolent empire, the private exercise of beneficent cupidity, the efficacy of grass-roots democracy. All, we were told, were untruths, or at least now exhausted and eclipsed. Everything we knew was now wrong, or too late, or both: we felt that the American stories had been twice told, once as heroic historical narrative and again as nostalgic reminder of past glory days. Figures such as Reagan could re-invoke the past but not restore it, only remind us of the wondrous way we once were. Was our future now behind us?

These popular concerns intensified as we approached the *fin de siécle*, with not much hope that the "American century" would persist in the new age. We were aware that now intellectual oracles talked of "post-modernity," as if the values and institutions that characterized modernity were now doomed, to be replaced by unknown arrangements in a future that holds no promise for all that we cherish. The many changes in our world to which we were witness—the change from a goods to a service economy, the internationalization of the corporate world, the movement of jobs abroad, the collapse of health care and other social systems, the influx of foreign labor, and so on—all seemed threats rather than promises. The political system seemed helpless to cope adequately, and so we turned to this or that political *guru* who promised to restore the way things once were, hold the barbarians outside the gate, revitalize the institutions that we thought were eternal, and imbue our lives with the certainty of the popular mythology of normalcy. Before the tides of history and economy and culturology, many of us felt helpless.

This sense of "helplessness" stemmed from our feeling that something was wrong, and that maybe it was too late to reverse the tides. Taken together, these sensibilities added up to what we might term *popular malaise*, the nagging and sometimes overwhelming feeling that both individual and systemic effort to right wrongs, reverse entropy, and overcome helplessness through common effort towards functional goals was beyond our reach. The American political system, which we had believed to be the shining beacon of democratic self-rule, now seemed a corrupt network of compromised politicians, selfish interest groups, and cynical news media. American capitalism, which had produced great wealth and productivity that benefited so many people, now exhibited the accumulation of stupendous wealth in a few, while real income and generational upward mobility for the many now was stagnant. If current trends continue, most workers will soon be temporary, with no retirement, health, or promotion benefits in the offing. Too, the American popular culture displayed, for many, discordant and subversive messages that threatened to undermine "tradition," or at least our myths of a stable cultural experience; in any case, as century's end neared, we feared popular culture as a disruptive and explosive social force, a source of instability and even nihilism. Popular malaise, then, had many root causes and popular expressions, but was in the final analysis a stubborn fact of the American condition at the millennium: there seemed to be no immediate "cure" for our mordant condition, since malaise as an attitude seemed to resist satisfaction. No amount of good news could satisfy us, nor did rhetoric by various authorities urging us to believe in the future of our national story. Malaise is often defined as "an indefinite feeling of debility" and "a vague sense of mental or moral ill-feeling," a discomfort of the spirit stemming from the sense that things aren't quite right, predictable, or amenable to control. As Americans surveyed their world approaching 2001, they had great difficulty sustaining faith and hope, faith in the myth of progress and hope that the historical gods will make things turn up roses. The persistence of the condition of malaise can have serious consequences. Schoolchildren, for instance, growing up in an atmosphere of "cultural pessimism" might well conclude that scholastic effort is folly, since the world, and their own lives are deemed beyond redemption. If the future is a threat rather than a promise, then why bother? This can lead to descent into anomie, acts of rebellion, or eat-drink-and-be-merry play. If wrongs are deemed irredeemable, if it is thought that it's too late to act, and that positive action doesn't get you anywhere, then the motives for action may be gone. The consequences for a society imbued with a state of malaise are obviously considerable.

THE PROLIFERATION OF CRITICISM

A major indicator of the American mood of this period could be found in the extent to which we engaged in constant, and often niggardly, self-criticism. The habits of civility and deference, gentility and good will, that had characterized previous "eras of good feelings," disappeared as the millennium neared and the world changed. The malaise of the populace found expression from individual criticism of social trends and institutional powers to media voices who expressed these popular fears and resentments. Criticism of society and government, power and wealth, culture and religion, races and sexes became more uninhibited and virulent. We seemed intent on savaging each other in the various forums, informal or formal, open to us. In a thousand different forums, we expressed our criticism of each other and the way we thought things were—of the powerful and powerless, liberals and conservatives, straight or gay, male or female; of institutions from President to Post Office; of the rich and the poor, of the immigrant and the native-born, of the young and the old, of those who teach and those who write. Everyone seemed to think that there was something wrong with everyone else, and was quite willing to say so in public.

The proliferation of criticism indicated an aggressive response to popular malaise. We were not willing to suffer in silence; like the deranged character Howard Beale of the prescient movie *Network*, we were as mad as hell and not willing to take it anymore. There was a ready audience for virtually every form of expressed criticism, from talk radio to newspaper letters-to-the-editor to public speeches to punditic forums to mass rallies. One could tune in TV talk shows from morning to night and see people—often friends, relatives, spouses, but also people who were different—savage each other. Oprah, Phil, Geraldo, Sally Jessie, and so on presided over "degradation ceremonies," wherein people voluntarily expose their secret lives or desires so that they may be degraded before a vengeful audience. No matter what social category one belonged to, someone else was sure to attack it. If you were a public figure, both press and public were sure to find fault; lawyers advised celebrities of any stature that they were sure to be libeled, sued, ridiculed, hounded, and hated by someone. Every day, the President and Congress had to attempt to govern in an atmosphere of savage attack; no matter how well-meaning or even successful, they were bound to be subjected to rumor being taken as fact, their every past act scrutinized for wrongdoing, their every political act suspected of foul motives and hidden agendas, their private lives intruded by every possible means (the British royal family knows all about it). The professional cynics of talk radio daily shout home the message of the untrustworthiness and culpability of the American governing class. At this moment in the American story, the audience for contemptuous criticism is far greater than that for either serious discussion of choices or optimistic and supportive rhetoric. We have become a "culture of complaint," intent on the frivolous invocation of domestic demons that must be exorcised by our collective resentment of them.[1] Everyone, especially those with power or prestige, was suspect, their motives impugned, their character questioned, their actions found wanting. Simply put, at this time in American history we no longer *trusted* each other.

6 Phony Culture

The reasons for Americans' distrust of each other seem clear enough. For one thing, after the end of the Cold War, we suddenly had no Great Enemy, no demonic Other, to fight. With the organizing principle of our national mission gone, our focus shifted to what was wrong with ourselves (or more particularly, people other than ourselves). Most of the popular criticism that emerged in America during this period was not thoughtful self-criticism, but rather recrimination and accusation, finger-pointing at someone else who was at fault. It was other people who could not be trusted. We no longer trusted the authorities to do the right thing, for systems to function properly, for social services to protect and serve us, for the media to tell the truth, for schools to educate our children, for our neighbors to care about us, for society to be a place of peace and plenty for all. When Rodney King asked of us, "Can't we all just get along?" during the Los Angeles riot, he was expressing the Hobbesian idea that society is only possible if we can get along; but if there is no trust, the danger exists that we may deteriorate into a state of nature, a war of all against all.

The proliferation of criticism, then, meant that we had reached a state of no trust. But why was there no trust? Some of the contemporary American viciousness, as we have suggested, emerged in reaction to sudden temporal change, which we did not anticipate or understand; so we lashed out at each other, in a cacophony of blame and complaint. It was curious how much the "big ideas" of America—popular democracy, consumer economics, and popular culture—came under attack from ourselves! At the precise moment of its historical triumph, we savaged our own political system as unworkable, ineffective, a bore, and not worth participating in; we proposed term limits to undermine democratic rule; we sought technocratic or charismatic solutions to "solve" the problems of democracy. We didn't quite trust democracy. Similarly, despite the cornucopia of the great engine of capitalism, we now were uneasy with the "cultural contradictions" and consequences of American enterprise. The exaltation of greed, the persistence of poverty and a middle class desperately keeping up, the cruelty of "market forces" that destroyed businesses and careers and communities, the strain on families of overwork and overconsumption—all led to a feeling of distrust of the system, and astonishing enough, in polls considerable popular agreement with the proposition that "the rich get richer and the poor get poorer"! We didn't quite trust our own vaunted economic system: it now seemed remote, international, threatening, even unstable, a complex of big organizations that didn't care. And we didn't quite trust popular culture, for one reason because it had become a critical force itself in American society. There were plenty of people who so feared popular culture that they wanted to shut it up—violent depictions on TV, rap singers, adult movies, stand-up comics, talk show hosts, tabloids, heavy metal, and so on. We no longer quite trusted popular culture to the extent of urging censorship, condemning performers (Madonna was a favorite target), and damning the media organizations that carried the plurality of messages that tormented us. (We were variously told that the TV character "Murphy Brown" was responsible for out-of-wedlock births, that MTV's "Beavis and Butthead" were responsible for antisocial acts among children, and that rock lyrics promoted satanism.)

The proliferation of criticism suggested that we were engaged in a culture war, an unruly and vicious debate about what the larger culture of the United States should be like in the new world of the twenty-first century. We were debating whether the political culture of the country should be pluralistic or monolithic in political life, who the economic culture was supposed to benefit, and how tolerant we were of an expressive and experimental popular culture. We were in a sense at century's end back to fundamental questions: Who rules? Who benefits? Who gets to say what they want? So in a sense cultural criticism dominated the debate, driving us down to the emotional level of arguing over the basics as to what kind of country we wanted, what are people like, who should get what, what is allowable and desirable, and so on. This acrimonious debate revealed the extent to which trust had deteriorated, and what "symbolic poverty" devoid of social agreement we now lived in. A culture war threatens to rend a society asunder into warring camps, political factions, economic enclaves, and cultural competitions and conflicts. It is not yet a Hobbesian war, but at its worst it could divide us into factional tribes, since cultural divisions are fundamental for the cohesion and differentiation of groups. What seems to evade us is cultural unity, especially in the wake of our something-for-everyone popular culture. Maintaining or re-establishing a cultural hegemony over such a diverse and multifaceted populace seemed difficult at best, no matter how much powerful elite factions might so wish it. Many people distrusted elite factions—conservatives, liberals, pundits and the press, the military, the political parties, the entertainment media—and consequently were not likely to accept easily some monolithic definition of what was officially sanctioned. After all, for much of the populace the people who "ran things" were the most untrustworthy of all, the object of the most savage criticism of all, since they are the most to blame for our curious and puzzling condition.

The proliferation of criticism was symptomatic of a society going through difficult changes, to be sure, but it also pointed up something at the heart of our malaise: the extent to which our distrust of each other, and disgruntlement with the state of our society, stemmed from a very basic realization. This is the fact that all of the social criticism, all of the earnest rhetoric, policy debates, partisan propaganda—all seemed fake. For complex reasons we shall explore below, at the very root of our malaise was the strong sense of "fakeness," that something about our condition was unreal, that all the things that were said were not serious or true, that all of the things we saw were somehow ungenuine, that much of what was done was insincere. Every day we were in contact with the fake, the deceptive, the counterfeit, the make-believe, the illusory, the sham, the pretentious, the inauthentic. We did not trust other people because we suspected them of being dishonest, putting us on, feeding us a line, acting as an imposter or charlatan, double-dealing, faking us out, doing lip service, play-acting. The list of our vernacular terms that characterize distrust of other people's actions is endless, but they add up to our belief that people are untrustworthy: they must be saying, doing, or feeling in our presence for some kind of ulterior motive. We distrust them because we believe that they are trying to *con* us.

THE WORLD OF CONFIDENCE

The sense of fakeness—that more and more we live in a society that is somehow fake—emerged from an awareness that our relationship to the world—of nature, of society, of human relations—is not "natural." For more and more of us, we had little direct contact with nature, in the way farmers or ranchers might: nature was experienced second-hand, in parks and zoos and TV specials on endangered species. We lived in dwellings and places that controlled nature, in asphalted urban areas or mowed suburban ones, hoping to escape the rhythms and vagaries of nature. Children grew up having no idea where meat or milk or bananas came from, nor any contact with the agricultural or pastoral life of nostalgic remembrance. Our reference was not nature but society, the complex of institutions, roles, and rules that characterized the conduct of organizational relations, and more informal interpersonal relations such as friendship or courtship. We lived increasingly in an "artificial condition" wherein one's life was a matter of negotiating relationships, in business, school, sexual relations, and informal group relations. The definition and conduct of relations became the nexus of society, and mastery of relations became the primary method of social advancement and power. People in the professions, for example, could successfully conduct institutional relations if they could elicit a degree of trust from other social actors. Those people interested in sexual adventure could successfully conduct amorous relations if they could gain the trust of other potential partners. Politicians engaged in democratic politics succeeded to the extent they could evoke trustworthiness. In American life, in many different contexts involving negotiated relations over who gets what, people were constantly communicating the "metamessage" (a message about messages): "Trust Me!" In other words, they were seeking the *confidence* of others in order to achieve some individual or social purpose. At the core of American life was the exercise of relations based on trust. To the extent that one gained the confidence of people, one could rule in social relations.

A glance across the spectrum of American society reveals the extent to which relations are based on trust, and how relations are ruled by the use of confidence. We have confidence in people if we feel sure of them: "I have faith in Pastor Smith"; "I trust my money to Investor Jones"; or "I believe in Candidate Martin." Confidence may be well placed, if the preacher is, or at least continues to be perceived as, honest and effective. The pastor produces faith and hope; the investor produces capital gains; the politician rules well. In such social situations, the placement of confidence creates a transaction that is a mutually beneficial exchange. Confidence is asked and confidence is given, and in both cases is not misplaced. In the nostalgic model of the American town of yore, the myth reminds us of the norm of honest deals and sincere pacts. The banker who absconded with the funds, the pastor who ran off with the church organist, the politician who sold out to the railroad were all deemed aberrations rather than the norm.

In the present and more doubtful day, we as a society place even more effort in the attempt to gain other's confidence. The massive efforts of propaganda and public relations organizations to convince the public to have confidence is obvious. Advertising daily bombards us with a message of trust; PR spokespersons attempt to influence us in our attitudes towards their clients. Economists fret over "consumer confidence"; labor leaders fret over the confidence of their rank-and-file; corporations are uneasy about the confidence of stockholders; professionals such as lawyers and doctors are concerned about public confidence in them; and politicians daily examine polls to see how they are faring in the confidence, or lack of it, of the voters. Social elites of various kinds spend a great deal of effort in order to elicit our confidence in them and what they do—to buy things, to trust those who run organizations, to believe in what they say, to have faith in professionals, to vote for politicians. It may be the case that as as our social confidence wanes, elites have all the more interest attempting to shore up our trust. Without trust, they and their enterprises are in grave danger of the loss of confidence and the decline of support for who they are and what they do.

The grave danger is that we will perceive all social actors who are eliciting trust as frauds, charlatans, deceivers, dissemblers, tricksters, swindlers, mountebanks, impostors, hoaxers, fixers, cheats, pretenders, cynics, hypocrites, hoodwinkers, four-flushers, welshers, and liars. In a word, we are afraid that people seeking our trust are *confidence men*—con artists who are manipulating our confidence for their own secret purposes. In a cultural atmosphere of distrust, we are more likely to be suspicious that social actors attempting to exert influence are in fact confidence men (and women, since there is a long tradition of female "operators"). This new and apparently sustained climate of distrust signals perhaps a turning point in American life, since so much of what we have been has been animated by the exercise of confidence.

It is our thesis here that the confidence man and woman has played an important and pivotal role in American life. We would not be what we have become today without the use of confidence. By the late twentieth century, the reliance on confidence had become a cardinal operating principle of social enterprise. There is even considerable evidence that eliciting confidence has always been central to the national experience. Gary Lindberg, in his magisterial survey of "the confidence man in American literature," convincingly shows that we are a "culture whose presiding genius is the confidence man," and that such a social type is someone who celebrates "the delight of entering a series of roles and making them work." The confidence man is a role-player who moves in and out of social roles at "role distance," views life as a challenge of marketing one's current image, and sees society as a fair field for confidence gaming. The confidence man proceeds on the basis of our belief in promise, and it is his promissory character that allows him to "make belief."[2] His language is the rhetoric of make-believe, since he must demonstrate that make-believe makes belief. His or her metaphor is the game, a game of confidence-building that produces desired results. Whatever he or she is selling, they are in fact selling themselves in order to sell it. The confidence person's social function is to "con" people, for good or ill, for his benefit or for theirs. His social ethic is whatever works. In consequence, the philosophy of pitching—making a pitch—permeates everything, from religion to politics to education. In a world moved by confidence, what matters is getting things done through the arts of persuasion, selling whatever needs to be sold, from sermons to snake oil. The confidence man makes a necessity out of virtue, converting needs into wants, the merely functional into the magical, the useless into the absolutely indispensable, the sow's ear into the silk purse. Most of all, the confidence man promises us the future.

The confidence man and woman fascinate us because they have so often made us believe on the basis of little more than their ability to persuade. It may be undesirable to believe in something of which there is not a shred of evidence to support the claim, but people armed with the arts of confidence-making can do so. The confidence man appeals to what philosopher William James called "the will to believe" (James once said in exasperation that Americans will believe anything; they would believe everything if they could). The con artist exploits the uncertainty of social relations through the act of conning, convincing people to think, feel, or do in ways they might not have otherwise. Conning is not necessarily criminal or evil; but it is persuasive on the basis of the con man's word. Con artistry is a rhetorical skill, not necessarily an exercise in truth; facts become factualities, truths useful for persuasion, metaphors ways of framing the pitch. Conning is a highly pragmatic art, with the artist bent on the practical project of achieving results. The "conner" makes things happen through his or her mastery of our minds, shaping attitudes with the power of "pitchery," making the pitch. But we are the other party of the conning transaction: the persuader has to have someone who is willing to be persuaded. The arts of social confidence proceed on the *principle of credulity*, the willed ability to take on trust the assurances of confident communicators. The social game of confidence may not necessarily be a deception, but it only "works" if belief is given on faith rather than logic and evidence. The credulous are ready to believe. Boorstin notes in this connection that P.T. Barnum, one of the pioneers of the pitch, discovered "not how easy it was to deceive the public, but rather, how much the public enjoyed being deceived."[3] Deception always involves self-deception, a "leap of faith" that puts trust in the purveyor of confidence. Perhaps since we do not completely trust our own judgment, we are willing to trust someone more confident of their ability to decide and act for us. (It was Jonathon Swift who said, "Happiness is the faculty of being well-deceived.") Credulity allows us to take the shadow for the substance, the promise for the delivery, the ebullience of confidence for the security of contract. Every area of social life—political, economic, and cultural—involves the invocation of confidence and the exercise of credulity, or else no one would vote, invest, or attend church.

It is our contention here that in the late twentieth century the American people are going through a crisis of confidence. In the social world, the artifices of confidence have ascended to the status of primary importance. Although the use of confidence has always been important, it is more so now because of the potential for mass communications, "scientific" methods of persuasion, and organizational power sustaining persuasive messages (ranging from advertising and public relations to promotion to "spin doctoring" to salesmanship). The confidence man, and the attendant values he or she represents, is firmly in charge. The con men have so mastered the art of making belief that we now live in a world of make-believe. But now we have every reason to know what they are about, so we vacillate between the will to believe and the will to doubt. It is likely more comfortable to believe and have trust; but we also cannot ignore the feeling that we are being had. The popular malaise stems from this confusion and suspicion. The will to doubt sees the appeal to confidence as a social game that is not worth playing, since the game is rigged by the conners; in that case, a fundamental tenet of American civilization is in deep trouble. The confidence game is seen as a fake.

THE CONFIDENCE MAN AS CULTURAL HERO AND VILLAIN

Not only are social games of confidence seen as a fake, so too is the confidence man himself or herself. Thus the crisis of confidence we face as a nation involves not only our suspicion that various social pitches are fake, but also those who are pitching them are fakes also. This then means that the status of the confidence man as a cultural hero is in serious question. The many social enterprises involving the use of confidence require a corresponding social role that is accorded the status of cultural heroism. The conduct of advertising, for instance, must be seen as a beneficial and legitimate enterprise for it to proceed; the corollary is that the enterprise is conducted by a heroic role. The advertiser who succeeds is thus extolled as an exemplar of cultural virtue through his or her ability to con the consumer. But if the enterprise comes under suspicion as social fakery, then so too does the practitioner of the art. The advertiser, for instance, becomes a social villain rather than hero if what he does acquires the negative status of a nefarious enterprise that is essentially an exercise in fakery.

We should remember that the confidence man has a long history as a cultural hero. He and she are part of the American tradition of cultural heroism. It is useful to distinguish between these "role traditions" in order to illuminate the expectations and uses of the confidence man. He may be distinguished from the republican idealist and the charismatic adventurer. The *republican idealist* is the cultural heroic type of American romantic myth. He is rooted in the Jeffersonian model of the yeoman, an other-directed individual who leads the community in a social project of conciliation between people and institutions. The mythic world of the republican idealist is typically the town, wherein he uses his good offices to create the therapeutic conditions for romantic democracy. His leadership brings peace and happiness to the community, helping it to realize the ideals of the benevolent democrat of Monticello. The republican idealist has been celebrated in many popular forms, perhaps most famously by Frank Capra in such films as *Mr. Deeds Goes to Town, Mr. Smith Goes to Washington, Meet John Doe, and It's a Wonderful Life*, wherein James Stewart or Gary Cooper played republican idealists struggling to make the democratic promise of an American community come true. A figure such as Stewart's "Jefferson Smith" of *Mr. Smith* is a kind of amateur Cincinnatus who reminds the national political class of its responsibility to the community's ideals, and to the republic for which it stands. The republican idealist in politics gives representation to the goal of creating one out of many, a community of virtuous democrats led by him or her who sought the promise of American life. Similarly, republican idealists in business advocated the ideal of benevolent capitalism and the cooperative spirit, that out of competition came social exchange and harmony devoid of class envy or widespread exploitation. In the realm of culture, the republican ideal led to campaigns of moral improvement and social aesthetics (learning, the arts, public architecture, parks, conservation). The republican ideal remains a social role type of great power, and presidents from Truman to Reagan to Clinton attempt to portray themselves as such.

The American heritage of the frontier gives us another heroic role type, this one less sociable and nicely civilized: the *charismatic adventurer*. If the republican idealist is an other-directed figure of the mythic town, the charismatic adventurer is the inner-directed loner of the various American frontiers. Rather than a social conciliator, the ruggedly individualistic adventurer is a figure of conquest. Reality for him or her is not a conciliable community, but rather brute nature that must be conquered. He is not responsible to the town, and so is free to roam the frontiers of individual achievement. He does not persuade, he overwhelms; his power is in his inner strength and iron will. He is a figure of violence on the natural frontier, and force on the social frontier; his credo is Jacksonian on the former, and Hamiltonian on the latter. If the mission of the republican idealist is social therapeutics, the goal of the charismatic adventurer is punitive enforcement of his will. In the Western myth, he is Natty Bumppo or Ethan Edwards (John Wayne) of *The Searchers* or Clint Eastwood; in the myth of the Town, he is the sheriff or leading citizen who gets his way, ostensibly for the good of the town, but nevertheless it is his will that prevails; in the myth of the City, he is often a private detective (a male like Phillip Marlowe or Mike Hammer, but also a female like V.I. Warshawski). In the world of capitalist adventure, he is Charles Foster Kane of *Citizen Kane* or Howard Roark of *The Fountainhead* or Gordon Gekko of *Wall Street*. The charismatic adventurer is willing to command, and in so doing creates organizations out of the wilderness, from the natural wilderness (John Wayne in *Red River*) to the social jungle (Big Daddy of *Cat on a Hot Tin Roof*, J.J. Hunsecker of *Sweet Smell of Success*). We like to believe that a socially benevolent function flows from his dominating individualism, and that his intervening creativity serves the cause of civilization. The Western hero creates the conditions for community, but makes himself irrelevant; the industrial magnate creates a corporation that eventually does not need him. And he clashes with the republican idealist (Mr. Potter conflicts with George Bailey in *It's a Wonderful Life*), and with civilized or organizational interests that would constrain his will (as in the mutiny led by republican idealist Montgomery Clift against John Wayne's imperious rule of the cattle drive in *Red River*, or the political defeat of Charles Foster Kane by Boss Gettys in *Citizen Kane*). The uncivilized and often bullying nature of such a leader makes him an ambivalent and often tragic figure, even to the point of criminality. The gangster (Tony Camonte of *Scarface*, Don Corleone of *The Godfather*) is both admirable and repulsive, what we fear unrestrained charisma can do. The charismatic adventurer achieves results by any means necessary, and thus may be drawn to the uses of evil; in the end he may be excluded from the legal-rational or moral community (as is the gunfighter in *Shane*, or the charming but evil entrepreneur of *The Third Man*) as a threat to the common life. He can never settle down to legal-rational authority stemming from organizations and public-regarding sociability that characterizes the peaceable community, so he often must leave, become an outlaw, or die. His radical self-reliance and inner strength eventually become his fatal flaw and defining weakness.

The republican idealist and charismatic adventurer are familiar figures in American popular culture. They have taken many forms, and have occasioned many uses for politicians, celebrities, and others as role-ideal models. But as we have indicated, there is a third strain or tradition in American cultural heroism, manifest in the figure we call *the confidence man*. While the republican idealist is associated with the town, and the charismatic adventurer with frontiers, the confidence man is typically a figure of the city. In the spirit of Melville's original conception in his great novel *The Confidence-Man: His Masquerade*, he is notable in cosmopolitan masquerades. (The snake-oil salesman and carnival showman of the frontier represented himself as an urban sophisticate.) He is the quintessential opportunist, the role-player who is constantly on the make; like Willy Loman of *The Death of a Salesman*, he is a man way out in the blue, riding on a smile and a shoeshine. The republican idealist lives in and for the community he serves, and speaks the language of social conciliation; the charismatic adventurer lives for the enterprise he leads, and speaks the language of conquest; the confidence man lives by his wits, and speaks the language of imposture. Reality for him does not exist in a settled community or the edge of a surmountable frontier, but rather in the mastery of negotiable relationships in a fluid world of changing attitudes and actions. Such relationships involve the constant process of defining situations and outcomes, the talents of social artifice and relational persuasion become crucial. The confidence man is engaged in a project of masquerade, a creature of artifice whose ability to play roles before social auditors is designed to produce desired results in shaping and directing thought, emotion, and action. His auditors know him only through his public *persona* as the social actor who appeals to their willful credulity, making belief and believers work for him. He is not so much other-directed or inner-directed as he is "performance-directed," eliciting compliance through the quality of his performance that defines and directs the new relationship he desires. In the contemporary world, a prototypical republican idealist would be a young city mayor, a crusading newspaper editor, or an earnest college president; a paradigmatic charismatic adventurer would be a financial speculator or "high-tech" computer tycoon; but the confidence man would more likely be an advertiser, promoter, or political "spin doctor" media advisor. If the republican idealist excels at being a conciliator, and the charismatic adventurer is notable for being a conqueror, then the confidence man is distinguishable for being a performer.

The confidence man is not a descendant of Jefferson or Hamilton, but rather P.T. Barnum. Barnum created "great realities" for people to believe in temporarily, until the next scam could be propagated. Although American conning had been around since the first land deals and promises of riches lured people here, Barnum gave scope and daring to the art of the bamboozle. For the republican idealist, reality was something made harmonious through Lockean social agreement; for the charismatic adventurer, reality was something overcome and bent to will through directed effort in a Hobbesian or Darwinian world; for the confidence man, reality is made up, remade, insubstantial and manipulable, amenable to dramatic representation, and easily discardable for new and greater realities. The republican idealist creates substantial communities; the charismatic adventurer creates palpable results; the confidence man creates a pageant of "pseudo-events" and similar contrived and synthetic realities which are insubstantial and impalpable. There is nothing permanent or essential in this world of manipulated and transitory appearances. The immediate and novel experience is the focus of attention, to which we are directed by the purveyors of confidence. The new reality is not objective but virtual, a momentary and fleeting place of perceived images. The confidence man is engaged in the promulgation, revision, and even destruction of the "great realities" of the imagistic world. He deals in perceptions, and how they can be shaped, changed, and directed. His good office is to give us confidence in the images he shows us.

The confidence man is at home in the world of communications, for such ephemera as entertainment, news, and advertising are typical stocks in trade. The con artist is at work in both Hollywood and Washington, where the practitioners of the art forms of persuasion and image management are at work in the both cooperative and competitive enterprise of working their magic. The shared art of the confidence man is his ability at social seduction; the competitive art is the effort to seduce people away from other seductive messages. The competition between Hollywood studios for Academy Award recognition of their movies is fierce but expected, an effort to confer on one film rather than another the mantle of Oscar, and thus bigger profits. The competition between party and presidential spokespersons to control the "spin" on an event (or more likely, a pseudo-event such as an interview or news rumor). involves the seductive message to have confidence (or, alternatively, to have no confidence in what they say, but confidence in what I say). The confidence man asks us "to take it on faith" as a matter of trust, but his job is not to leave trust to chance. Faith and trust are matters of confidence gained through communicating trustworthiness and hope, be it a movie we are urged to see or a president to support. If the republican idealist is a conciliator, and the charismatic adventurer an enterpriser, the con man is a seducer. He finds not only those who can be seduced, but also the larger group of those who *want* to be seduced!

The rise of the con man ironically corresponds with the increase in cynicism and doubt in America. For everyone who can be made to believe, there is someone else who has been made to disbelieve. The work of those adept at selling confidence has succeeded in getting many people to suspend disbelief; but the presence of conning has likely gotten just as many to suspend belief. St. Paul, one of the first great confidence men, urged people to believe in "the substance of things hoped for, the evidence of things not seen"; but confidence in secular hopes has become difficult to sustain, despite the massive and sophisticated efforts of the purveyors of confidence. The ascendancy of the confidence man as the powerful figure in our culture brought the reaction of revelation of and revulsion against what he does. Many people sense that what they are told to believe in is fake, and that the seductive communicator who invites them to believe is a fake himself or herself. Sensing that, we feel uneasy with the propagation of messages that are fraudulent, and with the duplicity of those who propagate them.

Much of this dis-ease stems from our difficulty in sustaining belief in republican idealists and charismatic adventurers. The former heroic figure now is suspected of affecting a stance, of not really believing in the faith he professes. Presidents as various as Carter, Reagan, and Clinton gave rhetorical representation to the values of republican ideals (democracy, bourgeois normalcy, reform and renewal), but they came to be widely doubted, and even accused of being frauds who didn't really believe what they professed. Similarly, the charismatic adventurer has been transformed into unappealing figures such as corporate raiders who destroy companies, careers, and employee prosperity for pure greed, notorious celebrities whose criminality or antisocial behavior is traded on for profit and fame, or political entrepreneurs who raise money or create organizations for their own self-serving ambitions. Both the idealist and the adventurist now seem to be opportunists, since we suspect that they are equally con men out to manipulate us through the assertion of public values or organized creativity, creating unwarranted hopes and unfulfilled desires.

In large measure, the ascendancy of the confidence man occurred in the wake of the collapse of social authority. The authority of traditional institutions and values, and of charismatic leaders and movements, has come under great suspicion. Low turnout in elections, low approval ratings for government and politicians, high rates of alienation, skepticism of new leaders with big claims and plans, all indicate our disaffection with the ability of either old or new ways to suffice. In a world being emptied of authority, the confidence man moves into the vacuum, attempting to garner all the techniques of persuasion and manipulation in order to create new, albeit temporary and largely fake, authority. The confidence man attempts to confer authority on whatever and whomever is convenient and useful, so authority may reside in a new candidate, product, slogan, or pleasure. These are, to be sure, fake authorities, perpetuated by the arts of seductive lure, but they serve as substitutes for the lost authorities that are perishing.

The confidence man, and his projects in attempting to sell new authorities, is suspect because his skill is not in discerning what is valuable, or who is potent, but in technique. Jacques Ellul and others have identified the general trend in our time towards the triumph of technique—how to do things efficiently and efficaciously—without much regard for inherent value or personal wisdom.[4] The confidence man is supremely gifted at means, not ends. Technique in itself is a social force, and in the service of fakery—attempting to make new authorities where there are none—it becomes the tool of confidence-making. Contemporary techniques—advertising, promotion, press relations, news gathering, catering celebrity events, and so on endlessly—are confidence games that succeed among the credulous as an appeal to new, improved authority. But these new authorities are not authentic, lasting, or substantive. They are transient and ephemeral symbols rather than mosaic codes carved in stone. They are made and unmade by technique, so that we are the auditors of insubstantial pageant of authoritative claims, all of which make a dramatic pitch but none of which have any lasting value or permanence. The confidence man succeeds in a society of skewed values, in which the techniques of seduction replace the affirmation of principle and even achievement.

The popular malaise of our time, then, has emerged in the wake of the triumph of the confidence man. We fear that everything of importance presented to us is inauthentic, that the masters of artifice are trying once again to get away with something. We are now ambivalent and restless about being well deceived, no matter how happy it seems to make us. There seems to us to be ample evidence that fraudulence has become the ethical and procedural norm of our culture, and that matter-of-factly every enterprise is undertaken on the assumption that we can be easily had. We have difficulty distinguishing the real from the surreal, the authentic from the inauthentic, the sincere from the insincere, the actual from the apparent, the true from the false. To use the vernacular, we now suspect that we live in a phony culture.

PHONY CULTURE

There is no other word for it: in the late twentieth century, the culture of the United States is becoming *phony*. The vernacular term "phony" is an American word but of uncertain origin, coming into common usage about 1900. People would speak of how you could "phony up," or "phony it up," or say "you can phony anything up," i.e., make things up, fake it, talk your way out of it, use a false excuse or alibi, and so on (interestingly, one proposed origin of the term is from the appearance of that new invention, the telephone: using talk "over the phone" to influence people, or actions such as "phoning in an excuse"; another theory is that it emerged from an itinerant salesman known as a "fawney-man"). Phony quickly came to mean a wide array of attributes and behaviors: the false, fake, sham, counterfeit, insincere, inauthentic, affected, the not genuine, the pompous, the punctilious, the snobbish, the histrionic, or anything whereby outward habits and actions do not reveal one's true character or nature, or whose words and actions are made to impress.[5] Phoniness soon became associated with other vernacular terms on the same track, such as bunk, baloney (one great early term was "the phonus-bolonus"), buncombe, sham, shilling, bamboozle, flim-flamming, chisel, welsh, snake oil, bluffing, a bum steer, rook, flummox, selling a bill of goods, the put-on, a raw deal, diddling, swindling, the snow job, the come-on, the gambit, the royal shaft, the set-up, being fleeced, getting burned, the ream job, and of course, conning. All these terms speak to the sense that in important human relations, both personal and social, all too often "the fix is in," the game is rigged, the cards are stacked, the deal is off the bottom of the deck, and we are the "mark" who is to be "stung."

The vernacular language of the American people indicates an awareness of phony behavior. Now as social psychologists tell us, people anywhere and anytime are quite capable of phony behavior. The social dissembler is someone who puts on false appearances, conceals facts, tells lies, affects a pretense, and so on. The sociologist Erving Goffmann has recounted the many ways in which we can use phony behavior to advantage. The "rational" phony is someone who is likely engaged in a form of activity that conceals from his auditors what his "true intentions" or "real motives" might be, as well as what he or she hopes to gain out of the transaction. Further, the social actor may try to give an impression of infallibility or superiority, to "show" only the finished product of what he is using to impress others, and to omit or deny disturbing or disconfirming elements from a performance. The task of impression management necessitates the use of concealment, deceit, and seduction, what Machiavelli called *froda*: fraud. Goffmann was interested in the operation of "the interaction order," but we here want to expand the investigation of phoniness as a major trend in American society.[6]

It is our contention that *phoniness has emerged as a social principle*. Phoniness in the contemporary United States is much more than an interactive strategy of the con; rather, phony behavior has become a central organizing principle of social activity, an integral part of concerted institutional and organizational enterprises. We have come to expect, and for many to resent, the utilization of phony behavior in virtually every legitimate (and certainly every illegitimate) activity. Dissembling and fraudulence permeate our society simply because *phoniness works*. We now expect social leaders to be phonies because we know that to get to the top of organizations one has to be a phony, to con others into believing in you. We expect the claims of an organization or a product to be fraudulent, because the organization is quite willing to lie, or at least to not tell the truth, in order to get what it wants. When a public relations "shill" speaks on behalf of an organization or personage, we assume that this indentured spokesperson is lying, since the truth is not useful in maintaining the advantaged social position at stake. When we see an advertisement for a product or a candidate, we suspect that the claims are exorbitant and the truth is absent. For many Americans, society seems to be a network of falsities, phony messages propagated by interested parties in order to achieve results rather than promote the truth. The more that social organizations say, the less what they say can be trusted.

Nevertheless, the social practice of phony communications has now become for too many Americans part of their world-taken-for-granted, the social "ground" not often reflected upon. But the pervasion of phoniness exacts an awful price, for many of us no longer can discern the genuine or authentic from the fake; many of us now take the fake to be real, the artifice to be natural, the false to be true. The French intellectual Baudrillard writes cryptically of the American as the new pioneer of "the age of simulation" wherein we "substitute signs of the real for the real," because "artifice is at the very heart of reality." The term "simulation" means "to copy, represent, feign," to show off sham objects or replicas, to commit a histrionic act as if it were real (as in "simulated sex"). America, says Baudrillard, is "weightless," a country wherein "the imaginary and the real are fused and indistinguishable. Disneyland is authentic! Television and movies are real! America has created an ideal world from nothing and consecrated it in the cinema." For Americans, "...the only context is its own mythic banality."[7]

Baudrillard's views are controversial, but he has focused our attention on the idea that we are becoming creatures of artifice, a society immersed in its own virtual "hyper-reality" increasingly devoid of concrete referentials. We are losing contact with memories of a past dominated by substantial facts—depression, war, industries, stable careers—and live in an eternal present of insubstantial artifices—entertainment, malls, suburbs, theme parks. But what he does not discuss is that this historical development emerged because of the utility of phoniness: in a world where it was becoming increasingly difficult to deliver the real thing, instead social powers could deliver the illusion, or image, of "the real thing," as if it were the real. In the wake of declining social expectations and morale, it became necessary to sustain the extant system with appeals which substituted or complemented real rewards with symbolic ones. Even though the appeal to confidence had always been important, with the threat of the loss of support for established social systems (consumer capitalism, political normalcy, and cultural pluralism), the appeal for acquiescence in if not enthusiasm for the existing system is now crucial to sustain social "development" and "progress" on the lines and terms of powerful institutions and organizations.

As a social principle, then, phoniness has become ascendant at the time we are being transformed into the "post-modern" world of change and confusion. The social phony has an advantage because he or she knows how to affect a stance that is impressive and often persuasive. Since we now live in a world defined by the mastery of artifice, his grasp of the superficials of communication and the sycophancy of self-presentation make such fraudulence a powerful mode of effective action. The phony acts at role distance, communicating influence through the use of the aesthetics of social interaction, and utilizing the ethic of expedience. The phony is committed to communicating rather than veracity, since veracity is only useful until the benefits of dissembling outweigh those of truthfulness. The art of the phony is *social pretension*, the ability to exalt make-believe as a credible reality for credulous auditors. The phony's work is to give shared credence to fictive states, raising "extravagant expectations" for a populace desperate to overcome malaise and to believe in something.

The social consequences of the phony principle is that it creates a phony culture permeated by pretense and fraudulence. Everything becomes transformed from a real, thriving, functionality into a pretentious and dramatistic symbolicity. The great impulse of the creators of phony culture is to transform everything into a pretentious and preternatural thing to which is attributed playful meaning. A classic example is the transformation of a community into a "tourist trap." Consider, say, a town in the mountains. The town in its original state had some functional relationship with nature and society, with farms, shops, industries, and so on. But let us suppose the town is "discovered." In a short time, it becomes something different: the town is no longer an original community; rather, it has acquired attributes through the intrusion of play functions. The instrumentality of the town as a complex of institutions and habits is superseded by a new symbolic significance, the extent to which "developers" can dramatize the place as a playful paradise worthy of visiting and living. A general store, for example, may have served the rural area for a long time as a place for farmers to buy cheap goods and congregate for communal fellowship. But in the phony play world, the general store becomes a place of dramatized nostalgia for people who have no memory of a real general store to visit and buy imported goods at inflated "tourist" prices. The general store, like the town, has acquired a new function, as a place that is pretentious (claimed to possess attributes that are phony) and preternatural (exceeding what was natural or normal for the original place). The town is now a "resort town" devoid of community and real and thriving social exchange among local neighbors; rather, it has a become a dramatic set with histrionic features (the general store is a stage which we may enter to see how original life was once lived, even though we have no experience of it that exists as an object of play). As the "upscale" housing developments, fancy restaurants, boutiques, and so forth proliferate, the town loses any semblance of contact with the old world of real functions and people, and acquires the ambience of the artificial, the pretentious, and the superficial. A preternatural world exists outside of nature, and so too does the newly phony town. For older residents or people who lived there and return, it is now unrecognizable: it has taken on fraudulent attributes that are beyond their original understanding of what the town was. The place has become an imposture, the fraudulent representation of a actual town that is lovely and charming; instead it is a contrived stage for paying audiences who wish to visit a symbolic setting created for their playful pleasure.

In the late twentieth century, the culture of the United States is now increasingly defined by what we might call *derivative features*. We have "progressed" beyond the original social forms of instrumentality (e.g., an economy of needs, a politics of material benefit, and a popular culture of mass entertainment) to a state of expanding forms of artifice and dramatistics. Rather than practicing the sensible economics of needs, we have moved toward the symbolics of an economy of wants, with an ever-expanding manipulation of consumer demand through advertising and public relations that, for instance, turns towns into "concepts" for development and tourism. Rather than practicing a politics of real benefits, we now engage in the histrionics of "symbolic politics," the monitoring and manipulating of public opinion, and the personality cult of the political personage as hero-celebrity. Rather than sustaining a popular culture of mass entertainment, we have progressed to the stage of ever-increasing multiplicity and outrageousness, with the celebrity expected to become ever more bizarre and unusual for our enjoyment or revulsion. In all cases, the social consequence is to create a society dominated by derivative functions that diverge ever further from the original functions of the system. When an economy of needs is superseded by an economy of wants, then the consequence is to make us into addicts of change and novelty, for whom new experiences, no matter how phony, become primary. Politics becomes an exercise in creating the illusion of well-being rather than providing well-being. To use a cultural example, the primary function of religion, one might think, would be the primary goal of theological enhancement, relating man to God; but with televangelism, the derivative function of entertainment and fund raising, not to mention enhancing the celebrity status of the televangelist star, becomes more important, in the process debasing the quality and mission of original religion. In a phony culture, it becomes normal and easy for those with organizational goals simply to use the art of the con in order to achieve newly defined purposes. But it has the consequence of further "phonying up" the society, creating the conditions for both credulity and malaise.

The derivative activities of the new American society underwrite the new "service economy," media politics, and proliferating popular culture. In these kinds of conditions, the results that are sought and gained differ from older forms of social life. In the new American order, the phony culture gives impetus to the values and practices of the confidence man. The republican idealist, we may recall, was traditionally a man of words, and for that "a man of his word," representing the political and moral ideals of democratic community in political honesty and ethical integrity. The charismatic adventurer was a man of action, conquering the not insuperable objects of some frontier, and representing the social ideal that individual action guiding concerted effort could produce desirable results. But the ascendance of the confidence man means something a bit different. Even though he uses words and conducts social action, he operates on the basis of a somewhat different principle, one based on symbolic manipulation rather than political coalition or material production. *The operative principle of a phony culture is hype.* "Hype" is a term (perhaps derived from "hyperbole") related to the tradition of Barnumian showmanship, expanded now to include all those manipulative activities which utilize appearances as if they were reality. The principle of hype operates in a culture for which reality is not an objective condition, but rather an existential creation. The hype artist makes up things which are then marketed and sold by procuring confidence in their phony merits. Like all con men, they do not politic nor do they produce; rather they procure. They procure belief through hyping make-believe. Whereas the republican idealist strives to make community real, and the charismatic adventurer works to make conquest real, the hype artist makes confidence real. Since appearance is reality, then ever-new appearances can be sold as the latest "new and improved" reality. Reality is, as Lily Tomlin joked, a matter of anxiety for those in active contact with it; thus more pleasing appearances—resort towns, planned communities, theme parks, awards shows, political ceremonials, testimonials, the list is endless—can be procured to allay anxiety and supersede quotidian gloominess through play. We do not have to work at understanding hard reality, when we can be diverted and amused through play with soft realities. If the mythic home of the republican idealist is the town, and that of the charismatic adventurer the forest or financial market primeval, the true home of the contemporary hype artist is Hollywood.

We live, then, in an expanding universe of phoniness, constantly created and re-created by confidence men using the artifices of hype. The habits and practices of phoniness are now so familiar to us that we accept them as commonplaces, the way things are done, without reflection on what they mean for our lives. Here we wish to point to the three major characteristics of a phony culture: immediacy, frivolity, and artificiality. The phony culture of contemporary America is characterized by *immediacy*. The constant emphasis is on the now, the new, the fashionable, the thing of the moment, what's happening right now, what's hot and what's not, where it's at, the immediate experience. What is current and hyped is what is real. Reality is momentary, the symbolic focus of the ephemeral now. In a phony culture, not only do people have no sense of place, they also have no sense of time. Time and the sense of temporality—memory and projection—lose importance. People have little sense of temporal placement, of the continuity of national past and present, of the legacy of history and the promise of posterity, of breadth of perspective. The narrow focus on "now" reinforces the ascendancy of the ephemeral: what is happening now is what is real and important. The unreal and unimportant is associated with what is past, which is easily disposable, yesterday's events or celebrities or music. Everything becomes unmemorable and quite forgettable just because it is old and passing out of the new immediate moment, and thus is boring and spent, "history" in the pejorative sense. The new is always something that can be hyped: the next experience, thing, or personage is given allure and thus desirability. One is hopelessly "out of date" if you don't yearn for the newest, and think that nothing old is worth having. As Christopher Lasch noted, "make it new" is the great message of modern consumerism, expressed through advertising and programming (such as soap operas and tabloid news), making us into "addicts of change" who constantly seek "novelty and fresh stimulation" and exercise "restless mobility."[8] All things old—cars, clothes, presidents, spouses—are potential throwaways. But confidence in the new is something that has to be created, through the good offices of hype artists who "phony up" futures of newfound pleasures and delights. Without either a sense of history or a coherent view of the future, people are easily lured to the phony object of interest at the moment, drawing attention towards the plaything of the now but diverting attention from a larger view of the temporal world which invites self-placement. The news, for example, is hyped to draw our attention to the "hot story" of the moment, but does little to place events in the larger context of historical process; news is sensational in that it plays to immediate interest, and uninformative in that it makes little attempt at more comprehensive understanding. News is hyped "new" information that is sold like any other hot commodity, and there truly is nothing as old as yesterday's news.

A second characteristic of a phony culture is *frivolity*. Democratic culture has long been accused of favoring the lowest common denominator, quantity over quality, and vulgar mass tastes. The quest for, and hype of, the immediate experience intensifies that activity. If people seek the newest thing that is hyped, it is likely to be a frivolity, something of little weight or importance, the amusing trifles of daily play. Consequently, people find it difficult to take things seriously, to consider matters of weight and importance rather than the glittering but banal entertainments of mundane leisure. In a phony culture, people lead lives of endless diversion, which draws them away from serious or earnest considerations. The frivolous is deemed more fun and less demanding than the serious, so we obey the injunction to be happy, and don't worry. And like immediacy, the impact of frivolity on culture and personality becomes cumulative: The superficial, the flighty, the trivial, the sensational, the gossipy, the shallow become the fare of cultural experience; people lack depth, the capacity for reflection, a commitment to values or ethics. A phony culture lacks what the Romans called *gravitas*, the willingness to discern the serious and consider matters of gravity. The grave is fraught with ponderable significance, which major cultural forces array against: we respond to the hype of the light and irrelevant, but not to the appeal to get serious. A phony culture cannot take anything seriously, including its own grave problems and drift towards decline. Since in such circumstances people can no longer distinguish between the important and unimportant, everything is treated as a frivolity, even war, love, and death. If life is presented as a big party, then the "party" extends to turning the serious into play. Everything becomes a big joke, making fun of politics, religion, education, indeed all institutions as frivolous and passing trivialities. The stand-up comic who savages everyone and everything becomes a model opinion leader in such a society. Everything, even the most awful and primal events and relationships (murder, love, charity), translates into the insubstantial and merely amusing or diverting. Thus a political campaign loses all its seriousness as both the campaign organization and the media hype personality, charges and countercharges, the "horse race," revelations about the candidate's past, and so on. What is lost in the glib and weightless shuffle is any sense that the campaign means anything, since political trivia drives out the importance of the choice. Indeed, the principle of frivolity affects all news in the era of "tabloidization": not only does the news have to be immediate, it also tends to be frivolous, banal, and shallow reporting that focuses on "playful" rather than serious elements. Indeed, there is a sort of Gresham's Law of News by which the trivial becomes equal to or superior to the serious and consequential, in a kind of "equality of all stories." (A melodramatic squabble between two skaters, a trial involving malicious wounding of a spouse, and a peripheral scandal take precedence in the news at the same time a major disarmament agreement is reached, the Warsaw Pact essentially joins NATO, and the president reaches an aid agreement with Russia.) All such social exercises in frivolity give impetus to the ascendancy of the phony. In a phony culture, frivolity becomes a social principle that supersedes seriousness. Since frivolity can be hyped, it becomes more important than matters of importance.

A third characteristic of phony culture is *artificiality*. A phony culture not only lacks a sense of temporal placement and relative significance, it also devalues rootedness in the past and tradition and the habit of seriousness and deliberation in favor of the sweet cheats of artifice. Since our lack of attention span and interest focuses us on the immediate, and since our flippancy and frivolousness will not allow us to sustain seriousness, we then are drawn to artificialities, social fabrications which hold our immediate attention and fill our moments with amusing diversions. Thus social experience tends us to artifices, the dramas of simulated life that characterize our politics, economics, and culture. Immediate amusements we deem to be "lively," when in fact they are synthetic creations which separate us from our natural condition and unite us with artificial conditions. A phony culture creates an environment of artifices, so much so that we come to believe that ephemeral fabrications constitute what is meaningful and real in our existence. In a phony culture, art does not imitate life; it supersedes it, exalting the status of "created actualities" as the things most real. A walk in the mall is better than a walk in the woods. A board game at home is mundane; a game show is hyper-real. A perfume is just a smell until an advertisement for it explains its magical powers to transform you into a creature of irresistible sexual allure. A political convention is of no interest until media managers transform it into a television show. Pseudo-events—events staged for their staginess—are more real than actual events, which tend to be messy, complicated, and inexplicable, lacking in histrionic structure and dramatic force. A televised briefing by a public relations spokesperson comes to be equated with action, since it lives up to our media expectations: the pseudo-event becomes an event, an "actuality" that has ontological status. Similarly, a meadow is not lovely until it has been developed in an expensive housing project, hyped as a "richly appointed" and "naturally appointed" place for the rich to live in prestige. A place is "nowhere" until it becomes a pseudo-place engineered for conspicuous living. The natural meadow is not valuable until it is denatured. When it becomes a pseudo-place, it then has the aura of environmental dramatization and is worthy of substantial investment. Finally, the news has become the purveyor of the pseudo-fact, "factualities" or "factoids" that fit the currently fashionable or ideologically correct story line, or "take" on what's happening. Much news is phony, focusing on "well-founded rumors" or best-of-authority "inside dope" gossip rather than substantive processes (the vaunted national press, recall, celebrated the personality cult of President Reagan, but a Middle Eastern newspaper broke the Iran-contra story, and they missed entirely perhaps the biggest story of the 1980s, the wholesale looting of the savings and loan industry). The ephemeral artificialities of news now have become so irrelevant to people's lives that newspapers and TV news networks are endangered journalistic species.

A phony culture, then, is characterized by immediacy, frivolity, and artificiality. To a large degree, this emerging culture is the creation of the confidence man, who succeeds to the extent he or she can manipulate our penchant for immediate experiences of play in environments of artifice. Phoniness has now become a social fact and a cultural value, transforming the way we live and what we expect. It is our task here to point out the ways in which we have become a phony culture. To that end, we will discuss in turn phony language, phony people, phony places and things, phony events, phony deals, phony politics, and conclude with reflections on the future of phony worlds. We might note at the outset that the popular malaise of which we spoke is a symptom that phony culture is ultimately unsatisfying, that underneath our widespread acquiescence in the pervasiveness of the phony is a desire for something more, what we might call "life in truth." We can only overcome malaise if we face the truth of phony culture, and confront the assertions of confidence which sustain it. Phony artifices sustain our illusions if we willingly suspend disbelief, and in so doing lose contact with whatever grip on the relationship between ourselves and the objective and dynamic world that exists beyond our hopes, fears, and fantasies.

FURTHER MASQUERADES

"Something further may follow from this Masquerade," Herman Melville concludes his great cultural tale, *The Confidence-Man: His Masquerade.* The new American culture Melville saw was one of guile and disguise, strangers who have in common their mutual effort to bamboozle, snooker, and swindle each other. Society on the metaphorical steamboat named *Fidele*, boarded on April Fool's Day, contains an array of Americans, including a mysterious stranger who quotes St. Paul about charity. This produces indignation, as does not a sign put out in the barber's window: "No Trust." As Lindberg notes, "Melville's hypothesis, then, is that American social activity is a confidence game. Cut off from mutually accepted authority, his characters play upon each other's credulity to find what can be made credible."[9] American society has long had the strain of confidence-gaming and the creation of authority through influence-peddling. But taken to its logical extreme, the dysfunctions of confidence outweigh its utility, for it makes for a society devoted to looting each other. The casualties in the masquerades of conning become trust in republican ideals, belief in adventurers, and charity towards each other. In a sense, a phony culture is likely inherently unstable, unable to appeal to the better angels of our natures. With that in mind, let us now examine some manifestations of the phony masquerades that now characterize American life.

CHAPTER 1

PHONY LANGUAGE

I ain't phoneying them woids.
—Jimmy Durante

We have stated the thesis that the major source of the contemporary American malaise is the pervasiveness of the phony in our culture. In order to specify what this means, it is worthwhile to begin with language. For if a culture is phony, then how and what people communicate with each other will be a primary manifestation of that phoniness. Those who seek the confidence of others will learn to use all of the resources of language that affect impressions and direct behavior—words, images, and gestures, all mobilized in the various modes and media of communicating in order to achieve a desired result. Language is our social instrument of illumination and truth, but it is also a means of mystification and power. At a variety of levels and for a variety of purposes, the confidence man and woman are constantly at work at the latter, making pitches that appeal to mysteries conjured up through language and which allow the conjurer to exercise power over his auditors. The language of trust can be used to establish the authority of honest and earnest truthing, or it can be used to establish the authority of dishonest and phony conning (and all the ambiguous shades in between). As Melville long ago sensed, American culture had the potential to develop into a phony culture, characterized by the ascendancy of those versed in the languages of confidence, all the communicative artifices that further the art of the con. *In a society dominated by the confidence man and the conduct of confidence games, the discourse of that society will tend to be phony.*

THE PERVASION OF DISCURSIVE EFFLUVIA

It is our stated thesis that America is becoming a culture of pretense, led by the confidence-seeking activities of pretentious

31

people. A culture of pretense is characterized by phony language, communications which are fake. Social pretension is a strategy of persuasion, wherein the resources of communication are put to use in the myriad contemporary activities of conning. Thus when a communicator "phonies up" language, he or she is utilizing the capacity of language to make belief. In contemporary America, an enormous amount of time and energy is expended in the attempt to make belief by telling us that we should believe. A moment's reflection reminds us of how many daily messages we get exhorting us to believe, to trust the source of the message and hope for the benefit of what is promised. From morning till night, we are surrounded by the language of advertising, ranging from radio spots to TV commercials to newspaper and magazine ads to telemarketers calling us at dinnertime. The news is filled with people speaking on behalf of other people—public relations specialists, press secretaries, lawyers, and indentured experts. Large organizations—corporations, universities, governments, and so on—are constantly involved in the propagation of the official version of things, the rhetorical "line" or "policy" to be taken. Various polemicists for whatever interest or ideology attempt to persuade us of the justice or wisdom of their cause. In all cases, they are using language so constructed as to further their influence.

The language of social influence can appeal to logic and reason by using the weight of evidence and valuation. But facts and values alone often are not always persuasive. In order to achieve a social purpose, one needs power over opinion. Thus it is often deemed necessary to utilize the language of confidence, to make phony pitches. The capacity of language to "phony up" a presentation is enormous, including such tactics as lies, white lies, and statistics; ignoring, omitting, or arranging facts to suit your purpose; deflecting attention through the use of straw men and other bogus symbols; character assassination; using stereotypes; appealing to emotive cliches, such as wrapping yourself in the flag; attempting to characterize something as "obvious to everyone"; all of the resources of propaganda (e.g., plain folks, bandwagon, card staking); the arsenal of informal fallacy (e.g., *argumentum ad hominem*); associationism, associating whatever you are pushing with something else deemed desirable (motherhood, sexual success, "financial security," etc.); and so on, endlessly. Rather than appealing to intelligence through logic and evidence, the pitch is in terms of credulity, attempting to seduce people into believing in propositions that "ain't necessarily so." For we may be skeptical of such pitches:

they go to great effort to attempt to persuade you through the use of dubious arguments and the other seductive charms of language; if there isn't something wrong with the effort to bamboozle you, then why do they use such misleading and alluring language? If they don't have an ulterior motive when they try to charm us, then why the phony pitch?

Phony language, then, is the *language of pretension*. The transactions of communication involve the use of languages as a histrionic resource which if effective has a dramatic impact on auditors. If a phony is a role-player, the social distance established in a relationship allows for the attempt to command others as an authority. The audience is in the presence of a *spokesperson*, a social performer who tries to speak as with authority. The "spokesman" or "spokeswoman" bespeaks a phony language for purposes other than the clarification of truth or the conduct of dialogue. The spokesperson is in the vernacular a "mouthpiece" (Chicago "front page" newspapers in the gangland era would say things such as, "Shyster Parillo, the mouthpiece of the Capone organization, said today..."). The mouthpiece is someone who speaks (or writes, or gesticulates) well and convincingly, but is a hireling concerned with "phonying up" what is to be communicated. A spokesperson is not a free agent, nor unconstrained in what they can say; but they are purposeful, shaping discourse that gains confidence and achieve compliance. They may be quite hypocritical and cynical in what they do, or they may be quite committed; but in either case, they are what George Orwell called a "doubleplusgood duckspeaker," saying the things that are designed to gain confidence and achieve compliance. A spokesperson may work directly for an organization, which dictates what she or he says (e.g., a public relations officer); or they may create their own audience by espousing things that appeal to some social grouping (e.g., a talk radio host). In either case, the mouthpiece has identified someone for whom he or she speaks, and says the things that please or persuade, always for a price.

In a phony culture, the chief utility of public language—those social messages communicated for widespread effect—is *mystification*. Those confidence men and women who make belief communicate with blue smoke and mirrors, imbuing what they are saying with an aura of symbolic mystery. Their skill is in the use of language to convey mystery, seducing us with rhetorical flourishes and imagistic imprints that give their subject its mystique. They are masters of the technique of mystique, using the considerable resources of organized persuasion (advertising agencies, public relations offices, promotional firms, and so on) in order to mystify something. The mystifiers of the contemporary world serve the important function of attributing phony qualities to people, places, and things, transforming the ordinary into the extraordinary through the magical incantations of language. Their job is to make the profane into the sacred (or in their "attack mode," to profane what some other con artist has deemed sacred), making us believe in the otherwise unbelievable. The anthropologist Malinowski noted that the language of magic has "mystical effectiveness," evoking mystery in order to affect behavior.[1] The advertiser evokes the mystery of the product (the properties that produce magical effects, such as sexual attractiveness, financial success, or social prestige) in order to affect sales.

The pretensions of phony mystification have been legitimated by its success in affecting our behavior. Phony language works in evoking responses to its suggestions and commands. In the process, the pervasion of phony language has helped create a *culture of make-believe discourse*, dominated by the mystique of confidence-gaining communications designed to make belief. On the one hand, such a culture is pervaded by the high level of credulity that sustains the habits of such an order. If large numbers of people did not believe and act in the make-believe of advertising, promotion, and other forms of persuasive discourse, the system would collapse. The major cultural forms of economy, politics, and culture are driven by the constant sale and resale of propositions that may well not stand close scrutiny—that consumption makes you happy, that politicians are godlike, that education is the answer. Make-believe discourse makes us believe in a variety of mysteries, all magically conjured for us by the Merlins of persuasion. On the other hand, a culture of make-believe makes for disbelief, since most of the propositions sold turn out to be bogus. Since many people realize that the language games of making belief are phony, they suspend belief in the unbelievable and become functional skeptics or cynics (unless they are attracted to some alternative belief, which can be equally a scam). The great deluge of language directed at us by the purveyors of mystery may fall on deaf ears if we begin to see it as deceitful and extravagant, promises that cannot be kept. The success of phony language is directly related to the numbers of people who are willing to suspend disbelief, and exercise a leap of faith that the magical words are true and efficacious, promising to make our lives better. For the skeptic, then, phony language is something to be disbelieved, but also understood and revealed as fake. Ordinary people have long sensed this, and in often bitter vernacular talk about phony promises, they express themselves well: phony language is doubletalk, jive, guff, garbage, baloney, hooey, poppycock, balderdash, big talk, wind, trash, jabber, bunk, junk, nuts, horse manure, bilge, filth, and crap. These terms connote the sense that a lot of the language directed at them by would-be authorities is *discursive effluvia*, an "offensive exhalation" of communicative effluence that threatens to overwhelm us with its mysterious promises. But once seen as a phony pitch, the words and images come to be seen as a malodorous flow of offensive language. There is a vernacular term for phony language derived from another kind of effluvium, the foul excrement of the male bovine. In order to be delicate about this familiar, vulgar, and quite expressive term, we shall follow the advice of Professor Ned Hockman and use the inverted word "tihsllub" (and also the familiar abbreviated term, "B.S.") in the discussion of this key concept.[2] The concept of "tihsllub" has been developed by Dr. Harry Frankfurt, chair of the department of philosophy at Yale University, who wrote in 1986:

One of the most salient features of our culture is that there is so much (tihsllub)...(Tihsllubing) involves a kind of bluff: Unlike plain lying (bluffing) is more especially a matter not of falsity but of fakery. This is what accounts for its nearness to (tihsllub). For the essence of (tihsllub) is not that it is *false* but that it is *phony*. [A]lthough it is produced without concern for the truth, (B.S.) need not be false. The (tihslluber) is faking things. But this does not mean he necessarily gets them wrong.[3]

The B.S. artist, then, communicates in order to gain other people's confidence, but this does not necessarily mean she or he is lying. Rather the communication is constructed to be phony, since the effort is a matter of fakery and not the expression of "truth-values." The discursive pretension is not exactly a lie; rather, it is an expression of discursive fraudulence, an artifice of language that persuades but does not enlighten. Truth and falsity are of interest to the purveyor of make-believe only to the extent they further his or her project of confidence-building. The imposture of the B.S. artist is a matter of faking it, of incorporating all discursive resources into the construction of an artifice that has suasive power. The confidence men who dominate our culture are not congenital liars, but they are manipulative phonies. They are, as Frankfurt observes, "neither on the side of the truth nor on the side of the false...[The tihslluber's] eye is not on the facts at all, except insofar as they may be pertinent to his interest in getting away with what he says."[4] Truth and falsity in language are of interest to the liar; but the B.S. artist is interested in what language can do for him or her. His deception is not so much immoral as it is utilitarian: what can language do for me in my enterprise of producing results through "getting away with" stated representations of what other people should do. In a culture of make-believe, the language of pretension is used to make assertions about the world that are pertinent to achieving pragmatic results. For the tihslluber, the large gray area of rhetoric between truth and falsehood is the range of discursive opportunity, for here language is a practical tool of persuasive enterprise. Language is here the repertoire of the con artist at work, translating all utterances into convenient dissembling.

The languages of convenient dissembling came to the fore in, and helped accelerate, a phony culture. In a world where the individual has to constantly make a wide variety of choices (consumer, career, relational, political, cultural, and so on) without clear moral or even pragmatic rules of selection, the languages of confidence can have a large-scale impact. For such a condition, the quest for confidence becomes equated with hope: the individual wishes to believe in a hopeful state for self and society, and thus is drawn to messages of confidence that hope is justified. Confidence-building language becomes the modal form of public communication, exploiting our lack of certainty and anxiety about choosing. But it does not invite critical analysis or suspended judgment; rather, it suggests that we engage in pretense, believing in the pretense of interested communication. Such a culture builds phony relationships, based on the ephemera of tihsllubing. Since its language is constantly redefined to meet new contingencies, its very instability heightens the exercise of phony role-playing. The world belongs to the phony who can best exploit language in order to affect confidence. We are what we communicate; if what we say is phony, then it furthers the phony culture we ourselves create and perpetuate.

In order to further our understanding of phony language, let us now look at some major manifestations of our national commitment to B.S.ing one another. Alternatively, we will briefly examine propaganda, most notably the "flack arts" of advertising; public relations; promotion; fashionable languages that define the rhetorical style of particular social or professional group, such as psychobabble, politicobabble, and academebabble; the rhetorical style of a particular class of journalists deemed "pundits"; and "politically correct" languages that characterize the lingo of various institutions.

PROPAGANDA: THE LANGUAGE OF PROPAGATION

If our thesis about the cultural dominance of the confidence man is correct, then we should expect that the culture he and she would create is one permeated by *the pitch*. The pitch, as Hugh Rank has noted, is an old American slang term, suggesting the range of persuasive talk, sales talk, high-pressure tactics, a line of tihsllub designed to appeal to "non-rational" aspects of the targeted audience. The pitchman dates from pre-Barnum America, and could be seen in carnivals, traveling road shows, medicine shows, and the like, and was embodied in such figures as the circus barker, flim-flam men, snake oil salesmen, riverboat and tinhorn gamblers, pool hustlers, indeed all the confidence men looking for the main chance through making a pitch to a potential sucker ("Is this a game of chance?," the rube asks cardsharp W.C. Fields in one of his movies; he replies, "Not the way I play it, no"). The hallmark of the confidence man of old was *fast talk*, making your play with such glib and adroit verbal dexterity that the element of chance is minimized or eliminated. "Bilking the suckers" involved outwitting persons who were designated as "the mark." The mark was subject to the persuasive power of the pitch, induced through fast talk ("the line") into doing something she or he might not otherwise have done without a little help from their friend.

In contemporary America, the spiritual descendants of these charmers of old are the agents of the pitch. For it is still the case that *bilking is a social principle*. The term "bilk" suggests the art of the con, doing what one can get away with, getting what the market will bear, burning the other party, stinging the mark, overcharging the freight, fiddling with the scales, fixing the game, and so on. In a commercial civilization, bilking is a widespread daily activity involving separating people from their valuables, be it money, allegiance, commitment, property, belief, or whatever. The wheels of commerce could not turn without the grease of bilking, but then neither could politics or culture. The confidence men who utilize fast talk are the facilitators of bilking so crucial to the operation of social organizations. For if people did not buy, invest, or go into debt, the economy would collapse; if people did not vote, contribute to political candidates or parties, or join interest groups, the political system would atrophy; and if people did not embrace popular culture, support the arts, or go to church, our culture would be greatly altered. The principle of bilk creates the energy for all these vital social activities, realized through the fast talk of those who propagate the messages of persuasion.

Modern propaganda is now more sophisticated, but its fundamentals are in the fast-talking pitchmen and con artists of old. For no less than its predecessors, contemporary propagandists—advertisers, public relations specialists, and promoters—are versed in the language, lore, and techniques of pitching fast talk in order to induce the behavior desired of latter-day marks, namely us. Even though the fast talk of old has been superseded by the dazzling efforts of professional propagandists, discursive fraudulence remains the communicative norm, and the principle of bilking remains the social norm. Pretentious language still has to be used to enhance the prospect of bilking, of working the con to sting the mark. The language of propaganda aims at propagating big talk in order to spread influence and achieve compliance. In the process, it furthers our cultural drift into phoniness by poisoning the discursive well: by exploiting people's credulity, it permeates society with phony pitches, and creates a widespread malaise stemming from the nagging suspicion of having been had. Social discourse—the very languages we speak and see and hear—can no longer be trusted. The pitch is by nature phony, since it has an ulterior motive of bilking something out of us through the use of the discursive con.

Propaganda, then, is a phony language that contributes to the pervasion of phoniness. In a sense, this form of communication is a demonstration of the maxim that talk is cheap. The cheap talk of propaganda allows the communicator to sway large numbers of people with an economy of effort. Some influence-peddling is one-on-one, such as a sales pitch by a car or insurance salesperson. But the true power of propaganda comes from the mass pitch, which if cleverly designed can overcome enough "sales resistance" among enough people to make it worthwhile conducting. Overcoming that resistance becomes the organized and rational study of the propaganda industry, those firms dedicated to the art and science of message propagation and mass influence. The skill of the master propagandists is propagating a message in histrionic "dress" so that it dramatizes something for mass auditors to the point of influencing future thought, emotion, and action. By, now the practice of propaganda is an ingrained cultural habit, with the daily bombardment of endless messages which appeal to our credulous natures.

The languages of propaganda are phony. They are based on the communication of pretense. The communicator pretends to be sincere or rational ("trust me!") when in fact she or he is discoursing in "bad faith": the audience is a target, an "it" to be manipulated, not a "you" to be considered with understanding or personal empathy. For the propagandist, you do not exist; the units of propaganda are those social objects to be manipulated in their behavior through the use of pretentious language. The art of the propagandist is to communicate dramatic messages that achieve pragmatic results. Since the language of pretense conjures up make-believe, that is what is utilized in order to manage mass impressions and affect mass behavior. Fast talk is designed to slip something over on you, not level with you; if it does, it is because its dramatic force produced efficacious results measured in terms of behavior—sales, votes, movie tickets, donations. The very success of propaganda proves that phoniness works, making more organizations and enterprises turn to its use in order to further their interests. Phony culture corrupts the very language we daily experience, and thus corrupts thought, both the thought of those who make language and those who receive it. Pretentious language breeds a culture of pretentious people, dominated by phonies who get where they are through tihsllub. For the skeptical amongst us, what they are communicating to us is foul language.

Not only is propaganda fast talk and cheap talk, it is also doubletalk. The propagandist is communicating at role distance, phonying up what she or he says in a social performance. So "in role" he is doubling: it is his public role, not his private self, that conducts the discursive con. He or she may profess to not like bilking people, but does it because it is his or her job. But in so doing, she or he propagates doubletalk, discourse that is not designed to clarify but rather to convince; it is not couched in terms of straight talk, but rather discourse that is not on the level. Doubletalk is language for sale, the arsenal of language put to use in order to alter behavior; since it is formulated with an ulterior motive, there is more to the message than might appear at first glance. The doubletalk of an ad, for instance, is the association of what is being sold with good things (cosmetics and beauty); the talk here makes a bogus association in order to sell the product on the phony claim that beauty will magically flow from its use. But the habit of doubletalking—phonying up logic and evidence to work the propaganda con—conditions the habit of doublethink. George Orwell invented the term "doublethink" in *1984* to point to the conditioned reflex of holding contradictory ideas that are logically incompatible but nevertheless are posited as quite compatible according to the fraudulent logic of doublethink. The propagandist constantly asks us to doublethink on instinct without reflection on the absurdity of a nonsensical claim. For thought is his enemy, since we will sense that the claim is phony; but if we doublethink habitually, we accept the legitimacy of propaganda as a source of knowledge and the validity of doubling together incompatible ideas as perfectly harmonious. Orwell feared that through doublethink, propagandists could doubletalk us into believing anything—that whales speak French at the bottom of the sea, that cosmetics make one beautiful, that $2 + 2 = 5$. Without our capacity to doublethink, the phony culture propaganda has helped to create could not be sustained. If we adhered to the principle that it is unwise to believe propositions out of blind habit, then the American world would be a very different place.

Let us now examine briefly, in turn, advertising, public relations, and promotion, with a view toward seeing them as forms of propaganda, and as major languages of our phony culture.

ADVERTISING AS PHONY COMMUNICATIONS

Advertising has been called "the permissible lie" propagated by "the uneasy persuasion" with "the image-makers" communicating through "hidden persuaders" and "subliminal seduction."[5] Even though most of us take advertising for granted as an integral part of our world, and think we are resistant to its lures, it is the case that advertising is so ubiquitous and relentless that it is a *major source of learning in the contemporary world.* We learn, for example, about fashion—how we are supposed to appear, according to the dictates of fashion propaganda, in social settings where we will be seen and evaluated. At an early age, we get the idea that the newest things— clothes, cars, entertainers, politicians—are "in," and one is "with it" if you are cognizant of the latest fashion trends, and able to recognize and abandon what is now "out." In the process we are not only learning what is fashionable, but also the value of fashionability. The language of advertising teaches us the logic of knowing and acquiring the "right" thing if we are to value ourselves. The doublethink of the commercial pitch is that we are what we have; therefore to be somebody you must acquire those things which make us important to ourselves and others. One's self-esteem is dependent upon constantly renewed acquisition and possession of the latest things which define fashionability. The consequence of this is to teach us the habit of identifying with the values and logic of advertising discourse, seeking glamour and sophistication, youthfulness and immortality, prosperity and conspicuous consumption, sensuality and the pursuit of pleasure, self-indulgence and living for the moment. Advertising doublethink gives impetus to the creation of cultural self-definitions that underscore the desire for more, and for the social *display* of those acquisitions. Such a quest seeks a mirage, a social self never satisfied and always anxious about how one appears. Advertising helps create the protean self, the mutable being who is forever changing shapes in response to new cues as to how one should appear now. Thus as a source of learning, advertising can be justly said to have considerable impact on how we think and who we are. The phony language of advertising helps create phony people who define themselves in terms of the fashionable appearances the doublethink of commercial interests has taught them. They are as they appear, enveloped in the latest objects of desire, obsessed with display but lacking substance beyond what they have to show.

Let us illustrate how advertising gets us to doublethink into conspicuous consumption. Most of us lead lives of routine conformity, but we all entertain fantasies of freedom and adventure. So many of us openly (or secretly) admire the social rebel, the nonconformists who dare to be different, be they poet or prophet, hell-raiser or hipster, radical or raconteur. Many popular heroes are admired because they appear to be rebels. The heavy-metal rock stars who engage in outrageous and bizarre behavior both on and off stage are presenting a model of rebellion most of us would not do but can admire because they get away with it. What we can do is affect minor rebellions in everyday life that do not seriously jeopardize our security. but which let us play with the fantasy of rebellion. Both the celebrity culture and the related advertising industry have long recognized the potential for representing rebellion to cater to this latent mass desire, and have developed services and products for us to consume to "be" rebels just like them. "In advertising, television, and all the other organs of culture," notes T.C. Frank, "hipsters are figures to be revered. They have been turned into a central symbol of the system they are supposed to be subverting."[6] One can be a pseudo-rebel by identifying with hip celebrities who hawk themselves or consumer items that appeal to our own play-rebelliousness. So we can have it both ways, affecting rebelliousness without really taking the risks of being so. But the celebrity-rebel does too: a Spike Lee can make a "radical" movie about true rebel Malcolm X for profit, and at the same time plug athletic shoes for corporate giant Nike for a large fee, but maintaining his image as a rebel. Rock stars can commit outrageous acts or sing lewd songs for the benefit of large audiences, and become wealthy in the process. A professional "bad girl" like Madonna can make a lucrative career out of appearing to be a sexual athlete. But their implicit message is also that they don't really mean it, that it's all for fun and profit. So they invite us to commit minor pseudo-acts of rebellion (wearing a Malcolm X ball cap, listening to heavy metal, wearing nose rings and fake tattoos to a party). Concomitantly, the advertising industry has commercialized this desire for "safe" acts of deviance by making a wide variety of acts of consumption as a way to express rebellion without risk. This can be as simple as harkening to the appeal of a franchise food ad: "Sometimes You Gotta Break the Rules." Or, a sporty car in an act breaks out of the crawling pack on the beltway at rush hour and speeds up western roads on the way to who knows what adventure. The tradition of dissent and deviance is translated by advertising and celebrities into commodities of play, wherein "rebellion"and "liberation" are given phony expression. Thus we, learning from advertising, come to believe that expressions of rebellion or freedom can be done safely, without any true danger or seriousness. We come to believe that rebels are phony, and that rebellion itself is phony. The hucksters turn social protest into a stance, displayed through consumption of bogus items of rebellion and admiration of celebrity pseudo-rebels. Advertising has the astonishing ability to transform everything authentic or fresh into a marketable commodity, thus taming and selling its newness. In such a commercial environment, everything is subject to the ability of the market to sense trends and create demands for products and services which cater to anything new. Thus the latest effort at youthful rebellion—hippie, punk, grunge, whatever—becomes a lucrative way to sell a "statement" of pseudo-rebellion, and be fashionable in so doing. In that way, rebellion becomes coopted through making it into a fashion statement. On the other hand, the practice of advertising makes all of those who participate in the consumer culture functional radicals, who learn that the old and established is bad, and that the new and novel is good. Although this message is propagated to stimulate cultural and economic consumption, it has affected political consumption too, transforming us from citizens into consumers of politics, expecting the commodities of politics to offer novel and satisfying experience. Advertising teaches us to rebel against the status quo of fashion, but it may well be that such phony rebellion has real consequences in reinforcing an attitude of expecting and welcoming change. The impact of advertising makes for constant cultural change, undermining the conservation of value by always holding out the lure of the new, the latest, the novel, the fresh. In consumer politics as well as consumer economics, there is nothing so out of date as yesterday's fad, so ideologies, politicians, and regimes may date fast to be replaced by today's "in" fad. The American "conservatives" who run economic, cultural, and political institutions are placed in the position of having to advocate, and sponsor, change because we now expect it.

Advertising has a concomitant, and again largely unintended, consequence for our culture. Commercial propaganda seduces us into "playing the role" of someone we would like to be, but have not the daring, skill, or looks to really be. So through consumption we can take on the role of, say, rebel as a form of amusement, and take it off again just as easily. Advertising gives impetus to us assuming fictive *personae* for public enactment, without our really believing in who we say we are. The advertisement lets us imagine ourselves as a kind of magical personage, with powers of youth, beauty, wealth, success, wisdom, and so on we do not in fact possess. But the ad allows us the fancy of legitimate phoniness, that role-playing as charming hostess, dashing executive, alluring lover, financial wizard, social rebel, or whatever in some sense makes us that. These phony roles let us dramatize ourselves as something we are not, but can play at being for the benefit of auditors.

The Prosperos of advertising conjure up these phony self-images through the use of magical languages of make-believe. Make it new, commercials tell us, through make-believe. Our capacity to believe, or at least half-believe, the language of advertising encourages the purveyors of commerce to expand its use, to the point now that billions are spent yearly on ads for virtually everything, and ads are everywhere (including, for instance, "product placements" in movies, on racing cars, at the Olympics, in parades, and on uniforms). The fast talk of propaganda is here applied in its ubiquity, constantly messaging us with slogans, jingles, montages, metaphors, indeed every discursive ploy that can be mobilized in the competition for attention, recognition, and action. One important theme, for example, in contemporary advertising is the "personal touch" motif that appears in a variety of ads. A bank chain will show a young couple becoming part of the "Gangplank Federal family." Restaurants will bill themselves as "family restaurants" that are "just like a family dinner at home." Restaurant chains will appeal to "country cooking" by "mom and pop" that is served in a "country kitchen dining room." An insurance conglomerate will assure you that through your friendly agent you are "in good hands." A huge financial firm will announce that "it invests in relationships" and serves its clients "one person at a time." A university will advertise itself to prospective students urging them to "become part of the Siwash family." In all cases, large impersonal organizations are trying to convince you that they are a small family business with a homey and friendly touch, as if they existed in a nineteenth-century rural town full of dear hearts and gentle people. This appeals to the contemporary anxiety about being lost in the crowd and treated impersonally by big organizations, exploiting this common feeling by conjuring up the phony image of the personal touch. Thus in the ad a "secondary" (I-it) relationship is given the phony frame of a "primary" (I-thou) relationship. Advertising here speaks to the fear of loneliness, which even if it is absent at home can be experienced in a mythical home away from home.

Advertising, then, uses language to let us dwell in the fantastic theater of wish. This colorful pageant of desire is a creature of confidence-building, manipulated by the sirens of wish-fulfillment. The advertiser knows the power of self-seduction, how we can always convince ourselves that what is wished for us is in fact what we wish for ourselves. The sovereignty of wish becomes a social principle that pervades not only the culture but also the language. Everything becomes a struggle of propagandas, of whose language of advocacy is to be believed, of whose wishes are to prevail. The common ads for fashion and cosmetic products and services speak to the wish for allure, that one can be beautiful, never age, and so forth. But more "serious" advertising uses the same hyperbolic language of wish. Political campaign ads, for instance, hold out the fantasy of hope, that one's wishes for self and country can be fulfilled through the heroic vessel of the latest candidate. The candidate is framed in the language of wishful thinking, that glory and riches follow for those who support him or her. Similarly, the fast-talking pitchers of the religious telemarketers preach the bogus theology of the "prosperity gospel," the good news that if one displays appropriate and conspicuous piety and contributes to the show, one will enjoy the earthly blessing of restored health and financial gain. The confidence men of advertising cannot resist framing advocacy with the language of hyperbole, and reducing their pitch to the level of popular gullibility.

We may see this even in public debates over earnestly held positions, such as the dispute over reproductive rights conducted by activist "pro-choice" and "pro-life" forces. Even though there are profound philosophical and social questions involved with abortion, the contestants for the approval of public opinion make their pitch in the hyperbole of advertising—evocative or shocking imagery, personal testimonials, moving words and phrases, simplistic but definitive choices. The very terms "pro-choice" and "pro-life" oversimplify and emotionalize the debate. The abortion ads on both sides of the issue are pitched in language that mystifies the subject but avoids equivocation and empathic appeals to compromise. Planned Parenthood and other pro-choice groups have run ads with testimonials from women (often from celebrities) who had illegal abortions in previous eras, conjuring up images of a return to an inquisitional dark age if abortion rights are curtailed. Militant anti-abortion groups have developed inflammatory ads, often with closeups of dead fetuses and characterizations of their opponents as evil people bent on "babykilling." A more soft-sell campaign was sponsored by the Arthur C. DeMoss Foundation, which ran a series of ads with beautiful children who were adopted rather than aborted by mothers who "toughed it out," extolling the "return to basic values" exemplified by images of uniformly healthy and lovely children whose cherubic presence rather than absence is designed to make us feel guilty about abortion ("Life: What a Beautiful Choice" is the DeMoss ads grabber) and virtuous about choosing beautiful life over ugly death. These ads suggest that everything would be just fine if women weren't so frivolous and selfish as to have abortions "on demand," and are designed to propagate guilt feelings among the immoral. All these ads have the effect of widening the polarity of the issue by the use of the hyperbolic language of moral rectitude and demonic attribution. Both "sides" can feel morally superior, since much of the advertising language casts their position as the moral one and the other as the demonic evil to be defeated. The ads wish for a world either free of abortions or free of constraints, in which their opponents have disappeared. But wishing is an emotional pitch, producing heat but little light. Both sides have made the issue less resolvable by resorting to the language of advertising, which tries to fast talk the issue in irreconcilable terms which are totally satisfying to one side but totally unsatisfying to the other. The temptation to use the fast talk of advertising is often irresistible in competitive situations, here in an intense competition for power over opinion and policy. But it puts a group committed to an ethic in the position of using language that is designed to "phony up" the issue, putting the issue under dispute in terms of language that persuades on the basis of irrational and monocular appeals rather than rational dialogue and debate. What is lost in the process is the claim to the moral "high ground," since the use of phony language in order to support the position compromises the claim to rectitude.

The language of advertising, then, is founded on the firm confidence that people are capable of being gulled. Fast talk may be simpleminded, coarse, and hyperbolic, but if it succeeds in talking us into something without thinking, then it is deemed by our society as valuable. Its value is in "phonying up" a variety of wishes we would not entertain otherwise unless conjured up by the magicians who design the advertising theater of wishes. The language of wishes fast talks us into an endless cycle of ever renewed desires aroused by the mesmerizing songs of the commercial siren. The siren sings a phony song, seducing us into patterns of behavior that become addictive for the gullible. Our addiction is not only compulsive consumption, but more fundamentally compulsive credulity in the faith that our boundless wishes can be fulfilled through acts suggested by advertisers. If some of us become disillusioned by the failure of these acts of faith, it is because we have become skeptical of the promises of phony language used to agitate very real wishes, including our pathetic hope that life can be better than it is if only we have the right things to stimulate us.

THE PHONY LANGUAGE OF PUBLIC RELATIONS

Public relations involves the effort on the part of some organized interest to relate well to the public. Corporations, unions, universities, interest groups, professional associations, and so forth all deem it necessary to hire "publicists," professionally trained hirelings who publicize the good works the organization is doing. The language of advocacy is here not put to work selling consumables, but rather selling the organization and its benevolent activities and leadership. The PR specialist is adept in portraying the organization or the leader as virtuous and effective, playing to our wish for organizational benevolence, that the big bureaucracies and elite leaders who run things are truly good, smart, and effective. They are charged with the job of portraying the organization in general in the best possible light, and when challenged with some specific event, to put the best possible face on things. Their effort is to polish the "image" of their employers, so PR personnel utilize phony language to shape the public imagination. The activities of public relations offices may not be inherently deceitful, but they may be inherently phony, since they almost invariably utilize fraudulent language in order to protect and further the interests of the organization or leader. The PR spokesperson bespeaks propaganda for an interest rather than a commodity. Their language is not oriented towards selling us something by fast talking us, but rather convincing us of something—

the good condition of the interest represented to the public and press. The advertiser asks us to trust his or her word on the product or service being sold; the public relations spokesperson asks us to trust her or his word on the organized interest being touted. The language of advocacy is here put to use advocating the social presence and activities of a specific segment of society as if they were the general interest. A corporation, for instance, uses PR "flacks" to justify its activities as in the public interest, that what it does is intentionally benevolent and altruistic.

The great pioneers of public relations, such as Ivy Lee and Edward Bernays, thought that modern organizations could not function properly without "the engineering of consent." The governance of organizations includes maintaining good relations with the public, through the use of languages of advocacy that are designed to shape favorable public opinion. PR discourse is not so much fast talk (talking people into doing something) as it is *slick talk*, talk designed to affect belief in the organization. Slick talk tries to talk people into believing something. (Ivy Lee defined PR simply as "the art of getting believed.") A PR "mouthpiece" is trained to be slick, using language skillfully to "talk up" and "talk around" things through the deft use of tihsllub. PR spokespeople for corporations are touting a social state (freedom of action for the corporation) rather than a product to be bought; thus the language must be a rhetoric that is clever and wily, using nimble wit of tongue to protect and further the interests of the organization. PR teams are sent out in communities to "talk up" the organization (Wombat Oil is a good neighbor, responsible citizen, doesn't pollute, contributes to the economy, sponsors community projects, and so on). When some trouble arises, they are also trained to "talk around" the problem (Wombat Oil is "concerned" about pollutants, working on the problem, and will "take appropriate action"; the company regrets it has to "downsize" (fire) so many workers, but felt it necessary in order to maintain its "market viability" (profits); the company "vigorously denies" that it broke any laws in the bribery case now in federal court). Talking up the organization propagates the pretension that Wombat Oil or whoever is a paragon of virtue that is indispensable to community progress, and talking around bad things (accusations, accidents, firings, bankruptcy) often allows the organization time to ride out "firestorms" of controversy or get off the legal hook. In all cases, public relations offices are at work phonying up the image of the organization, effectively engineering that acquiescence that passes for public consent.

In contemporary lingo, public relations specialists are often referred to as "spin doctors." The term is revealing: their expertise is in "doctoring" situations so that their discursive ministrations produce a healthy image of the organization or its representative. With a mission of talking up something—a policy innovation, plant opening, merger, and so on—the spin doctors mount a campaign out of a "war room" which attempts to give positive spin for public and press direction. With a more troublesome mission of talking around something, the job is to apply the medicine of slick talk to the problem, attempting to restore to health the image of organization or leader. If, for example, a corporate spokesperson is charged with putting the best face on things, he or she may use such rhetorical tactics as evasion ("A complete investigation is under way"), denial ("We categorically deny all charges of misconduct"), passing the buck ("The company takes no responsibility for the actions of irresponsible individuals"), poormouthing ("Excessive government regulation and taxes force us to pass the costs of cleanup on to the consumer"), and stonewalling ("It is not our policy to yield to hysteria and irresponsible charges by extremists and lunatics"). Public relations mouthpieces live in the linguistic world of euphemism, more auspicious terms that conceal an unpleasantness or make something more agreeable or inoffensive. Thus firings become a "career enhancement program," massacres become "free-fire zones," bombing as "air support," neglect of decaying areas "deferred maintenance," losses as "nonperforming assets," and so on endlessly. Spin doctoring is deemed a necessary rhetorical charade, since the wrong phrase or metaphor can damage the apparently fragile image of that which is being protected and nurtured.

Similarly, spin doctors expend much energy grooming the image of the boss. Slick talk here is applied to transforming the president, CEO, university president, or whatever into a giant in the earth. The chief as the public is supposed to imagine him or her is always on top of things, is the font of initiatives, the soul of wit, an awesome intellect, the cause of our present happy state, a person of nobility and purpose but also humble and unassuming, a dynamo of energy and charismatic leadership, someone committed to both principle and pragmatism. The most obvious example of this is the personality cult maintained by the White House communications operation, which elevates the president they work for into a demigod with superhuman powers but who is also someone supremely human, a regular guy who is called to lead because of his vast abilities, both Clark Kent and Superman. The object of the PR enterprise is to create a phony personage, a looming and gigantic presence that is the artifice of imaginative representation through slick talk that enlarges him into greatness. The president is known through staged "photo opportunities," the media events, the partisan testi-monials, the "town halls," the policy speeches, the convention extravaganza—all dramatic devices to showcase the great man of both heroic and democratic virtue. The president's flacks are often akin to witch doctors, conjuring up through sympathetic magic a variety of angels and demons, and making credulous believers cringe before the shimmering image of the mighty one they magnify. These latter-day Wizards of Oz may also be creating a humbug, only now the machinery of image and word mystifies the image all the more. The difficulty is that the president can be revealed as merely human, with all the fallibilities and foibles of the common run of humankind, which deflates the carefully constructed image of a phony personage. The astonishing discovery that the president is human demotes him from an exalted status, making him quite amenable to attack and scorn. Like other celebrities fallen from public grace through the collapse of their public *persona*, presidents recurrently have to face the cruelty of a fickle press and public easily disenchanted by revelations of their mortal limitations and human failings, not to mention political mistakes. The press and public are tempted to believe that the president is a phony, and now we are seeing the emperor without his clothes, a raw and reduced image we don't like.

There is a deeper difficulty with the use of public relations by important organizations. Even though a good bit of PR work is routine, the use of slick talk can become an organizational principle to the extent that *problem-solving is defined primarily as a matter of public relations talk.* In an era of mass communications and opinionmaking, it becomes easy to think that a problem is solved if it addressed through the language of PR. The temptation is great to approach matters of substance as something which can be resolved by image management, "damage control," and the like. A problem—environmental disaster, health care, employee or student discontent, job loss, racial tension—comes to be seen as something that can be dealt with by slick discourse itself, a more insubstantial if immediately less costly approach. But the PR ploy "bakes no bread": the difference, say, between a public official showing up at the site of a riot, industrial accident, or the home of a family stricken with bankruptcy through medical bills to show "concern" and "commitment" and then leaving it at that, and an official trying to redress substantive grievances through policy changes is considerable. PR discourse becomes doublespeak designed for the manipulation of public opinion but may be little more than a phony dodge of responsibility and response. For this reason, many people come to feel that the PR ploy is a trick, the use of mystifying language to "fix" a problem but that effectively does nothing other than spread discursive effluvia to cover things up.

Public relations language, then, can be used to phony up things, turning leaders and organizations into creatures of fabulation, and announcing that problems have been solved by being addressed through magical words of reassurance and gestures of concern. Although the use of public relations is widespread, its major social uses seem to be in defense of established institutions, professions, or industries. The general tendency for such organizations seems to be: when there is trouble, don't call for reform, call the PR squad. For instance, a profession under social fire—doctors, lawyers, teachers— will now typically respond not by reform of their practices but rather refurbishment of their image. We are asked, through their PR propaganda, to regain confidence in them as a profession because the "collective representation" of them in magazine ads and the like depicts them as worthy of admiration and deference, especially towards their lucrative professional rewards. During the extended health reform debate of the 1990s, many of the groups involved— doctors, pharmaceutical companies, the insurance industry—tried to affect the outcome in order to protect their interests and privileges. One major way was public relations programs which essentially depicted them as benevolent and caring groups committed to the public health. The American Medical Association mounted a campaign of magazine ads which portrayed doctors doing the hard, and often unpaid, work of healing the poor (one ad showed a pediatrician who volunteers for *pro bono* work in a slum, treating babies addicted to cocaine at birth). The effort seemed designed to restore the mythic image of the kindly country doctor of yore, the tireless and sympathetic healer of the community who made house calls and sat up all night with sick children by lamplight in a farmhouse. Such image refurbishment does little to redress the medical grievances of the public at the present, but it may do much to defend the professional prerogatives of doctors. Or then again it may not: a public increasingly dissatisfied with the medical system may disbelieve the PR pitches designed to shore the image of the profession that runs the system. If so, doctors may be forced to make house calls again. For the severe limitation of PR ploys is that its linguistic embellishments and glorious depictions may not cohere with people's experience, to the extent they suspect the "line" they are being fed is bogus. In that case, all the king's PR men cannot elicit confidence in what has come to be seen as a phony image.

PROMOTION: THE PROPAGANDA OF HYPE

One of the primal figures in the tradition of American confidence is the promoter. The promoter was, and is, a quintessential user of language in order to pique people's interest, eventually getting them to pay cash money to see sights hitherto unseen by civilized man. Promoters mastered the arts of public tihsllubing in order to promote whatever was coming to town—a new medicine, the circus, the latest revival, the hottest politician. Indeed, the history of the settlement of the American nation is one of promotion, with con artists promoting the "promised land" of real estate by conveying the "magical sense of confidence" through what Henry Adams had called "the hyperbole of enthusiasm." In the American mind, "confidence will create its own object."[7] When the promoter became a townsman, he was no longer a land speculator but a developer, no longer a circus barker but a politician, no longer a medicine man but a Rotary booster, no longer a Barnum but rather a Babbitt. In the ever-new American promised land, new objects of confidence are promoted—celebrities, theme parks, televangelists, media politicians—but the arts of promotion still utilize the hyperbolic language of enthusiasm for those magical objects of desire.

Promotion proceeds with the language of *hype*, persuasive propaganda that works through conveying a magical sense of confidence in the object being promoted. If advertising tends to hype products and services, and public relations hype organizations and leaders, then promotion tends to hype events and processes, those "pseudo-events" to which they hope to draw attention and ticket sales (this includes the "human pseudo-event" of the celebrity). A real estate promoter (such as the salesmen in David Mamet's *Glengarry Glen Ross*) is hyping the concept of living in a pseudo-country paradise. The promotion of a new movie aims at creating a "bandwagon" of enthusiasm for this colossal! stupendous! marvelous! production. The promotion of a beauty queen involves hyping the *persona* of this beautiful and talented creature as the rightful winner of the fabulous event of the beauty contest. The self-promotion of a movie starlet or presidential hopeful may include an endless round of media appearances in the effort to hype one's own fame or political aspirations.

Advertising, public relations, and promotion are all related propaganda activities. But with promotional ventures, the emphasis is on inflated language puffed up to generate excitement. Rather than fast talk or slick talk, the language of promotion is *big talk*. The promoter talks big in order to make something seem extraordinary, special, momentous, and important, too big an event or process to miss out on. Big talk is the language of enthusiastic advocacy, evoking the pretension that something happening or about to unfold right now is a unique and once-in-a-lifetime chance. Advertising can be soft-sell or subtle, and public relations evasive and circumlocutory, but promotion tends to the bombastic, the titillating, and the effusive (the word "hyperbole" derives from the Greek word for excess). Like the title of the old movie trailers, promoters shamelessly tantalize us with "previews of coming attractions." It is often the case that the actual event doesn't live up to its hyped promise—the movie may not be as exciting as the previews pledged, the Super Bowl may be a big bore after all the "build-up," the Academy Awards show may be interminable. But the task of promotion is to "phony up" the coming attraction by making it attractive through enticing language. If we are disappointed afterwards, it is we who are the suckers. Promotion cheerfully proceeds in a culture with a general toleration of such fraudulence, and we rebound with the hope that the next hyped thing will this time satisfy.

The habit of credulity conditions us to ignore previous experience and trust that this time the thing promoted will live up to its advance billing. The promotion of a coming attraction involves the use of a wide variety of attention-getting devices, ranging from publicity stunts to testimonials. Publicity stunts offer a way of directing attention towards a newly marketed desire. The fabled Edward Bernays was hired by a tobacco company in the 1920s to hype the desirability of women smoking, hitherto a social taboo. Bernays hired debutantes to march in New York's Easter Parade defiantly smoking cigarette "torches of freedom," an act he arranged to have widely reported; although the acceptability of women smoking was already changing, Bernays' stunt did dramatize for the nation the desirability of the change, associating sophistication and female equality with lighting up.[8] Testimonials include the use of "blurbs"—testaments as to the worthiness of a book—in order to hype sales. Blurbs are words and phrases lifted from the reviews of the book, often taken out of context to give the impression of a wholly favorable opinion. Added to the back cover of the book, the blurb gives the weight of critical approval to the work. The book becomes "extraordinary," "definitive," "seminal," "a dramatic and harrowing account," "amusing and provocative," "thoughtful and disturbing," and so on. Blurbs are verbal previews of the attractions in the book we simply must buy. (This practice extends to academic books also: potential classroom adopters are hit with brochures and back cover fare that touts the merits of the text: one of the author's previous texts was plugged, for its second edition, as an "innovative attempt" and a "highly readable, entertaining, and useful introduction" to the subject by authoritative academic names.)

Promotional showmanship is sometimes big talk that ballyhoos a show everyone knows is a con, but we love it for the utter audacity of the hype. Such is the case with professional wrestling, wherein the considerable audience is fully aware of the con, enjoying the media event for its popular histrionics. The many hyped rivalries, grudge matches, and intrigues of rasslin' amuse us for their colorful melodramatics, and the fact that we are in on the gag. We may rightfully condemn phoniness as morally suspect in contexts wherein it does harm, such as advertising for harmful products such as tobacco or public relations that lies and evades. But the promotion of professional wrestling strikes us as charming if juvenile fun rather than something sinister. Who, after all, can object when heroes such as Hulk Hogan and Sgt. Slaughter defend right against such villains as the Legion of Doom and the Ultimate Warrior?

Propaganda, then, involves the use of talk—fast talk, slick talk, and big talk. It is language that takes advantage, seeking openings in our psychic defenses to appeal to a credulous suspension of disbelief. Propaganda phonies up things, fast-talking us into buying things, slick-talks us into accepting things, and big-talks us into hyping things. The artifices of language are mobilized in the interest of propagating a message. The message requires, but does not necessarily deserve, our trust, since without gaining credulous faith the "modified" truths of propaganda would fail. The language of propaganda removes many of the rough edges from life, offering us a vision of the world that is prettier than it is in fact. But it portrays phony worlds, presented to us as if they were true, beautiful, and good. We cannot live in phony "as if" universes all our lives, but the propagandist proceeds on the assumption that we wish to.

FASHIONABLE LANGUAGES: PSYCHOBABBLE, POLITICO-
BABBLE, NEWSTALK, ACADEMESE

The principles of doublespeak are not confined to the purveyors of propaganda. People will use phony language in order to convey their status as among the fashionable. Pretentious people will use pretentious language, associating themselves with the "in" talk of the moment that is impressive to social auditors. Fashionable babble mystifies the individual as smart enough to know what kind of talk is momentarily the thing to say, so we may label such babble *smart talk*. Smart talk is the language of fashionable babble, what people currently "in the know" are saying. Smart talkers know both what to talk about (the currently fashionable subjects) and how to talk about those subjects (the "buzzwords" of linguistic style). Smart talk is the rhetoric appropriate to the fashion situation, how one talks in order to command the respect and admiration of those impressed by fashion. Smart talkers are a variant on the social type known as the "inside dopester," the person whose claim to superiority or notoriety is that they possess privileged or secret knowledge of what's happening now. The goal is enhanced social reputation, increasing one's self-importance in a status hierarchy. The smart talker is showing off, pretending to be fashionable. The show-off is exercising vanity in the guise of knowledgeability. Acquiring the right language becomes as important as wearing the right clothes; the show-off "wears" language for the same purpose that they wear designer clothes. Their language, like their clothes, is not for utility nor durability, but for show.

Phony languages appear in many forms, but let us point to three major and familiar ones: *psychobabble, politicobabble, newstalk and academese.*

PSYCHOBABBLE: THE LANGUAGE OF SELF-DISCOVERY

In the 1970s, observers of the changing social landscape began to talk about a retreat from the social concerns that characterized the 1960s, and the extent to which people were interested in self-absorption. Terms such as "the Me Decade," "privatism," and "the culture of narcissism" appeared, suggesting a general focus on the quality of one's own life rather than society. This new self-interest took many forms, from a rediscovery of fundamentalist Christianity to the "new conservatism" to religious or philosophical cults to the "human potential movement." It is this last movement that is our subject here. For the various psychological and self-help theories that abound among educated upper-middle-class circles is called *psychobabble*. "Insight," wrote R.D. Rosen, "packaged as psychobabble, has become a commodity...the verbal rent we pay to contemporary American life..."[9] Psychobabble emanates from pop psychology, and has become an argot, the special vocabulary of those "up on" the latest psychological chatter. Since the 1970s, an endless array of psychobabble has come and gone—Est, rebirthing, primal therapy, scientology, codependency, the inner child, and so on. They have in common the "therapeutic ethos," the conviction that whatever is wrong with individuals can be cured by the proper medium of psychic therapy. And perhaps these popular therapies can and do. But fashionable phonies use the language of psychobabble not for purposes of cure but rather for display. If you can display your knowledge of the latest therapy, you can then impress people with the quality of your psychic (and often also physical) health. These "canned" expressions of self-understanding are expressed by people with the smug assurance of fashionability of cure. They are most fashionable because they are "in tune" with the latest psychobabble, which lets them pretend and proclaim that they are more psychically perfect than their peers, who are hopelessly *passé* if they haven't grasped the latest pop psychology lexicon and stance. Asserting yourself as a healed initiate into the mysteries of codependency, "wellness," or whatever gives you status as trendy and ahead of the pack. (Such psychic self-assertion seems to concentrate in service-industry professionals located in precious enclaves of wealth and leisure, such as Marin County, California.) Human potential psychobabble makes a phony pitch for people to buy a psychic magic bullet, that in spite of the constraints of a bureaucratized and consumer culture, one can assert one's individual "self-development" as a kind of secular salvation achieved through the recommended psychic regimen for sale at the local bookstore, encounter group, or weekend seminar.

Postmodern psychobabble is actually a later version of the self-improvement movements that are a continuing part of our popular culture and literature. In the American search for confidence, self-confidence has long been a salable commodity. Our desire to transform—or "help," "fulfill," "improve," "develop," and "under-stand"—our selves into something better leads us to buy the pitch for quick and easy results in making our selves over. But like psychobabble, these earlier confidence games emphasized the extent to which that self-help was an act of will, as if one could overcome the constraints of society and create a new, improved self as an act of will alone. Outside of the precious circles of wealthy psychobabblers, more common babble is sold as therapeutic and reconstructive; like cosmetic surgery, the self can be made over into something fresh and exciting, and most of all, impressive on display. The most obvious programs are physical strength and weight control. But most relevant here perhaps are the programs of bourgeois confidence, that one can succeed in business, church, and local society through the exercise of "educated" will. If one mastered the axioms and advice of social friendliness (Dale Carnegie), philistine theology (Norman Vincent Peale and Robert Schuller), or capitalist metaphysics (Ronald Reagan and Zig Ziglar), one could gain the power of babble that guarantees worldly success, winning friends and influencing people, adopting positive and possibility thinking, and gaining personal wealth while feeling quite moral and beneficent about it. The objective conditions of society can be mastered through the invocation of the power of "the right stuff" that elevates one's social status. Making big money through real estate investment or direct marketing becomes a matter of self-transformation. "The popular psychology of positive thinking," writes Donald Meyer, "...flourished among people able, for reasons of culture and politics, to imagine that the only thing wrong with their lives was within themselves."[10] Learning the language of success makes for at least the display of success, if not the fact of riches, social standing, and peer admiration.

The purveyors of psychobabble of whatever stripe make the pitch that the only thing that stands in the way of the individual's quest for fame, fortune, or psychic health is lack of commitment to and mastery of a language of success. The clever cop-out for the sellers of confidence was that if one didn't succeed in social or psychic endeavor, it was your own fault in not truly grasping the linguistic discipline that was supposed to lead to success, and not the language itself (or the unforgiving marketplace or social structure). But the promise of success through linguistic assertion gave impetus to phony expressiveness: even if one didn't succeed in doing or feeling better, you could always fake it, showing off for others by asserting your familiarity with and adherence to the rhetorical principles laid down by the psychobabblers. You risked being labeled a brag and a bore, but you could also impress with your grasp of the language of success.

POLITICOBABBLE: THE PHONY LANGUAGES OF POLITICS

It has long been argued by political critics that the languages of politics are phony, masking interests and misleading the public. Indeed, it can even be argued, as some interpreters of Machiavelli have asserted, that political language is inherently phony, that the only possible way to rule is through humbuggery and expressive fraudulence. Language is used by political spokespersons in order to "clothe" the exercise of power in terms and images that make rule acceptable. Political language "phonies up" situations and policies, allowing politicians to define a situation in the best possible light and conduct policies that are justified as beneficent. It may well be the case that situations (crime, for instance) are out of political control, and policies are ineffective or unbeneficial, but one cannot say so. Quite the opposite, politics is one area of social action in which the successful politician has to tihsllub his or her way through. For a wide variety of reasons of power, political groups have to create forms of talk we may call *politicobabble*. If the art of government is maintaining or changing the facade of government to advantage, the artifices of language are the discursive forms that effectuate the holding or gaining of power.

Aside from propaganda, politicobabble also includes such forms of talk as *ideologese, policywonkese*, and *bureaucratese*. Ideologese refers to a fashionable form of political talk associated with a political ideology. Like those drawn to psychobabble because it makes them feel attractive and trendy, people also learn a language of politics in order to become part of a political movement because it is the current fashion. Ideological movements obviously include many sincerely drawn to the ideas (some quite fanatically), but they also include those who are there to associate themselves with the political smart talk of the moment. Political phonies enjoy being able to spout the litany of a political ideology for the same self-aggrandizing reasons of psychobabble, to be able to say the politically "in" thing for the right audience. This is not so much ideological articulation, the forensic development of ideas, as it is ideological self-assertion, the display of fashionable ideas the phony has had the trendy good sense to embrace since they are "hot" at the moment. This was the case with the "conservative" movement of the 1970s and 1980s, which became the intellectual driving force behind the Reagan ascendancy. Along with the many committed conservatives were the political phonies who leapt onto the political bandwagon and asserted themselves as "new conservatives" or "neo-conservatives" when it fact they had no interest in conserving anything, but did have great interest in advancing their own self-importance. Thus the new shibboleths of ideologese could be mouthed as meaningful concepts or meaningless jabber, depending upon one's motives. The fashionably phony conservative associated herself or himself with emotive terms such as "family values," "empower," "magic of the marketplace," "pro-life," "Christian America," and "rewarding success," and dissociated himself or herself with pejorative terms such as "liberal," "anti-America," "corruption," "welfare cheaters," "tax and spend," "babykillers," "secular humanism," and so on. Such smart talk becomes for the phony a vehicle of expressive rather than political power, increasing personal ego strength rather than political dialogue. Conservative rhetoric becomes a form of Orwellian doubleplusgood duckspeaking, mouthing the "right" phrases for the purpose of political showing off.

Similarly, political phonies can pick up on the pretentious use of the language of policy formulation and articulation, turning it into a pretentious exercise in expressing knowledgeability. Policywonking became fashionable in the 1990s with the proliferation of think tanks, conferences, and policy journals, not to mention "wonks" (people devoted to talking about public policy). But policy talk can serve phony purposes also: one can weasel into the good graces of powerful people by bespeaking the currently fashionable policy jargon: "reinventing government," "information superhighway," "community policing," "managed competition," and so on, as well as the more arcane lingo of policy studies, such as "opportunity costs," "regressive effects," "fiscal discipline," "micromanagement," "visceral policies," and "intervention strategies." For the astute political exhibitionist, a new phraseology must be mastered with the change in political fashion; policy terms, like ideologies, are abandoned like yesterday's ties or skirts when they are out of vogue. For the political phony, political vocabularies are just one more resource to be used for public display; the words they utilize have no inherent but have much exhibitory meaning. Political phonies are the camp followers of the political wars, changing loyalties and rhetoric easily and cynically to exploit the latest smart talk.

Bureaucratese is smart talk that serves a variety of political functions, including phonying up things. A situation unmastered or policy that has been a failure calls for the use mystifying language that couches things so as to dodge or hide the truth. Diplomatic or military language will often speak of unmastered situations in such terms, that "frank and substantive talks are under way but many issues remain to be addressed" (the talks are deadlocked) or that "a tactical redeployment was called for under the circumstances" (we had to retreat). The phony languages of diplomacy or war mystify rather than clarify. War, for example, is bloody business that no one likes to talk about baldly. So euphemistic and jargonistic language is used to make the awful sound not so bad. In recent wars, we have had "weapons systems" which "visited" the enemy with "ordnance," which "suppressed their assets" and "degraded" their abilities, although occasionally there was "collateral damage" with "incontinent ordnance." In other words: we shot at them with our weapons and killed a lot of them, but sometimes we also killed civilians with bombs that didn't work right. In the appropriate year 1984, the U.S. State Department decided that in its annual reports on human rights around the world it would no longer use the word "killing" and would use instead "unlawful or arbitrary deprivation of life," apparently to avoid bald discussion of government-sanctioned killings among governments supported by the United States. Bureaucratic smart talk sanitizes bad situations, and it also sugarcoats policies. A tax is a mechanism to finance government through levies on the citizenry, extracting money from them that accumulates in government treasuries for official use. But taxes are burdensome and onerous, and no one likes to say they're for them. So for the bureaucracy they become "revenue enhancements," "rate adjustments," or "user fees." Bureaucratese, or gobbledygook, then, becomes a language of phony terms, since their inception is an act of design that obfuscates the truth about taxes, war, or whatever. (Legalese is that branch of bureaucratic language that mystifies the law, making it forbidding and arcane, beyond the capacity of ordinary people, and thereby maintaining control of the legal system with lawyers and their powerful clients.) Phony language becomes a misleading and obfuscating defense of what is done in the corridors of power, phonied up in words that don't tell us what is actually happening. It should be noted that bureaucratic language, especially the technical languages of such government enterprises as space shots and warfare, can become fashionable. Phonies can master the lingo of NASA or military adventures such as the Gulf War to display their grasp of the techniques of Mars probes, Patriot missiles, and the like.[11]

Ideologese, policywonkese, and bureaucratese are all political languages that have phony uses. The Orwellian argument that political language can corrupt thought is true enough, to which we may add that it also corrupts discourse. Phonies are a corrupting influence in politics, since they are using language for deceptive purposes. If phony language becomes the dominant discourse of politics, then people may be excused for believing that politics is a phony enterprise designed to con us into subjection and manipulation. Phonies do not either mean what they say or say what they mean, and if we believe that politics is dominated by such people, it may be the case that we may "tune out" the pretentious smart talk of political spokespersons for something more edifying.

NEWSTALK: MEDIA GOSSIPING AND OPINIONATING

The phony languages we have identified in some measure are all the creation of professions. Fast talk emanates from professional advertisers, slick talk from public relations professionals, big talk from promoters, and smart talk from various babblers pitching some kind of phony argot. Below we will examine a linguistic creation of academic professionals, "politically correct" language. Here let us look at the creation of phony language among professional journalists, what we will term *newstalk*. Newstalk does not refer to the strict objective reportage of facts, difficult enough to do in itself. Rather it refers to the trend among visible news professionals to become commentators on the news, becoming gossip and opinion leaders. Newstalk is professional talk about news in media forums, in which more and more celebrity news reporters become "analysts," "discussants," or "pundits," interpreting the news for our benefit. As it has developed over the last few years, newstalk is a form of mass-mediated smart talk, wherein the reporter-interpretant humanizes, and largely trivializes, the news by placing it in the context of "human interest" gossip and celebrity-reporter "take" on unfolding events and processes. Professional journalists are acquiring a juridical and doctrinal mode of expression through mediated newstalk, whereby they pretend to speak as with authority.

The development of newstalk came about for several reasons. For one thing, the national news has changed: news is now extremely competitive, threatened by the multiplicity of channels with the proliferation of cable TV and alternative presses and publications, and desperate to attract and maintain news audiences. For another, "tabloidization" has invaded the respectable "mainstream" press, since a public eager for gossip, inside dope, and scandal has been increasingly fed this by news tabloids (*National Inquirer* and the like); tabloid TV (*Inside Edition, Hard Copy*, and so on; talk radio and talk TV; and news programs that purport to be "investigative reporting" (*60 Minutes* and its many copiers) but in fact are tabloidistic sensational stories. Finally, national reporters in key positions (e.g., covering the White House, writing a column) have become celebrities whose fame gives them a kind of communicative status, wherein they have the wisdom and authority to speak on a variety of important matters, and indeed define what is and what is not important. In all cases, the reporter acquires the air of a judgmental and social authority, for whom the world does not live up to his or her standards and expectations and which must be exposed and condemned. The world is deemed thoroughly postlapsarian, devoid of inherent social merit or moral worth. The celebrity-reporter stands above and apart from this fallen and irredeemable world, but like a newshawking grand inquisitor, must pronounce her or his verdict on the miasma of iniquity that bedevils the wicked world.

The difficulty with this development is that the celebrity-reporter is very often a phony. Because of the collapse of moral authority elsewhere, journalists have taken on an authoritative role for which they are not qualified nor able to sustain without challenge. For such roles as celebrity-reporter invite the ascendancy of the phony who sees such a social opening as a chance to exalt his or her own ego before the world. The phony celebrity-reporter has no interest in the traditional functions of newsgathering and reporting, or uncovering the truth; rather, the interest is in using one's position in a role of news authority to aggrandize one's public fame and reputation as a social authority. To do so, the celebrity-reporter cultivates the arts of smart talk in the context of the "news cycle," becomes a communicative practitioner of *smartspeak*, the ability to sound to mass audiences, and to one's reporter-peers, as someone who speaks as with authority. Smartspeak is a matter of tihsllubing, using the rhetoric of various media forums to promote oneself as both social and moral authority. The goal is self-promotion, which can be gained by using the forums available to impress audiences and peers with one's insight. But the typical media forums—the news talk shows, newspaper columns, talk radio, etc.—favor glibness and not thoughtfulness, instant "sound bites" or clever phrases rather than logical development, topical focus on today's happenings rather than the larger view of historical and social change. The successful celebrity-reporter is a discursive artist pretending to be an authority figure to whom we must defer and listen; but the ability to smartspeak doesn't mean they are smart, only able to make the superficial sound profound.

The newstalk of pundits, commentators, and reporters arose in the social context of large-scale and complex processes, such as the growth of bureaucracy, the innovations of technology, and vast demographic and economic changes. In the popular press, this created an opening for news personages to become famous for speaking about current affairs without actually knowing what they are talking about. Frankfurt notes that "(tihsllub) is unavoidable whenever circumstances require someone to talk without knowing what he is talking about. Thus the production of (tihsllub) is stimulated whenever a person's obligations or opportunities to speak about some topic are more extensive than his knowledge of the facts that are relevant to that topic."[12] Celebrity-reporters are given the opportunity to speak on a variety of subjects of which their qualifications or research efforts are scant; thus they have to *appear* to be authoritative, which requires that they B.S. their way through. The practice of journalistic commentary and opinionating becomes a con job, something that attracts phonies trying to make a name for themselves. The contemporary celebrity-journalist is undaunted by complexity or scale, since she or he is not burdened by knowledge of history or social science (not to mention philosophy), nor much research into their contemporary subjects. (It is not uncommon for well-known reporters to publish books about current affairs that were in fact ghost-written by other writers; the publication is designed to support their claim to punditic status, to illuminate themselves rather than the world.) Ignorance of subject matter can be faked through the clever expression of pretentious smartspeak that allows one to talk impressively without knowing what one is talking about.

Let us point to three outcomes of the proliferation of the celebrity-journalist commentator: the spread of "take journalism," the gossip allowed by "lateral attribution," and the popularization of commentary with the growing centrality of the journalistic pundit. Contemporary celebrity-reporters pride themselves not on their research or sources but on their "take" about things. Fact or historical context is now regarded as ephemeral and irrelevant; what is relevant and important is the celebrity-reporter's perception, judgment, and conclusion about things on his or her own. Ambitious journalists (there are more than 17,000 in Washington alone) trying to make or advance a name for themselves see themselves as "professional explainers" who draw attention to themselves, and achieve commentator or punditic status, by constructing plausible arguments made up of metaphorical "sound bites" and quick logic that affects the "conventional wisdom" of the capital's press corps and gains national attention. They realize that they must operate in the news cycle "context of no context" and make news from nowhere if they are to succeed; they are in a "perception competition" that usually vastly exceeds the significance, or endurance, of the event, person, or whatever under press consideration. News, after all, celebrates newness; news commentary must be equally produced to remain fresh and maintain the reputation of the commentator. John Taylor notes that the "competition among pundits to see whose view prevails depends less on the inherent validity of the position than on the rhetorical skill with which it is put forward."[13] The celebrity-reporter can thus demonstrate intellectual superiority impressive to popular audiences and peer groups by smartspeaking his or her "take" on things, on the pretense that such an uninformed but glib "take" is authoritative and not self-serving. The "take" of the celebrity-reporter is thus a phony stance, motivated by the fierce competition among such pretenders to become the center of attention and achieve the status rewards desired, often by staying one step ahead of the rest of the press corp and saying something new if equally preposterous. A related practice that facilitates the legitimation of gossip is "lateral attribution" (sometimes called "rubber glove journalism"). In this practice, the journalist affects not a pseudo-authoritative "take" on things, but rather attributes to some unnamed and vague source the existence of a story ("a story is circulating") that has no factual base or perhaps any relevance to anything, except the fame of the celebrity-reporter. Thus the existence of rumor, real or created, is legitimated as newsworthy, and placed in the "inside dope" context of "people are talking about X"; since they allegedly are, the intrepid investigative reporter knows about X; this then allows the discussion of the most outrageous and unsubstantiated rumors, and of course "my take" commentary on what this does to X. Gossip becomes not only newsworthy, but also the core of news, further "tabloidizing" the news by focusing attention on, for example, soap opera politics (who is mad at whom, who's "in" and "out" at the White House, what politician is dating what celebrity); destructive accusations that public figures have to defend, undermining their reputation and effectiveness whether they are true or not; and a penchant for scandal, going into a "feeding frenzy" over rumors of high-level intrigue and malfeasance, again true or not. The "Whitewater" affair that emerged in 1993-94 was a classic example of rumor-mongering through lateral attribution; press careers were advanced by reporters who constructed elaborate and sinister conspiracies—vaguely resembling the plot of a John Grisham novel—based on nothing more substantial than rumor-mongering ("people are talking about Vince Foster's death") and endless competition for a new "take" ("this new charge raises questions for this reporter about the Clintons"). Such practices are the product of phony journalism, a virtual pseudo-reality of non-existent relations and events unburdened by the leaven of fact, now deemed irrelevant by the celebrity-reporter.

The competitive quest for status rewards among celebrity-journalists is evident in the coverage of campaigns for president. Thomas E. Patterson studied the coverage of such campaigns from 1960 through 1992 and discovered that news coverage of presidential candidates has become increasingly more negative in tone and portrayal, to the point of suggesting the candidates are unworthy to become president. Secondly, he discovered that the journalist had superseded the candidate as the focal point of election coverage, elevating the journalist's voice as more important than the candidate's words. Finally, Patterson found that journalists covering campaigns saw the introduction of policy proposals as a strategy of the election game rather than an effort to discuss and create alternatives to problems. All these changes occurred during the time that news reporting moved from description to interpretation, with the celebrity-reporter becoming the hero of communication, thereby becoming increasingly negative and cynical in tone, focused on melodramatic controversy, and calling positive attention to the celebrity-reporter himself or herself. In order to self-cast the celebrity-reporter as the hero of the drama, it is necessary then to altercast the candidate as the villain or fool, someone who is beneath contempt and who must be exposed and condemned. The campaign press's celebrity-reporters thus ask us to mistrust everything the candidates do, but to trust them as sources of truth and guardians of right. However, the introduction of such cynicism poisons the well, since the public becomes distrustful of all parties to campaigning, including the press, which it ranks lower in trust than the candidates, the talk show hosts, and even the political consultants![14] Perhaps people sense that the celebrity-reporters are phonies who represent themselves as juridical and doctrinal authorities deserving of trust, when in fact they are self-glorified news readers trying to "phony up" news stories that will promote their own careers. In historical fact, all this savaging of the political system and its leading figures comes at a time not only when news competition has become more intense but when the "mainstream" press (TV networks, the national news-papers, the news magazines) has dwindling relevance for the public or for the attention of media consumers. The dynamics of "take" journalism and "lateral attribution" occurs in an atmosphere of Hobbesian conflict between celebrity-reporters for attention and status, making their reportage all the more focused on phony stories emanating from gossip, rumor, hearsay, and the like, and manufacturing stories from virtual news reality of scandal, conspiracy, malfeasance, corruption, sexual misconduct, and apocalyptic predictions of doom. It is no wonder increasing numbers of people, knowing phony stuff when they smell it, tune out.

These transitions in the rhetoric of news are most evident in the proliferation of the professional smartspeakers of the media, known collectively as *pundits*. Originally a "pandit" in India was a wise man steeped in wisdom, but the word has been corrupted into referring to anyone who does media commentary. In the contemporary media culture, wisdom is a matter of successful self-promotion, conning peers and audiences into believing that you know what you are talking about. The scam is that reporters, somehow by dint of their professional experience and status with a news organization, possess some kind of superior knowledge that gives them superior insight into the contemporary world. The TV punditic groups, the newspaper columnists, the talk radio hosts, guest pundits that appear on business, political, or cultural shows—all are supposed to communicate "expertise," thoughtful reflection on current affairs. Instead, they have demonstrated the principle that phony language tends to drive intelligent language out, and have tended toward shouting matches, egotistic self-exaltation, rumor-mongering, partisan or ideological duckspeaking, and cynical self-promotion. Thoughtful language is replaced by pretentious language. Rather than draw attention to ideas to be reflected upon, increasingly the pundits perform to draw attention to themselves to be celebrated as famous media authorities. Less and less are they journalists in the traditional sense, and more and more are they media figures whose expertise is in rhetorical tihsllubing about the news. They are not well-informed or even intelligent, but display talent in evoking emotional assertions, polarizing debates, name-calling, indeed the whole range of pitches that appeal to glandular responses among their auditors. The popularity of radio talk shows is the paradigm case: intellectuals like David S. Broder or George Will are heeded less than populist cynics such as Rush Limbaugh and Howard Stern. The TV and radio punditic shows are organized increasingly around the conventions of entertainment rather than high-level policy or situational discussion. Like the celebrity-reporter making himself or herself the hero of the campaign and the candidate as the villain or fool, the pundit seeks to dominate a forum wherein she or he can vilify the politicians of the moment and what they are trying to do. The tone of punditry becomes an arrogant exercise in wild speculation, personal attack, and contemptuous bluster. The forum becomes a medium to display the ego of the pundit, not to illuminate the political process; the celebrity-pundit looks on opinionating about politics and society as a way to increase ratings and fame. Punditry becomes entertainment, a way for the commentator to aggrandize fame and make big money. The scam is for the pundit to accuse everyone else of being a phony, and thus a legitimate object of hate and distrust. Limbaugh has excoriated everyone from the president to inner-city schoolteachers, conjuring up wondrous and apocryphal fairy tales about those we should distrust (e.g., expenditures per classroom is such that we could provide chauffeured limousines for teachers, or that the hated "liberals'" espousal of ending discrimination is "phony"). Limbaugh and Stern are only the most egregious examples of the deterioration of public discourse into savage and puerile nonsense, but they augur the future. The difficulty is that such figures are themselves phonies whose egotistical and hypocritical quest for fame and riches will impel them to say anything about anybody if it benefits their own careers. (Limbaugh, for instance, expended much smart talk about Bill Clinton's draft record during the 1992 campaign, without mentioning the fact that Limbaugh himself avoided the Vietnam draft allegedly through the intervention of his rich and influential family in Missouri, with the convenient discovery that he had a polonoidal cyst—ingrown hair on his considerable backside—which gained him an I-Y classification from his local draft board and avoidance of combat service.[15]) Celebrity-pundits, then, may be usefully understood as media phonies who gain fame and fortune by offensive and sneering pretension, setting standards they cannot themselves live up to and making social observations they themselves cannot defend. Their lucrative smart talk enjoys success among those who are equally as ignorant and distrustful, but it does little to elevate public discourse or encourage enlightenment or trust. The celebrity-pundit is a pure and simple confidence man, enamored with the power to destroy reputations, policy innovations, and perhaps even rend the fabric of society through the poison of his or her widely exhibited cynicism.

ACADEMESE: THE LANGUAGE OF POLITICAL CORRECTNESS

Much of the phony language discussed above comes about through its exploitation by phonies. The language of ideology or policy, for instance, may have merit in political discussion, but it is badly used by phonies with the ambition to make themselves the center of attention. Many celebrity-reporters and pundits have no convictions outside of their own advancement and wealth, so they use language to self-promote rather than advance a cause or enlighten the public. But it is also the case that phony language may be created by people who are quite sincere, in an earnest attempt to deal with a sensitive social problem. Such is the case, at least in part, in the emergence of "politically correct" language on college campuses in the form of speech codes and other official mechanisms designed to impose a kind of "sensitive orthodoxy" of speech, and by extension, of thought and emotion. Faced with growing diversity and the "politics of identity" on campuses, many college administrators responded with the imposition of such mechanisms to deal with a difficult situation. Most of the people who designed "politically correct" languages were in dead earnest, but what emerged became the object of scorn and ridicule, both by libertarians who saw such codes as a restriction of freedom of speech and thought, and by cynics and reactionaries (such as Limbaugh, who found them great sport, but erroneously thought their designers just as cynically motivated as he) who felt apparently that racist and sexist speech was still quite legitimate. In any case, the spread of "political correctness" (P.C.) on college campuses and elsewhere demonstrates how the road to discursive hell can be paved with good intentions.

The difficulty is that P.C. is a phony language, a "sensitized" alternative to traditional or more direct language. With the substitution of "correct" terms for the usual ones, the language becomes a form of doublespeak, a way to not say what you mean but rather say what is approved as correct. When imposed by academic or other authorities, it becomes a new kind of orthodoxy. It is one thing to enforce a rule that one cannot call other people who are different a dirty name (which is punishable under assault laws about "fighting words"), but it quite another to insist that some social group be given an official title and status that demonstrates official sensitivity to their problems and plight. By such linguistic logic, minorities become "people of color"; a young girl is a "prewoman"; pets are "animal companions"; the stupid are "cerebrally challenged"; one does not fail a test, but rather "achieves a deficiency"; the bald are "hair disadvantaged." Such language reforms enforce a sensitivity that, if nothing else, is downright precious. (Some colleges have even attempted to punish people for laughing at the "wrong kind" of jokes, saying the "wrong thing" in class, or having the wrong kind of emotional responses to other people.) The movement extended to attempting to have P.C. Halloweens which eliminated the figure of the witch, since that image reflected stereotypes of gender and age, and somehow enforcing sexual harassment rules down to kindergarten level (one college instituted "may I" rules, insisting that in sexual encounters, the one party to the passion had to ask the other permission to proceed to another level of intimacy!). Somehow the establishment of rules of sexual or social etiquette and the magical language of euphemism will eliminate conflict, prejudice, and exploitation. For academicians in particular, it commits them to a program of curtailing freedom of thought and expression that one might have thought they would ardently defend; instead they developed a substitutionary language that is so phony that it invites ridicule from the very people who oppose their agenda of change. Like the pundits, the academic bureaucrats who made up P.C. vocabularies didn't know quite what to say or do in the new academic situation of diversity, so with all good intentions they tried to turn plain language into more "sensitive" tihsllub. Phony languages do not invite thought about real social problems and choices; rather they sugarcoat the world in a more pleasant and orthodox form of talk that restricts rather than enhances critical and careful thinking. P.C. is a synthetic language that is predicated on the preposterous assumption that formal rules of speech change the world. If one says things in a sensitive way, evil and injustice are magically banished. This is the kind of mystical attribution to the power of language that propagandists, babblers, and pundits have used and exploited. The P.C. advocates are "discursively challenged" (to invent a P.C. term): they need to recall the Orwellian task to make language precise and clear, and do away with any political or academic agenda that turns their greatest tool for understanding into phony doubletalk. They should also remember the contemporary graffito: "Nothing political is correct."

CONCLUSION

Phony language pervades our culture. Many people for a wide variety of motives speak in phony tongues, using the magical resources of language in order to "phony up" something. Phony language builds facades, discursive Potemkin villages that allow the perpetuator the leeway to tihsllub his or her way through. Language is a matter of discursive display, telling people what form of snake oil they should buy this time. Whatever her or his intentions, the communicator has an interest in giving linguistic shape to the thought of others for reasons they are not supposed to fully understand. Even the sincere P.C. terminologists are propagating a message of sensitivity they well know is not fully understood or shared by students, but which they are sure will be edifying for them. Language becomes an agency of pretension, making the word and image mystifying forms of discourse that spread influence but not enlightenment. Our penchant for phony language indicates our dissociative state, since phony language describes a world in which meaning has been eroded and discourse has become poisonous. A phony culture is not without consequences, and it remains for us now to outline some of the ways in which our phony thought and language have become manifest.

CHAPTER 2

PHONY PEOPLE

✦   ✦   ✦

We have developed the argument that the source of malaise in American society is the pervasion of phoniness, and that this is exemplified by the use of phony languages. A phony society gives credence to games of confidence, with language used not to illuminate but to convince. The theory and practice of confidence-making, and the ingrained use of the languages of confidence, make for the creation of the conditions of phoniness. Thus the "human condition" in America becomes ripe for the ascendancy of the phony person, the "operator" whose triumph has been one of the most important developments in American culture. In order to understand contemporary America, we must understand the phony, the con artist who exercises the most fundamental entitlement in our society, the rationalized self-interest that provides "moral" justification for the right to win, and to display that winning by "showing off" in public. We shall here examine various cultural manifestations that incur the presence of phony people.

We might begin by invoking one of the most acute observers of the American social scene, J.D. Salinger's character named Holden Caulfield in *The Catcher in the Rye*. Holden's adolescent odyssey through New York's nighttown brings him in contact with various people he deems "phonies." Phonies are everywhere, using language to display their own beauty, intellect, and wit, be they piano players in a bar, the attenders of a play, celebrities being conspicuously seen, actors overacting and hamming—all in all a social collection of bores and snobs and frauds putting on a facade. Society is an ecology of affectation, phony people trying to gain some kind of advantage or make some kind of impression.

Holden's phonies were limited to urban dwellers attempting to appear urbane. But we may here note that the social ecology of phony people extends more broadly. Economic phonies, for instance, include those people trying to con us into buying goods,

71

services, or ideas that we might not otherwise desire. Political phonies are trying to persuade us to "buy" some kind of political message of dubious benefit. Cultural phonies are trying to sell some cultural object, either themselves or something equally bogus. Phonies can be found everywhere, from local people "putting on airs" for their friends and neighbors to celebrities attending a big event covered by the media to con artists making up the latest advertising or promotional scheme. All phonies share in common the effort to gain other people's confidence, when it may not be warranted. Beyond that, they display a variety of motives and actions.

Many social phonies that Salinger's hero observed are motivated by a kind of narcissism, whereby the individual hopes to attract people's attention and admiration through dramatic posturing. In its extreme form, this is manifest in shameless and often lurid exhibitionism; in its more socially acceptable forms, this behavior appears as "legitimate exhibitionism," in which the individual desires to be seen as someone to whom social groups or society in general should pay attention. Through self-dramatization, the individual becomes the center of attention, the star of the show, the one others wish to observe. Such individuals are usually "on," self-conscious of the role they are playing and hoping to make a good impression. As Laurence Oliver remarked to Dustin Hoffman when he inquired why Oliver became an actor, Sir Laurence replied, "Look at me, look at me, look at me." Social narcissists are actors who are definitely on, exhibiting the "public self" they wish to present to "significant others," those whose attention they wish to command. They may very well enact their part in social dramas at "role distance," separating a private and unpresented self from the public self they want the world to see. But the common impulse is to invite the social gaze, urging through performance a sustained and impressed "look at me."[1]

But that is not the only thing that phony people do. There is often another message, "Look at that!" rather than "Look at me!" A debutante, an athlete, a society matron, a playboy, a new professor—all may want to command attention from impressionable audiences. But others may want to call attention to what they are doing or "hawking." The salesperson or spokesperson is selling something, and wants to make the thing rather than the self the object of others' desire: "Look at this!" A car salesperson may be "on," presenting his best role behavior, but his effort is to direct our attention at the car of our dreams. The spokesperson for, say, a corporation or politician puts on a happy face for the press, but the object of a "press briefing" (after, for instance, an event such as an oil spill by a corporate tanker or a breaking scandal) is to call attention to the message, in effect "Look at this explanation of that!" The social narcissist wishes to dramatize the self through exhibitive behavior; the social messenger wishes to dramatize the message through behavior that exhibits not the message, "Look at me" but rather "Look at that." The former asks you to trust your eyes and ears as you look at them; the latter asks you to trust your eyes and ears as you see and hear the message. For the narcissist, the public self is the message; for the messenger, the message delivered is the point of self-presentation. The narcissist is self-serving; the messenger serves the boss. In the latter case, the message is often "Look at him" or "Look at her," pointing out why their employer should be the object of our attention and admiration. The boss is the "this" that should be gazed upon, as the "mouthpiece" for this paragon of virtue, wisdom, and power tells us.

In all cases, the language of trust is used to invite us not only to believe and admire but also to have confidence. The narcissist asks us to trust them as deserving to be the center of attention; the salesperson asks us to trust their judgment in directing our attention to things we should want; the spokesperson asks us to trust their explanation of things, including events and personages. In all cases, the role-player is dramatizing something, either self, object, or exalted person. We are asked to suspend disbelief and accept the role as presented. The difficulty is that we are being asked to trust something that is patently phony. The role-player here is constructing a theatrical facade through the use of the languages of histrionics. What we are seeing lacks authenticity. The person becomes a personage, a construction that displays phony characteristics. Salinger's urbane phonies, for instance, are trying hard to dramatize themselves as having the characteristics of cosmopolite urbanity—sophistication, fashionability, knowledgeability, wit and charm and grace as defined by New York culture. The narcissist is often driven to peacock displays of personage, communicating to others the surface beauty of the self-loved being. But the salesperson or spokesperson is equally committed to direct our attention to the beloved object, be it a foreign sports car or a presidential candidate. The advertiser urges us to love the beloved object that we should wish to buy; the press secretary frames the politician as a worthy object of popular desire. Such personages and things are deemed to be trustworthy (or with specifically sexual objects of desire, lustworthy), as ones in whom, or in which, confidence can be placed. But here confidence is sought:

the phony seeks trust for manipulatory purposes by projecting an inauthentic being-in-role. With the phony, what we see is not what we get. The phony is a *poseur*, and the pose has a purpose beyond the magic associated with the personage or object.

With Holden Caulfield, we observe phonies everywhere, from the exalted ranks of the rich and famous to more modest folks in towns and neighborhoods. American life has increasingly given credence and opportunities to phonies, since it is not nature or industry but rather relationships that must be mastered. In an organizational and artificial world of uncertain and negotiable relations, phoniness can pay off. The Goffmannesque "presentation of self in everyday life" involves the use of histrionic resources in order to achieve desired results in human relations.[2] Rather than the conquest of nature or of the brute objects of production, increasingly our efforts are directed at the conquest of negotiations. In both work and play relations, we are much interested in mastering the arts of persuasion and inducement, since social payoffs emerge from convincing people to believe in us and do our bidding. In a relational universe, we all become social entrepreneurs, selling ourself and our wares in the marketplace of relationships. (This is one of Tocqueville's great observations, as when he notes that in America "no natural boundary seems to be set to the efforts of man.")

The widespread pursuit of the confidence of others gives rise to a pattern of behavior ingrained in our social beings. There have been various attempts to codify this phenomenon. One observer notes that the contemporary "self-process" gives rise to a social chameleon, termed "protean man" after the god Proteus, who could change shapes easily as the occasion dictated. The modern sense of "dissociation" gives impetus to a diffusion of identity, a sense of absurdity, and often a "protean style," wherein the individual *uses* the resources of self-flexibility in order to dominate situations. In a world of incoherence, those willing and able to project a momentary and attractive image give us the illusion of coherence, eliciting our confidence in them.[3] If we look at them, wonderful and magical consequences flow.

The protean style involves a principle of theatricality. In a world of negotiated relationships, advantages go to those able to enact roles with histrionic skill. Many of us are no longer "inner-directed," taking moral and behavioral cues from "inner gyroscopes," nor are we "other-directed," taking cues from other people in a reflexive way; rather, we are "performance-directed," relating to other people as if in dramatic roles, eliciting their confidence through performance. Performance-direction means that the confidence-seeker is not "on the level"; rather the effort is to influence without being influenced in return, using protean adaptivity to make people do one's bidding without significant reciprocity. The performer wishes to put others in the role of auditor, reacting rather than acting, and minimizing critical evaluation and maximizing uncritical approval of the performance. The social performer trades in confidence, gained through popularity, understanding that popularity is gained through people suspending disbelief and allowing themselves to be charmed by the performance. The "performance artist" is a fictive personage, acting out for auditors the impressions she or he wants to convey, aiming to maintain the fiction of self, of who and what I want you to believe I am.[4]

Such a social personality is a phony, characterized by the commitment to opportunism of relationships. The opportunist is rooted deep in American history, but contemporary opportunism involves not so much the mastery of industrial organization or other traditional power roles as it does the mastery of publicity. Rather than the will to power, we now speak of the will to fame. Reputation mattered in previous eras to those who sought high office or even merely local leadership roles, but it was the perception that one deserved power because of moral rectitude, distinguished social service, or familial distinction. Typically, cultural heroes were distinctive because of achievement, and reputation accompanied their social ascendancy. But they were expected to be authentic, "solid citizens" solicitous of their social standing and convinced of the legitimacy of the social order. Although they may well have believed none of the "great words" of the rhetorical order, they were expected (as Woodrow Wilson remarked) to believe all the things they told the children. They were not thought to be phonies. That would gradually change through the alchemy of mass publicity, and the ascendancy of the desire for fame. The resources of phoniness would serve well when it became important to become important in a new way, through the mastery of popular reputation.

THE CELEBRATION OF THE CELEBRATED

It is fair to say that there have always been phonies. In the Biblical account of Genesis, perhaps Satan was the first con artist. We have also noted that the confidence man is a major "character motif" in American culture. With our pursuit of "social goods"—wealth, status, power, conquest—becoming a phony has its uses. But what is different is that increasingly we admire and exalt phonies, expect people who pursue social goods to be phonies, and indeed have difficulty believing that anyone of consequence is not a phony. Much of this is related to the rise of the celebrity as a dominant social actor, and the spread of the principle of celebrated being into every area of social life.

In some measure, the astonishing ascent of celebrity is rooted in a shift from emphasis on class to status. As one famous study found, whereas formerly we admired "heroes of production" (including captains of industry, prominent politicians, clerics and academicians distinguished in philistine ecclesiastical or academic circles), we came to admire "heroes of consumption" (athletes, movie stars, "cafe society," even criminals if they were dashing and rich).[5] A prominent person with good reputation had class, either in the sense of social standing (the "ruling class") or was "classy" (in the sense of good taste or *noblesse oblige*). But in recent America, this was superseded in importance by a new kind of status. Traditionally, clerics or academicians might not be rich or positioned, so they lacked social class standing; but they did have status by dint of their social reputation as pious or learned. But with the rise of heroes of consumption, *popular status* become important. It mattered less about class standing and traditional status, and mattered more about popularity. One could acquire popular status—a reputation for fame—without having class standing or even respectability. As America became more democratic, it become a popular society; as it became a popular society, it increasingly valued personages who acquired popular status.

It is ironic that in large measure the celebrity originated in those American circles of wealth wherein their social anxieties led families to assert their social superiority. Veblen long ago satirized the "leisure class" as characterized by an early effort to appear prominent, through practices such as "conspicuous consumption" and "pecuniary emulation." The "idle rich" of the Gilded Age evolved into "Old Money" with ambitions towards aristocracy. But as the twentieth century processed, these pretensions became more well-known, and the great fortunes and families (the Vanderbilts, Rockefellers, Mellons) became the object of mass-mediated interest. Soon the lure of publicity was deemed useful both in business (the Rockefellers hired publicity agent Ivy Lee after the Ludlow massacre) and in the pursuit of upper-class reputation (the activities of "the season" at Newport or for New York's debutante balls became the subject of press reportage). Rather than defining themselves as superior to the common herd by being publicity-shy, the super-rich found that they could better communicate their exalted status by the use of publicity. Indeed, as pretenders to high social position—such as Joseph P. Kennedy and William Randolph Hearst—emerged, they actively sought publicity that enhanced their social reputation. Further, the categories began to collapse: the offspring of the "bluebloods" could not resist commingling with the new celebrities from Hollywood and Broadway in the public environs of cafe society. The activities of "poor little rich girls" (Gloria Vanderbilt, Doris Duke, Barbara Hutton) became notorious; the scions of "high society" went into politics and courted public fame (the Kennedys, the Rockefellers, the Bushes); the heirs to great fortunes became the "angels" of Broadway and the backers of motion pictures, hoping to acquire some of the allure of famous stars. Whereas high society had been for a time the focus of mass envy and resentment (as evidenced in the "screwball" movie comedies of the Depression era), slowly what Veblen had called the "radiant body" of society was superseded by a more popular and certainly more democratic class, the Celebritocracy.[6] The precedence of Old Money, and the pretensions of New Money, were replaced by the new class of celebrities.

The rich, both old and new, had plenty of phonies. Wealthy people often like to have around them an entourage of toadies, flatterers, yes-men, gofers, camp-followers, and various hangers-on who phony up to the boss. And there is nothing quite as pathetically phony as "new rich" trying desperately to "put on airs," acquire class and taste, and associate with (and even marry) people of breeding and station (this is a common tale in American popular literature). The comic effect of, say, Texas *nouveau riche* attempting to "buy class" through the purchase of a mansion, impressionist paintings, ballet lessons for the daughter, and admission to Harvard for the son is considerable. They believe, not without some justification, that the way to acquire class in the traditional sense, is to become a phony— being seen in the right places with the right people and saying the right things. The "play-form of society" becomes a constant and subtle parlor game for the rich, no less silly and dangerous than the gamesmanship of the old European court societies. Patrician classes seem universally to sustain themselves through studied and practiced phoniness, rituals that convey their own aloof superiority.

The rise of celebrity robbed the rich of a mass audience for their snobbery. If no one cares who is listed in the Social Register, then why bother to belong? The "radiant bodies" of celebrity were chosen by the plebeians, in a sense; one "voted" for this or that public personage by attending their movies, reading their novels, or whatever. Celebrities became a new aristocracy, a new kind of cultural hero, a god or goddess of plebeian origins and identifications but exalted to patrician status. Hollywood was the latter-day Palatine Hill, with the familiar radiances of Pickford and Fairbanks living in the palace named Pickfair. The new gods of the movies were soon supplemented by athletes (Babe Ruth, Red Grange), writers (Fitzgerald, Hemingway), radio stars (Rudy Vallee), celebrity reporters (Ed Murrow), and so on. Celebrities were the spiritual descendants of the public rich, in that they were the focus of social fascination as "the show of society." Bagehot long ago had identified the deferential value in the great show of the English royal family and the ceremonial dignity of government and high society.[7] With celebrities, the expectation is deference for popular icons and images rather than the old political class and aristocratic order. The "celebrity order" is more fluid and diverse perhaps, but it is no less powerful. The success of Ronald Reagan in collapsing the categories of politics and celebrity is only the most spectacular manifestation of our will to fame.

In an important sense, all celebrities are phonies. The celebrity is a public personage who exists in popular reputation. Whereas the figures of high society had reputation through exalted social position, the figures of celebrity had position through exalted social reputation. One became a celebrity by being recognized as famous, as in Boorstin's definition of the celebrity as "a human pseudo-event" who is "known for his well-knownness."[8] Celebrities are the personages who need no further introduction, are instantly recognized, and at the height of their recognizability, have "fans" among the multitude. But a human pseudo-event is, in our sense, not real. A celebrity exists by reputation, a being who is important only in the minds of other people. He or she exists as a Big Name, a momentary plaything of a mass audience drawn to the public figure for vicarious purposes. When the audience for a celebrity loses interest, then the Big Name no longer exists. Celebrity existence is ephemeral, and increasingly it is difficult to sustain celebrityhood beyond a fleeting moment in cultural time, Andy Warhol's fifteen minutes. In any case, the work of the celebrity is to remain in the spotlight, and the great fear is to be out of sight. (The rich fear being out of money; the political class fears being out of power; the celebrity fears being out of view.) What we see is a designed being, an image "projected" to attract our attention, a "star" whose defining characteristic is his or her claim to fame. But the famous are different from you and me: they not only have fame, they also "live" in a virtual world that is to a large degree our creation. They depend upon our reception for their existence, but we do not "receive" them unless they delight and instruct us; but as virtual beings, they are there because we make them up. To be sure, there was a real Marion Michael Morrison, but a virtual "John Wayne" (Morrison's stage name); similarly, there was a real Norma Jean Baker, but a virtual "Marilyn Monroe." Such incorporeal beings are a kind of "imaginative universal," in that they serve a variety of popular functions, from the merely amusing to the deeply pathological to the highly mythical. But they do not exist apart from our collective interest in them.

The celebrity industry is a vast and perpetual enterprise, employing agents, news people, propagandists and spokespersons, technical personnel, and so on. Some people are born celebrities (John F. Kennedy, Jr.), others achieve celebrity (movie stars), and still others have celebrity thrust upon them (anyone who sues a celebrity and wins, commits a bizarre crime that captures national attention, or fights a big corporation). And, as Jimmy Durante said, everyone wants to get into the act. TV talk shows (Oprah Winfrey, Phil Donahue, Maury Povich, Geraldo Rivera, and so on) offer us the daily spectacle of ordinary folks who bare their souls, deepest and darkest secrets, trashy behavior, or whatever, for the amusement of the crowd. People seem willing to suffer the humiliation and embarrassment of public self-exposure in order to have a brief and fleeting moment in the limelight, however degrading. For such "momentary celebrity" on such shows is a degradation ceremony, a ritual of popular humiliation in which bizarre or errant members of society are savaged by a forum (the studio audience and callers) reminiscent of a Jacobin assembly. At a slightly more pathological level, would-be assassins and terrorists (including people who shoot up public places) are often motivated in part by the desire for quick fame and "instant immortality," and the knowledge that we will respond in horrified fascination at their actions. Since there is popular response to infamy as well as fame, people on the fringes are willing to commit infamous acts in order to enjoy the infamy, even if it leads to incarceration, death, or execution. What they do is quite awfully real, but for us they exist in a mediated realm of symbolic infamy, creatures of our popular demonology.

The phony realm of celebrity, then, is largely a matter of our popular creation. As the philosopher Vico long ago argued, we can only truly know what we create. The celebrity is a creature of our imagination, a pageant of heroes, villains, and fools who personify the mythography of our cultural maps. They are the insubstantial product of the process of mediation, whereby we focus on those popular creations which we choose at the moment, using them to delight and instruct us. They are both amusing and interesting, offering us a way to express sentiments and learn behavioral patterns. We are quite willing to be seduced by celebrities, and share the fiction that they have superhuman qualities in a superworld. Nietzsche's superman turns out to be Michael Jackson. Our transaction with them is mutually beneficial: they con us into believing in their celebrity, and we acquiesce in the con by enjoying the celebration. Celebrities become our popular royalty, the play-show of society of our immediate radiant beings.

Celebrities belong to us as playthings. Their lives are not their own: they have to lead phony lives if they expect to remain worthy of celebration. The principle of celebrity taken to the extreme allows them no private life, no "offstage" self, no quotidian reality to their "real life" apart from their fame. Their attempts at privacy, suppression of embarrassing pasts or behavior "out of character" for their public role, or efforts at avoiding the expectations of celebrity make us all the more curious about them. We love to both exalt and degrade them, finding them at once both admirable and contemptible. Like any other plaything, we use them for our purposes and then discard them when we no longer have any use for them. Celebrities become the victim of their own phoniness, disappearing when we no longer think of them; as insubstantial beings, they cannot survive our ceasing to play with them.

The principle of celebrity extends everywhere. Politicians, for example, are now celebrities; if they do not utilize the resources of celebrity, they risk losing the acclaim of political celebration. They must submit to the scrutiny, risk the danger of exposure, court popularity, and dread unpopularity. Positive celebration involves cooperating with the organs of celebrity. First Ladies, for instance, cultivate a popular image through interviews with women's magazines, having a project, touring hospitals, setting fashion styles, redecorating the White House, and so on. If successful, they can then stay on "most admired women" lists, enhancing her husband's political fortunes. But they can become the object of ridicule or contempt, as Nancy Reagan did when it was revealed that she set the president's schedule and perhaps influenced decisions through consulting an astrologer. Negative celebration relegates the political celebrity to a lower status. A respected senator becomes the object of feminist scorn when he is accused of sexual harassment, changing his status to that of an icon of powerful male exploitation of vulnerable women. Political celebrity can benefit the political figure if it contributes to popularity, but it can be destructive if it leads to unpopularity.

The celebrity principle also extends to incorporeal beings who are not real or alive. Our popular culture is quite capable of generating phony representations or composites that serve a variety of needs or respond to a range of desires. Our popular mythology has been enriched by fictional cartoon and puppet characters— Mickey Mouse, Bugs Bunny, Dick Tracy, The Muppets, Superman and Wonder Woman, Doonesbury, and so on. One of the most remarkable such creations is the doll known as "Barbie," the tall and svelte blonde goddess who so dominates the female play-doll market (Mattel announced that one-year sales for Barbie dolls and accessories had reached $1 billion). Barbie was a phony representation of a "perfect" middle-American young woman, as she was originally conceived in 1959: tall, blond, and beautiful, engaged in high consumer activities, owning a vast wardrobe, and aspiring to be a fashion model. The range of acceptable female roles has expanded for Barbie over the years, and she has involved herself in a wide variety of trendy or glamorous activities, from candy striper to stewardess to fashion designer to animal rights volunteer. Through it all, she remains beautiful and unaged, communicating to those who play with her the value of beauty and youth, commitment to fashion, and perhaps more subtly, the legitimacy of hedonism and sensuality. She is an unattainable ideal, and we can only speculate how much she contributes to disappointment in growing girls that they are not as beautiful and rich, the epidemic of anorexia and bulimia in teenagers, and the desire to act like adults, including acquiring fashions, using cosmetics, alcohol, and having sex. In the last instance, we may note that Barbie's emergence as a phony icon was contiguous with the popularity of *Playboy*, and that the air-brushed "Playmate" ideal favored tall and willowy blondes (Hugh Hefner always said that all he did was find prototypical "girls next door" and take their clothes off). Both Barbie and the Playmates led lives of fun and frivolity, basking in the glory of their eternal youth and voluptuousness. But they are a consumer-era version of physical beauty and fashionability. Recently they have been supplemented by the model, who has achieved celebrity status. No longer anonymous, the model has become subject to the laws of celebrity, accorded quick fame, gossip-column mention, expectation of being seen at the right places with the most fashionable people, and so on. Like the Playmate, their celebrity "shelf life" may be short-lived, since it is based in that most transitory of qualities, youthful beauty. Barbie has the distinct advantage of being wholly fictional, and thus has attained virtual immortality.

It is often said that celebrities are the new gods, attributed powers and abilities beyond the gods of Mt. Olympus. But they are phony gods, gods sought by us to fill the many voids in our own lives. They are the creatures of our collective wishes, beings who populate the country of our popular imagination. They can even acquire cultic status, functioning for us as surrogate saints and martyrs. James Dean's hometown and burial site (Fairmount, Indiana) is a pilgrimage site, where the faithful come to "worship" at the grave of the departed but curiously immortal youth, now immune from time. Marilyn Monroe has become a feminist icon, the girl-goddess who was martyred by the system of exploitation that made her into a celebrity in the first place but could not make her happy. She was a victim of the phony love transacted between her and her fans, which brought her much lust and notoriety but no real love. In death, Elvis Presley has become a cult figure, and the tabloids regularly report the latest sightings of "St. Elvis," including his intervening to comfort the troubled and heal the sick. These extremes suggest that celebrity worship is a phony religious experience, an idolatry of fame that leads ordinary people to seek sacred experience.

The confusion of religious and celebrity worship stems from the fact that the famous exist in a kind of status of transfiguration. They live in "the context of no context," a mass-mediated world of play, figurative rather than literal existence. Celebrities do not work, they play; they do not live out textual lives, they romp in contextual limbo, the never-never land of nowhere. The celebrated country of Nowhere is their true home, the elysian fields of fame to which only the gods of celebration are admitted. (Michael Jackson built a fun park, complete with merry-go-round and miniature railroad, on a ranch he named Neverland.) But it is a phony world full of phony creations, all of whom are anxious about enhancing the one thing that differentiates them from other and unheralded human beings, their claim to fame. We should remember the fundamental concept of celebrity epistemology: if we the people do not see them, they do not exist.

THE POPULAR PRACTICE OF PHONINESS

The social practice of celebrating human beings by virtue of their exalted status in society began with high society and reached its fruition with the expansive use of popular celebrities by the mass public. The well-known figures of "society," and their successors in the worlds of entertainment, were adept at the arts of affectation, putting on a show that confirmed their status as public celebrants. Self-dramatization communicated the phony personage one claimed to be for the willing confirmation of amused and instructed auditors. The quality of phoniness worked to make one conspicuous, largely as a figure of play which people found interesting as a representation of the leisure class.

Over the course of the twentieth century, Durante's Principle—that everyone wants to get into the act—has expanded into a widespread social practice. The playful activities of the leisure classes of high society and popular celebrity became important sources of social emulation, and the celebrated figures of those exclusive and visible groups became "role models" of play. Everyone wanted to get into the act of elegant play, doing what the rich and famous did, even if it was a diminished and local version of the Big Doings of Park Avenue or Beverly Hills. Celebrities became style-setters, giving us knowledge of just which consumptions are conspicuous at the moment. More than anything else, many people simply want to be "in style," affecting the fashion of the moment. This ranges from country-club socialites who spend enormous amounts of money on designer clothes to inner-city children who kill in order to obtain name-brand basketball shoes. Those people for whom the affectation of the right style and fashion is paramount are phonies. They wish to dazzle others with the brilliance, and the only way they can think to do that is to affect a stylish image and fashionable display. This affected habit is not confined to those who attempt to emulate "high society." This can also include those people who wish to identify with a group, gender, or language. The assertion of identification with a minority group or sex, making much of one's superiority and oppressed status, can be a phony effort to appear conspicuous. Showing off one's "identity" can be a phony exercise of stylistics that does not display wealth but rather trendiness, of "how cool I am" to appear as part of a newly identified group or ideology.

Academicians are quite capable of the same kind of phony emulation that we associate with other social groups—the newly wealthy aspiring to position, people aspiring to show off identity, teenagers anxious to display that they are in style. Academic people often display both intellectual and personal trendiness. Those who enforce codes of "political correctness" or curriculum revisions are often asserting their own phony commitment to correct thinking and championing the oppressed, when in fact such displays are nothing more than a stance. Intellectual styles may dictate to some in academia to ape the trendiest language and thought of the moment, and lecture and write on the subjects that will call the most attention to themselves. If the current fashion in a field dictates that the thought of "old dead white men" is without merit, there will be plenty of phonies declaiming that position without reflecting on its implications or justice. If a new version of conservatism becomes both trendy and lucrative, there will be plenty of professors willing to espouse that position for the acclaim and the money. Like any other social group, some (perhaps most) academicians are people of integrity; but also like any other social group, phonies can take advantage of any new trend or situation to exalt themselves. Phonies are in it for the personal payoff, how this can be used to aggrandize themselves. The academic *poseur* uses ideas for career advancement and notability in professional circles rather than for the advancement of knowledge.

Phoniness is a quality that "chains down" social hierarchies. As we noted with leisure classes, the principle of display of self is emulated by lesser mortals. The local wealthy who display status symbols find suitable models of emulation in the activities of the cosmopolitan rich and famous, as seen in media forums (including profiles and advertising in magazines such as *Vanity Fair, Glamour, Cosmopolitan, Southern Living*, and *The New Yorker*). In academia, pecuniary emulation is more limited by group constraints on ostentatious displays of wealth by faculty (professorial families will own Volvos but not Cadillacs). Display is expressed through intellectual emulation, mouthing the latest ideas for effect or aping the trendiest academic guru. Critics of academic fashion accused the intellectual movement termed "deconstructionism" of this, noting that a founder of the movement, Paul de Man, was likely a Nazi collaborator and an academic charlatan, and that many practitioners of deconstructionism in the humanities used this method of inquiry as an ideological weapon to undermine intellectual traditions or as a rationale for a range of grievances with an academic institution.[9] The difficulty with such movements is that they attract phonies, people who want to use the movement for purposes other than intellectual. Rather than wishing to illuminate the truth, they want to illuminate themselves. The "intellectual property" of whatever "ism" is in fashion is what they wish to exploit, impressing their peers with their ability to be "ahead of the curve." Further, such movements become the occasion for the affectation of an intellectual stance, communicating either "how knowledgeable I am" or "how oppressed I am" to all in purview. Ideas become the status symbols of academic bores intent on self-display for everyone's benefit.

The affectation of a lifestyle is a major way that phonies let the rest of us know of their superior social worth. The academic "lifestyle," for instance, involves not only intellectual conformity, but also personal stylistics, affecting the dress and manner deemed suitable for an aspiring academician. For aspiring "yuppies" (young urban professionals), the affectation of a lifestyle involves conspicuous consumption without appearing to value more traditional status symbols associated with upper-middle class "keeping up with the Joneses." Yuppies affecting an upscale lifestyle were more prone towards newer forms of conspicuous consumption—the right wines, the trendy vacation spots, living in a "fun" place, wearing L.L. Bean clothes, listening to New Age music, and so on. The yuppie lifestyle typically connotes the idea of acquiring things without appearing to desire acquiring things, as if money and valuable trappings didn't matter (driving a BMW somehow isn't *gauche*, while driving a Cadillac is). Yet in all cases—local "new rich," academicians, yuppies—we may suspect that there are significant status anxieties that drive the acquisition of material or intellectual properties. Acquisition often belies a desire to reassure oneself of worth, as if such things can make one important or even immortal. But doing so often transforms the acquirer into a phony who identifies the self with the thing acquired. The phony thinks that we are what we acquire; by showing off the objects of acquisition, she or he becomes somebody.

A massive industry exists to support the desire for display on the part of phonies. This includes the body-shaping industry, catering to the fundamental narcissism of those who wish to be seen. Both men and women submit to the tortures of exercise and diet, body shaping and vitamins, cosmetic surgery and hair transplants, virtually anything that will make them look impressive. Phonies are excessively concerned with their own body image because they want to be noticed. Thus they seek to enhance their appearance in every way. They scan the fashion sections of newspapers and magazines to study the art of appearance. The phony is an avid student of the art of mimesis, of imitating what is being thought or said, worn or driven, felt or enacted at the moment. But the phony affects not merely the imitation of life, but rather the unauthentic imitations of the moment. His or her concern is to "be" whatever is popular and wherever the action is, so that those who matter may see them at the center of popularity and at the "cutting edge" of the action. The phony wants to appear at the times and places where his or her mimesis can do them the most good. In a world where everything is for sale, the phony is selling herself and himself where they think it will do them the most good.

As Holden Caulfield thought, there are phonies everywhere. In some measure, the phony style is something that derived from the popular image of high society and the celebrity world. The mimetic arts of social affectation practiced by phony socialites and celebrities spread throughout society. The histrionic resources of putting on an act in public were available to everyone who wished to command attention and gain other people's confidence. The phony always found auditors, people who could be "gulled." Without human gullibility, the phony would have no audience, no one to attract, no corps of admirers, no source of the confidence she or he needs to exist and prosper.

Unless there is some fundamental change in American culture, we may expect the phony to be with us. The fraudulent personality will seek out people to defraud. The fundamental pathology of the phony is likely a fear of loss of control, rooted in the fear of death. By gaining other people's confidence through fraudulence, the phony feels powerful: he or she has gained that most precious of possessions, the confidence of others. Further, the phony can be smug with his or her secret: they did it without sincerity or honesty, without really believing in what they did. Phonies withhold emotional investment in others because their total emotional investment is in themselves. By controlling others, they exercise their gift of self-control, the secret knowledge they possess. Being found out, exposed as a fraud, caught in the big lie—that is the phony's nightmare. It is no accident that many of the great confidence men took their secret to their grave, wherein they hoped to have the last laugh.

CHAPTER 3

PHONY PLACES AND THINGS

✦ ✦ ✦

We have made the argument that the phony is a major social type in American culture. Phoniness is rooted in the languages we use to conceal our true selves and real purposes. The phony is thus a major social force in our national life, helping to shape the nature and purpose of our society. In an ironic way, the phony is something of a creative talent, an artist who gives character and meaning to our social life. The phony gives social impetus to the aesthetics of pretense, making pretension into a popular art form. Phonies excel in those areas of social life we may deem the "play-forms" of society, wherein the social actor acts upon auditors for influential effect. But wherever they are in society, phonies wish to be seen by audiences. In those settings, phonies can then appear before others. A massive industry has thus come into being to cater to that desire, providing settings and objects that are designed to complement or encourage phony behavior. The fashion industry, for example, advertises and presents itself as the creator and harbinger of the newly made and decidedly fashionable without which one is hopelessly old-fashioned and out-of-fashion. We are made to believe that we must have these things, and further, to act like the fashionable people—models, the rich, the celebrities—who are fashion leaders deemed worthy of emulation. Such an appeal—buy the things that will make you fashionable—underscores the social value of being a phony, dressing in garments that "phony you up," and admiring famous people who are phonies. Phoniness begets phoniness by making the phony objects of social admiration seem worthy of possession and display. The "play-form" of fashion showings thus becomes the vehicle for the widespread phoniness generated by the value of fashionability. As a social principle, phoniness then becomes central to not only human conduct but also the surroundings and trappings of our lives. Our culture becomes increasingly phony not only in what we do but also in where we go and what we possess. Let us look at some phony places and things.

PHONY PLACES

If one drives across America, it is easy to observe changes in the way we live. The family farm is replaced by agribusiness; the mom-and-pop store is replaced by the supermarket; the corner tavern and grill is replaced by the franchise restaurant or fast food; the downtown stores are replaced by the mall. Many familiar staples of the common life of Americans have become a victim of the marketplace. But what they were usually replaced by was not something authentically rooted in the community but rather something that was connected to larger economic forces. The comfortable local restaurant had to compete with the franchise food; locally owned downtown stores had to compete with the "name" chains at the mall; even local bars now compete with franchised bistros. We deserted the local for more cosmopolitan environs, either more elegant, more gaudy, or simply cheaper.

Many of these new places are phony. Franchise foods are efficient and clean, even if the food and the decor are tasteless. The mission of such an establishment is to move the eaters through quickly, without their enjoying the small luxury known as dining. The surroundings are bright but uniform, complemented by "wallpaper" music designed to cheer the eaters. One is not expected to linger in such a place; McDonald's is no Parisian café. Even the more elegant franchise restaurant chains are standardized in their architecture and homogenized in their food: one can walk into such chains from Maine to California and the place is decorated exactly the same way, and the food is just as bland, toned down to appeal to the broad middle of tasteless taste. Too, unlike the local restaurant or bar, there is no clientele connected to the place. Local places used to be part of the community; the franchise serves the mass at random, and has no interest in sustaining a community of local folks. Both local restaurants and stores had the quality of "funkiness," of having local color and character. But the franchise food place has no social "color" other than corporate-mandated cheer, and the defining character of no character. Similarly, the local hardware store or dress shop has for us now a kind of nostalgic charm, since such enterprises have become difficult to sustain against large discount stores and mall shops. In the memory of older Americans, small towns and neighborhoods included such local places—small coffee shops, butcher shops, dress stores, and so on. These are disappearing in favor of more impersonal and interchangeable places devoid of the warmth and "personality" of the locally owned store.

Many phony places, then, lack community or clientele. If a place is devoid of humane feeling and communal understanding, it may well be an artificial and lifeless collection of individuals. This has often been observed about American housing practices. Many older neighborhoods and regions, including suburban ones, were characterized by stability and continuity. Several generations might live in the same house; neighbors on the same street were close friends; boys dreamed of marrying "the girl next door"; farm neighbors got together for revivals and barn raisings. Such relationships are now the subject of nostalgia, since communities have become difficult to sustain. "Development" often destroys or abandons such places in favor of planned phony places. Many settled and charming urban, suburban, and rural places have been ruined by development that is intrusive and ugly. The Amish community of Lancaster County, Pennsylvania, for instance, has been largely destroyed by housing developments that intrude upon Amish life. Whereas the Amish were a community that shared religious belief and farm life, the suburban sprawl that spread throughout the county is impermanent, interchangeable, and meaningless, destroying the permanence and meaningful existence of the Amish. The countryside has been "developed," bringing the blight of transience to an area that had been quiet and orderly, a shared community of "plain people" who had no interest in development.[1]

Much American housing development is intrusive, either on local communities or on nature. The idea is to use a locale or natural setting to impose an artificial development that appeals to the transient wealthy seeking a fashionable or "safe" place to live. One may drive across the countryside and suddenly come across a place where the farms and forests have been bulldozed to be replaced by an intrusive development, a place that does not fit in with the setting. The phony names of such places give them away: "Harbor Centre," "Buckingham Acres," "River Plantation," and so on, all suggesting the creation of some kind of elegant paradise that can be had for an exorbitant price. They have to have a pretentious name because they are developed to be sold on the pretense of buying into elegance, comfort, and safety in condominium or townhouse heaven. Their intrusiveness is made apparent by their placement in the midst of the unpretentious and inelegant, as in the many "exurban" places where the locals and the transient wealthy who moved or weekend there for the place's "charm." The irony of development is that it destroys what it wants to exploit; a place developed to appeal to the phony intrudes on the locale, and by so doing, transforms it. Phony developments are charmless, but are placed among what phonies like to think is charming. Soon such areas are "gentrified," with exurban or resort towns full of overpriced boutiques and antique shops selling manufactured "antiques" (pie cozies and spinning wheels made in a Mexican factory). For many local people, development means higher taxes, the loss of serenity with increased traffic, crime, and hassle; but mainly it means the appearance of the phony in what had seemed to them to be a "real" world. For the phonies who crowd into such desirable places, the locals are objects of art, part of the dramatic and "charming" world the developer promises. It is a tribute to how much we are committed to creating a phony culture that state and local governments are often complicit in the destruction of the countryside, the farm culture, and local communities. Tax money is used by states and localities for roads that destroy farms; mayors sit on the boards of directors of corporations bent on creating golf retirement communities in the middle of a stable farming community; ugly condominiums and rows of "mini-mansions" intrude upon historic districts, bringing with them development uglification—malls, gentrified areas, and ever more roads. A phony culture quickly makes the desirable undesirable, the stable unstable, the lasting transient, and the beautiful ugly. Aspen, Colorado, is a place where the billionaires have forced the millionaires out (not to mention ordinary folks), but it is no longer a pretty place where one would like to go.

At this level, housing development is a confidence game because it promises mobile and rich American upper classes a chance to live in the "great good place" of charm and grace. Rich "yuppies" among the professional classes, people in various entrepreneurial games, socialites seeking the latest "in" place, and their many imitators among the upper-middle class, are people cut loose from social ties and settled communities by their very success, which meant they had to be upward-mobile, willing to move, and attentive to fashionability. This restlessness and rootlesssness impels them towards such parasitic places, because there they can both associate with their own kindred professional and entrepreneurial kind and sustain the illusion that their "lifestyle" in a development close to rural, historic, or "old" wealthy areas will associate themselves with something lasting and "classy," the very things they don't have. Developments can only offer phony charm and grace to the charmless and graceless, but in so doing they destroy whatever there was of local charm and grace around them.

The rootless and transient wealthy classes who frequent such developments are often shamelessly proud of their phoniness, since the display of wealth places them in what they believe to be the fashionable place that the lesser of us would give much to be part of. They apparently see the phony as the latest and highest of lifestyle aspiration, and that their cosmopolitan display is not a parody of local, rural, or frontier life. A mountain, lakeside, or exurban house in the country complete with every possible amenity and creature comfort (central air, the latest communications and entertainment rigs, complete kitchen) is not exactly "roughing it." Even the apparel and paraphernalia of such outings are parodies of the actual life of outdoor work. A glance at L.L. Bean or Eddie Bauer catalogs reveals the extent to which this phony identification with the "natural" has been taken. Bean clothes all have phony names: "Shepherd's Check" flannel shirts; "Maine Camp" sweaters; "Powder Keg" parkas; Bean's "Snow Sneakers"; and so on. Such apparel is not authentic nor carelessly selected and worn; rather the clothing is worn for effect, evoking the image (and self-image) of being close to the earth, the frontier, or the great outdoors.

A tour through many planned housing developments in America reminds the observer not of their "homeyness" but rather their sterility. Many developments are "exclusive," formally or informally for people who are different. In some retirement communities, children or stay-over visitors are forbidden. As cities and older suburbs have difficulties with crime, congestion, and migration, developers offer the well-off the lure of living in a "safe" enclave. A visit to one of these developments is instructive: they have gates and walls, guards and police patrols, alarm bells and strobe lights, entrance buzzers and sturdy doors. The houses or condominiums are like fortresses. One may drive through the streets on a nice day and never see anyone. The people who live in such enclaves are often wealthy professionals, but they often have no idea who lives next to them. They are sold as a new kind of safe "community," but there is nothing communal about them; the people who live there are a collection of rich individuals. They share exercise classes, arts and crafts displays, and the like, but little else; all they seem to have in common is fear of the outside world. These latter-day "walled cities" are hopefully sealed off from the barbarians at the gate. Yet both physically and psychologically, this desire for secure environs also transforms the bourgeois fortress into a kind of prison. These enclaves are governed by corporate boards and homeowners' associations that enforce a myriad of rules over the inhabitants. Like many other planned societies before them, these "bourgeois utopias" allow for no messy individuality: no wash on clotheslines, no recreational vehicles parked in the driveway, no exterior lights; regulations govern the size of mailboxes, the number of dogs and cats, the placement of garbage cans, and the color of your home. Although the American wealthy like to believe in the myth of individualism, their own reward for achievement makes them submit to considerable uniformity and confinement. A place that is lifeless and jejune affects the people who live there, tending to make them into inhabitants who belong in such a phony place. The "great good place" of nostalgic charm did have pedestrians strolling and lounging in parks or front porches, did have neighbors talking over back fences when the wash was put out on the line, did allow for quirkiness and choice. But a phony development threatens to atrophy the individuality and the soul. As one observer notes, such places are a "simulacrum of a real place...a community devoid of improvisation, of caprice, spontaneity, effusiveness, or the charm of error—a place where the process of commodification has at last leached life of the accidental and ecstatic, the divine, reckless, and enraged."[2] (We might also recall the philosopher William James's visit to a Chautauqua, those nineteenth-century summery paradises of ice-cream sodas and intellectual discussion: on leaving, he breathed a sigh of relief for being out of such an insipid place.) The appeal of an artificial place that promises to guarantee happiness and comfort in a secure if sanitized environment remains great in a world of multiplicity and risk. One Toronto developer has even gone so far as to hire actors and models to play happy homeowners for the benefit of prospective buyers, conveying for all to see the joys of living in this latter-day Potemkin Village.[3]

Phony places tend to be designed in order to eliminate human variability and uniqueness, evoking the "proper" and uniform response patterns of inhabitants or visitors. Planned communities become *designed places*, wherein the planners attempt to structure and predict experience, leaving nothing to chance. The individual must fit the design, rather than the design being flexible enough to allow individuality. Uniformity in housing is designed to promote uniformity of experience, eliminating human idiosyncrasy and cussedness. But dwellings are not the only designed place: the same principle of designing a social form that eliminates depth and variation and promotes the appreciation of artificial surroundings can be observed in other places in contemporary America. These include the theme park, the megamall, and the megaresort.

The theme park is a designed place constructed for organized and directed fun. Theme parks are places of contrived amusement, a descendant in some measure of carnivals, circuses, and amusement parks such as Coney Island. But those older places had a kind of lurid excitement about them that most contemporary theme parks lack. Since the success of Disneyland, the theme park has become a place devoted to "good, clean fun" without the sense of slumming or cheap thrills. Rather the theme park is a sanitized and safe place to have fun, usually for the entire family. The amusements at the Disney parks and its many imitators and successors are not sleazy or titillating; rather, they are clean and orderly, mildly amusing and often uplifting. And they are everywhere—Six Flags, Dollywood, Busch Gardens, Great America, and so on. In a wider sense, places like Las Vegas, Hawaii, the French Quarter, and other "fun zones" transformed into tourist attractions have become theme parks manicured and made safe for mass enjoyment. Many cities and towns in the post-industrial age compete for tourist dollars by enshrining past glories, from coal towns making shrines of closed coal mines to "rust belt" cities enshrining former manufacturing plants (the Studebaker museum in South Bend, Indiana) to the Rock 'n' Roll Museum and Hall of Fame in Cleveland. But Disneyland remains the model of the theme park: a simulated world of idealized yesterdays and tomorrows, monuments and experiences of fantasy that agitate American mythic yearnings for nostalgia (the Main Street of Our Town, circa 1900, and Frontierland), technological progress (Tomorrowland), and childish archetypes (Fantasyland). Disney did meet resistance to the construction of an "historical" theme park in northern Virginia called "Disney's America." The objection came not only from local folks upset by the intrusion of a monstrous park in a rural area but also from people interested in historical preservation and the teaching of history. The president of the National Trust for Historic Preservation objected to the construction of an "amusement park" that was to include exhibits on the Civil War and slavery. Disney's America is to be set in the middle of one of the most historic, not to mention scenic, areas of the country, close to authentic sites of historic significance, such as Mt. Vernon, Montpelier, Monticello, and Civil War battlefields such as Manassas and Fredericksburg. The justifiable fear is that Disney's phony history will be more interesting to tourists that the "real thing." (They may recall Disney's mechanical Abraham Lincoln at Disneyland, a moving thing that simulates Lincoln, but only the Lincoln as self-made man and folk hero, not the mournful and brooding Lincoln who presided over a national calamity.) Worse, not only might the estimated 30,000 tourists who they anticipate will visit Disney's America daily prefer to come there rather than to Monticello or Bull Run, they may come away believing that "the Disney version" is the "true" history, something more upbeat and thus easier to believe than the darker versions one might get at a battlefield or slave quarter. We might find a phony history more palatable than an authentic one, just as the phony Lincoln is "nicer" than the historical one. Disney's America will promote a kind of pseudo-history that will be pleasant propaganda, but will not enrich our historical consciousness. A phony culture cannot deal with the complexities and darker aspects of history as lived; it wishes to substitute the phony history of a simulated and "smoothed" exhibit for the real and rough-edged history. Disney's America will not offer a reconstruction of the past but rather a reconstruction of popular myth, telling American stories not as fact but as fable. Disney, Inc., is the Great Fabulator, and undoubtedly sees no reason why history cannot be transformed into a charming and lucrative fable made available for the touring masses. (There is, however, no guarantee that Disney's America will be a success: Euro Disney, located outside of Paris, has consistently lost money and drawn disappointing crowds, inspiring one wag to comment, why would one want to go to Euro Disney and see a phony castle when you could drive down the road and see a real one? One French intellectual deemed Euro Disney "a cultural Chernobyl" with disastrous polluting effects for French culture; we shall see if American intellectuals find Disney's America just as phony.)

The theme park has become a place to go to during the free time people have. They go there ostensibly to play, to have fun and enjoy the outing. But in an odd way, the play is passive; one voluntarily goes to the theme park but once in, the exhibits, rides, and so on are largely passive. Everything is provided in the squeaky-clean environs of the park; there is no need for thought or skill, and the only obligation is to doggedly use up all of your tickets. In a sense, one is supposed to enjoy the theme park as a *popular shrine*, a place where values are displayed and celebrated. The celebration is planned and ritualized: the "homo touri" have entered a place of popular veneration of social and corporate values. The theme park is a funhouse of sanctioned and controlled fun, devoid of spontaneity or ecstasy but including the expectation of compliance with organizational rules of mass enjoyment. Therein are displayed social symbols and images in monumental form that invite us to celebrate their legitimacy. Tomorrowland, or the Museum of Science and Industry, celebrates the corporate order and the advance of social progress through technology; Frontierland perpetuates the myth of benevolent empire and original self-reliance. By displaying such values in a festive setting, social learning can take place easily and subliminally. (We might distinguish here between play and display: play is often creative, impulsive, and even downright anarchic, as in child's play or sexual play; but display, as is typically seen in theme parks, is planned and exhibited for a serious purpose but is presented in an ostensibly playful setting. Play originates in individuals, while display stems from organized effort to convey a message. The "metamessage" that says to people "This is play" is very different from the one observable at theme parks that "this is display.") Those who go to the theme parks enter a universe of contrived conviviality, phony places that ritualize the Barnumian ideal of a "sinless carnival." Leisure time is spent in the structured ceremonials which sacralize the values inherent in the park displays; herein one enters an eternal present, what one might do throughout eternity in a heaven where the faithful have been rewarded for their earthly pursuit of fun morality.

An interesting political variant on the theme park has become the presidential library. These enormously expensive and ostentatious monuments to past presidents are more than just a place to store papers and memorabilia; rather more they function as propaganda for the reputation for greatness of the departed or retired president. Presidential libraries are a pure example of phony display, since the visitor is invited to participate in the veneration of the Great One. (In the twenty-seventh century, archaeologists may dig up and study the ruins of these tombs as they now do the pharaoh's pyramids in Egypt.) They make an effort to simulate the presidential life, not only through artifacts but also films and recreations of the royal personage and palace. At the Reagan Library, for example, there is an "exact replica" of the Oval Office recreated to simulate "a sense of realism" as to how the Reagans "would know it"; the office includes facsimiles of the vistas from the windows of the office, and all the memorabilia that cluttered it. Indeed, the Library includes a doll house replica of the entire White House as it would have appeared during the Reagan "watch." Presidential libraries are also lucrative enterprises, since they maintain shops that sell a variety of goods with the presidential stamp on it. At the Richard Nixon Presidential Library, the gift shop's items for purchase include golf balls with the Eagle crest and Nixon's signature, a wristwatch with a picture of Nixon and Elvis, a frisbee with the presidential seal, and a poster of a smiling Nixon with the caption "Nixon in '96: Tanned, Rested, and Ready." (Watergate, however, is not in evidence, and one must ask the guides for mention of it.) Presidential libraries are shrines of political veneration, offering displays that are designed to convey the majesty of the prince and his court, and to sell baubles sanctified by the presidential *imprimatur* to the visiting tourist. The explicit "theme" of the presidential library is the glory of the honored president (who is often also buried there), and the implicit theme is the imperial majesty of the presidency, a memorial and tomb worthy of an emperor.

American popular shrines honor a wide variety of symbols, including contemporary or nostalgic objects deemed worthy of veneration. This includes the Barbie Hall of Fame, the Dillinger Jail, the National Atomic Museum, the Frederick's of Hollywood Bra Museum, and the Dog Museum. Many such fun places are merely "camp," put together quite tongue-in-cheek. But some of them have a didactic purpose or pathetic quality that reminds us of the potential for enshrining the phony. Henry Ford's Greenfield Village preserves a mythic American past by simulating it as it should have been, enshrining Ford's conception of the essential harmony and historical logic of preindustrial and industrial society, the "machine in the garden" (the Village includes Thomas A. Edison's reconstructed boyhood home moved there for the benefit of worshippers of technology; but then Heritage, USA, of Jim and Tammy Bakker fame, did the same for Billy Graham's boyhood home!). Similarly, the birthplaces of cultural heroes become shrines. One expects this for presidents, and places such as Johnson City, Texas; Whittier, California; Plains, Georgia; Dixon, Illinois; and Hope, Arkansas, exploit a thriving cottage industry on those tourists curious about the mythic small-town origin of American kings (Dixon's claim is a bit bogus: Reagan wasn't born there, the enshrined "boyhood home" was rented and lived in for about two years, and the family moved to less "Norman Rockwellian" towns, such as East Chicago; but then the Clinton family moved quite a bit also).

The astonishing array of shrines we have noted includes several that signify past social relationships or events that are deemed worthy of nostalgic celebration or remembrance. They are of interest to us here because they remind us of something that we have lost. An example that illustrates this is the charming Country Doctor Museum in Bailey, North Carolina. This tiny museum is a small house with the memorabilia of the practice of country doctors in the

American rural past. The shrine has the instruments, medical books, files and journals, and the inevitable rolltop desk of these hardy doctors who made house calls to farmhouses on winter nights. Visitors go there to see something that no longer exists: the memorabilia of doctors who were an integral part of a community that they served at great sacrifice. With the changes in American medicine, the "high-tech" and bureaucratized profession seems remote, forbidding, and uncaring to many Americans. Despite all the rhetoric about the "doctor-patient relationship," nothing seems more irretrievably lost. The nostalgic appeal of the Country Doctor Museum centers on that loss, the feeling that despite the relatively primitive equipment and knowledge the mythical country doctor of yore possessed, at least he (and occasionally she, as "Dr. Quinn, Medicine Woman" dramatized) cared. This sense of the loss of personal and therapeutic doctoring is due to the practice of contemporary medicine, which seems impersonal and uncaring, not to mention exorbitantly expensive. The myth of the country doctor offers us a nostalgic contrast to the "fallen" present. Our difficulty now is that we suspect that much of bureaucratized medicine is phony: unnecessary tests, "self-referrals" to a specialist or clinic the doctor is connected to, procedures (such as caesarean sections) that are excessive, outrageous hospital bills (the infamous "five dollar aspirin"), and so on. Whereas the country doctor was a respected member of a small community that we all knew and loved, the contemporary doctor is perceived as just another icy professional interested only in money. This may not be fair, but in the popular mind there is much suspicion that in the medical game the fix is in, and we are being had by a phony system. In an odd way, those who come to the Country Doctor Museum may well feel that they are entering a real place where once personal care was given, while at the same time when they enter a contemporary clinic or hospital, they are entering a phony place wherein impersonal care is sold.

There was even much discussion in this vein about the establishment of the Holocaust Museum commemorating the Nazi destruction of European Jews (and Gypsies, homosexuals, Jehovah's Witnesses and other religious minorities, and political prisoners). The Museum was designed as a solemn and reflective experience, including issuing "identity cards" to visitors which had the name and vital statistics of an actual Holocaust victim imprinted on it, in order to "humanize" the Museum's ghastly displays. Yet some critics, while supporting the idea of commemoration of the major ontological event of the twentieth century, thought the Museum came uncomfortably close to making the Holocaust into a "therapeutic mass-cultural experience," that it was one more American theme park for tourists to queue up and see, like a "horror ride" at Six Flags. The danger, one observer notes, is that the Holocaust Museum becomes trivialized by being made into a place for mass tourism, an "edifying spectacle" for the millions of visitors snapping pictures of crematoria and the other ghastly artifacts of the death camps. The Holocaust Museum was designed as a reminder of an event that invites solemn reflection and resolution; whether the many tourists come into it or take away from it the right attitude remains to be seen. The difficulty might be that touring Americans, especially young people, have been so long exposed to the phony that they miss the Museum's authenticity, its attempt to bring to attention the almost unbelievable. We may devoutly hope that it does not become just another roadside attraction, gone to for its horrific thrills, which are seen in some sense as not "real," a horror movie and not a horror. We are by now so used to seeing history "phonied up" (in popular novels, television specials, and movies) that we may only hope the Holocaust Museum can revive the distinction between the phony and the all too actual.[4]

Phony places can be identified because they fabricate vivacity. Those housing developments and theme parks that simulate the world also attempt to simulate liveliness. The officials and help in such places are ordered to put on a smiley-face cheer, as the norm expected of all who enter here: be cheerful or else. But not only the personnel convey the message of enforced cheer; the architecture and settings are all designed to convey a kind of phony gladness. The housing or theme park enclave appeals as a happy place wherein one can expect bright-colored and safe gaiety. Everything is contrived to convey an atmosphere of fun, of playful release from duty. This aim is also much in evidence in that related fun place, the mall. But here there is another motive: the mall is a place designed for the waltz of consumption, of walkers browsing and shopping in a fun place wherein the shared cheer leads them to express gaiety through buying things. The mall is a theme park for consumption, a variety of consumer "rides" that display in colorful and attractive manner those things that will enrich our lives. The banal goods therein displayed take on a vivacity of their own: shoes and skirts and rings are talismans of life, bringing joy to our mundane existence. The mall is the clean, well-lighted place to which we are drawn, and where we may find convivial people funning through the personal expression of prosperity. The mall is an enclave (cheerful and helpful guards here to enforce the good cheer) of consumer confidence, reassuring us that life is in the things we may possess and take home. The mall is designed to be a "confidence place," putting us in the mood to exercise the basic American right, the right to consume.

Like many other phony places, malls have long since transcended their original functionality as a convenient and comfortable place to shop. Malls began to display phony elegance— fountains, facades, fashion shows, art exhibits, fancy restaurants, and so on. Too, they began to display another disease of phoniness: the urge toward gigantism, building bigger malls to the point of dwarfing the individual who must wander through caverns of mall corridors in search of just the right item. The most gigantic of them, such as the "Mall of America" near Minneapolis, are more than just convenient malls, but rather "zones of entertainment" that depend on tourists coming to gawk in awe at the size of the immense place as much as shoppers looking for a bargain. The Mall of America is gigantic, with 330 stores, a seven-acre amusement park in the middle of the mall, four hundred trees, and approaching $1 billion in sales. The mall is five times larger than Red Square and twenty times larger than St. Peter's Basilica, with 2.3 miles of hallways. But one observer noted of the Mall of America that the place is an "endless promenade" of people who feel lost and diminished by the immensity and audacity of the place. The mall "exploits our acquisitive instincts without honoring our communal requirements, our eternal desire for discourse and intimacy." The mall attracts promenading strangers, all of whom shuffle through the expansive emptiness of a labyrinth. But it is a collection of individuals who do not interact; as in many megamalls, the visitors walk along in virtual silence, as if they were in consumer heaven and should remain hushed and reverent. But those who come there largely mill around, immersed in the overwhelming false grandeur of the place. Once in American life, the marketplace was the place for discourse and friendly intimacy. One went to the farmer's market or corner store or country market to find products, but also to meet people and engage in small talk. At megamalls, people are largely anonymous and alien, constantly moving from store to store, attraction to attraction, since stopping and observing might induce thought as to the immense phoniness of the place (and besides, loitering at leisure is not permitted). For all their glitter, such gigantic constructs are not fun places. They are built on an inhuman level, as monuments to the god of purchase. But they are not playful, in the way, for instance, of Asian bazaars or American flea markets, wherein part of the fun is in the bargaining over price and value. A bazaar or marketplace is a thriving place of free trade in the best sense, with both buyer and seller engaged in a bargaining game. But at megamalls, all the fun has been taken out of the process. Price and value are exorbitant, associated with prestigious brands ("designer jeans") and the elegance of the store and mall, a kind of mass-produced snob appeal. There is no spontaneous play, no ecstatic outbursts of joy; rather there is the organized and tame fun of a model railroad, log ride, eighteen-hole miniature golf, and so on. Tourists stay at the hotel for lengthy periods without ever leaving the mall. Similar megamalls are planned for other parts of the country, and around the world (a Mall of Japan is being built). No matter where they are built, they will be essentially the same: a commercial surreality without any functional connection to the community in which it is placed, standing as a gigantic monument that inspires awe in the ambling masses who tour its caverns. But it does not serve as a marketplace or bazaar; it is a "desolate substitute" for the vitality of the bargaining center.[5] Shopping centers used to be places to buy; now they are more places to be. The reigning motif of a megamall is not free trade, but organizational control (the Mall of America has 109 surveillance cameras that can focus on objects as small as a hand or wallet). The place has no contact with nature (a promotional brochure touts the Mall of America as a place wherein "snow never falls, streams never freeze...where the feeling of summer lasts all year round"), no vital link to the community, no effort to include the many less-than-affluent who are effectively excluded from the sacral act of consuming. It is simply an expression of mammoth organizational power, the ability to make a place that is huge (never mind that it is also ugly and superficial). Gigantism in architecture always seems to be an expression of the phony, as evidenced not only by megamalls but also buildings as various as the Sears Tower in Chicago, the Nation's Bank building in Charlotte, or the Astrodome in Houston. The megamall is merely an example of the proliferation of phony places of gigantic and inhuman proportions that characterize the "postmodern" world. Postmodern architecture in particular seems to express the lack of objectivity in design and functionality in purpose. We now speak of "generic cities," urban areas that all look the same: a collection of "international style" buildings that are everywhere ugly, boring, and nondescript. The dominant theme seems to be their inaccessibility, expressing the power of those who do have access to the exclusive upper floors of offices and suites. One is reminded of the "fortress mentality" of the early medieval period, when castles and walled cities were built to protect people from barbarian incursions. The "megacenters" one sees on the fringes of cities in "edge cities," proliferating office and meeting centers in suburban enclaves, are equally fortresses—inaccessible, surrounded by security fences and guards, with careful screening of who can enter. the "silicon valleys" of the country, centers of high-tech businesses, exist in a paranoid state about industrial espionage of new discoveries (computer chips are a major item for theft). The prevailing imperative is security at work (and many of the same people live in similarly "protected" housing projects, like the ones we discussed above). It is ironic that in the "information age," many of these edge city businesses are housed in buildings and enclaves wherein the free flow of information (and movement) is severely inhibited; the purveyors of information live and work in barricaded centers that exclude the madding crowd. Cities have lost their core of the talented and rich who gave it leadership and money; now in a sense the talented and rich have seceded from the city, abrogating responsibility for its decline into penury and chaos. The elastic and vital metropolis of 1950 has become a decaying inner city with insoluble problems surrounded by suburban enclaves whose secession has left it to its own devices. In reaction, one urban strategy is to fortify spaces within the cities: in some troubled areas, police stations, courthouses, expensive high-rise apartment and penthouse builds, and office buildings look as if they are constantly under siege. Another is to create phony spaces in "public areas" within the city. Public spaces such as open malls, parks, or river walks are developed as "themed spaces," with a planned motif to attract tourists; such places are often corporate designs with some sort of phony atmosphere in mind, such as San Antonio's river walk or Los Angeles's CityWalk (a project of MCA). Typically, such places are characterized by control and exclusion, creating a phony atmosphere safe for tourists through architectural design that creates "crafted spontaneity." But they are in no sense public spaces, modern *agorae* that promote civic life, such as debate, conversation, demonstrations, and lounging. Such spaces are swept clean of "undesirables," making them safe, clean, and predictably sterile. MCA's Citywalk in L.A. is actually in the Universal Studio lot in the San Fernando Valley rather than in the city it celebrates; it offers a shopping mall in the guise of idealized L.A. streets, replicating the architectural facades of Venice Beach, Melrose Avenue, Olvera Street, and the Sunset Strip, importing sand, palm trees, minstrels, restaurants, and shops selling celebrity memorabilia. Distinguishing between L.A. the "mall" and L.A. the "real," they omitted simulation of riots, drug- and gang-ridden *barrios*, earthquakes, and the homeless. On the other hand, it should be admitted that Los Angeles has always been associated with the phony: it was the great film director Jean Renoir, after working in Hollywood, who said he had seen Paris, France and Paris, Paramount, and on the whole he preferred the latter. Like the mall walkers, those who visit theme spaces in cities are expected to admire the place and keep moving.[6]

The difficulty for both suburban and urban areas is that this fortress mentality, mania for security, and secession from the city as an organic whole combine to destroy a vital and authentic civic life. If the professional classes who populate these secluded areas of work and play continue to "drop out," as it were, from social leadership, then the American project of civil democracy will likely continue to flounder, indeed finding leadership elsewhere. (We may wonder whether in some subtle way this self-exclusion is related to the catastrophic decline in the popular reputation of the professions over the last several decades: whereas once doctors, lawyers, bankers, and academicians were held in high esteem, now they are held in great contempt and distrust. The doctor, for example, is now typically a specialist ensconced in a plush office in one of these suburban enclaves, and a trip there for the patient is difficult and expensive, often involving long waits and personal humiliation.) The professional classes no doubt believe themselves to be justly rewarded, and also justified in caring for their own safety. For as one acute observer has pointed out, the professional upper-middle class projects onto the working class and the poor the very attributes it most fears in itself—the belief that the lower elements are childishly hedonistic, unable to defer gratification, and addicted to drugs, all mythic practices that symbolize the professional class's fears about itself going into debt to live the upscale lifestyle, lured into the soft life of creature comforts, travel, and vacationing rather than working, and becoming addicted to the drug of consumption, all of which stems from the deepest fear of all, the fear of falling in status.[7] The professional middle-class is quite willing to live and work in phony environs if it protects them from those outside the gate who most threaten their pristine existence. The gigantism of the architecture of protected suburban housing projects and megacenter office buildings offer symbolic protection, a class Maginot Line that defends the professional's lives, fortunes, and self-image. (The future of such latter-day castle keeps seems assured: in Japan, there are ambitious plans for high-rise buildings that are "self-contained urban complexes," one with 500 stories and another taller than the Sears Tower; another corporation envisions cities tiered underground or under the sea, all connected with rail lines. All envision a world without contact with nature and with controlled contact with the human race.)

The problem is that choosing to live and work in such places forces people to lead a phony life. The doctor who cares not for the health of his or her patients and resists reforms that makes the country a healthier place is not necessarily vindictive or mean, but rather is living a life of enclosed fear, surrounding himself or herself with environs of work and leisure that guard against involvement or compassionate altruism. Phony surroundings protect, but they also enclose; the fortress is also a prison. But the soul becomes a prisoner of the same self-enclosure act. One only works and plays with people of the same status, all of whom are quite content with their lot in life and sense of their own social superiority. But in so doing, they lose touch with the real, the authentic, the raw edges and rough contradictions of life outside the enclaves of conference rooms and pleasure-domes. More to the point, they lose touch with their social function, which includes making the world that pays them so handsomely a better place. But if one is a professional who knows only the phony worlds of protected lives, then we can expect that such people will be phonies. If people live in a dissociative universe, their environs will help determine who they are. If there is no there in the place one lives and works, we can figure that there is no there in the people who occupy corridors of emptiness.

PHONY THINGS

One of the classics of American social inquiry is Thorstein Veblen's *Theory of the Leisure Class*, published in 1899. Veblen hit upon something fundamental about modern America: that ownership of property and the accumulation of wealth were not merely functional. Rather they were also symbolic, conferring honor on those who owned property and possessed things. In order to impress others with one's status, it was necessary to display things, objects that evoke admiration and envy of the displayer. The world is divided between the "haves" and "have-nots" in more than just material goods and advantages; it is also divided between those who have the means to display status through flaunting the things that distinguish them from the rest of us, and those who only can wish they had such means. Veblen understood that things acquired have symbolic meaning, reassuring us of our self-worth by displaying that "worth" in worthy things. Things displayed are not simply functional, but more somethings to serve as emblems of worthiness. Thus they have be noticed; the things have to be conspicuous for significant others.

Veblen observed the super-rich of his day and saw what they did with things. His terms have entered the language: "pecuniary emulation," "conspicuous leisure," "conspicuous consumption," "pecuniary decency," "conspicuous waste," and so on. The visible social display of wealth and opulence becomes a signal for emulation of one's equals (outdoing them in mansions, antiques, servants, vacations, mistresses, parties, and philanthropy), or of one's betters (middle-class folks attempting to emulate the lifestyle of the rich and famous). For all who are caught up in the display of things (goods and services designed and shown to enhance one's social reputation as a person of status and means), the goal is to be seen as a gentleman or lady of leisure. One's "conspicuousness" among those from whom you wish to elicit admiration and envy is measured by how much they are impressed with your ability to do nothing worthwhile. What Veblen discovered has now become a larger social principle: whereas once achievement was measured by functionality (what one did at work to produce worthwhile things of use), now achievement had come to be measured by non-functionality (what one did at play to consume unworthwhile things of uselessness). Leisure and play are no longer a secondary reward for hard work; rather they are becoming the primary social activity of those who wish to display themselves as admirable. Conspicuous play is more important for social reputation than conspicuous work. It is still true that people ardently seek achievement in the world of work; but seeking those rewards (money, free time, early retirement, access to the elite pleasure-domes) is now motivated by the desire to afford conspicuous leisure. Play may well be replacing work as the ascendant social principle, replacing work at the core of American civilization.

This quest for conspicuousness in social relations that Veblen first identified is a major manifestation of the phony. For the people who engage in expensive self-display—the self among one's glittering things—are interested in acquiring a superior status based on a false and manipulated reputation. In a sense, the status seeker aspires to the phony because that is now perceived to be the way to be impressive. As Veblen saw, it is not enough to achieve for its own reward, or merely to have wealth and power; status is a matter of reputation, and it is only by being phony that one achieves admiration and envy in the eyes of other. If they wish to emulate you, then you have achieved your goal of conspicuousness; but you have also become a phony, someone who defines themselves in terms of their possessions. The phony status seeker is possessed by his or her possessions. But if one aspires to being impressive, there may be no other effective way to achieve conspicuousness without intrinsic merit. Conspicuousness becomes a standard that invites phoniness, since a phony can fake much of the symbols and artifacts of status. Recurrently we read about someone who has passed themselves off as European royalty or a learned professor, flaunting fake heraldry or degrees; and it is easy enough to pass fake diamonds or antiques off as "the real thing." Indeed, as status seeking and pecuniary emulation proliferates throughout American society, we can observe the pervasion of phony things which are sought and purchased with a view to shoring up one's status anxieties. At the bottom of society, this can include little more than the acquisition of personal items—gold jewelry, name-brand sports shoes, or a "boom box"—but among one's peers, it gives you status. Among inner-city youths, status is so important that some few will kill to acquire such outward signs of worth. At the top of society, the quest for the things that symbolize status is equally ardent, if more expensive and occasionally more refined. Art, for instance, is sought by many wealthy people for its status value rather than because of any deep and genuine passion for art. Art is sometimes an investment, but more often is likely a way of self-display. Owning a Renoir or Picasso becomes an act of conspicuous consumption that identifies the owner as having both good taste and a great deal of money. Art in this context has become both invaluable and worthless, since it priced beyond all reason and made the private property of someone who likely appreciates it only in terms of self-enhancement. Art has no intrinsic worth, and is not available to be seen by those lesser beings who might appreciate it on aesthetic grounds. Similarly, rich mature men who have reached the apex of their careers have acquired the habit of marrying a beautiful young woman, termed a "trophy wife." (Apparently this "reward" involves a kind of marital potlatch: older wives can be callously thrown away when they have served their purpose, a new twist on Veblen's "pecuniary decency.") The trophy wife, we may suspect, is acquired for her youth and beauty, which like art may be admired for its aesthetic value. But she is also an object of admiration for the rich man's circle (and if he is a celebrity, for the envious male public), and in that sense is no different than any other work of art or other valuable object displayed to elicit admiration and envy. Such a "beautiful young thing" is, like the art object, both invaluable and worthless, in that she is priced beyond all reason and has become the private property of someone who appreciates her only in terms of self-enhancement. Both the painting and the young wife are conspicuous status symbols, but they are there in the penthouse or mansion to "phony up" the place for their owner.

A similar process seems to happen with some people towards their children. We are all familiar with the legendary "stage mother," referring to parents who attempt to make their children into movie stars. The principle has expanded to include those parents or other associates who are willing to do almost anything to have their offspring become rich and famous in some context of achievement (examples include the Texas cheerleader mom who allegedly plotted to kill her daughter's rivals for cheerleader slots, and skater Tonya Harding's associates who tried to cripple her rival). The common practice of many such parental Svengalis is to make the child over into a performer. The father who drills his child to become a great athlete or chess player may be living out a vicarious fantasy—my child will be what I am not—but by so doing, he robs the child of the joys of childhood. The child skater, dancer, musician, or whatever has no childish existence; rather children are trained to perform as "little adults," like Mozart playing the violin for the Pope. More commonly, rich parents try to insure their child's future by bribing school officials to guarantee his or her admission to an Ivy League college eighteen years hence, arranging for the kid to meet "the right people" at private schools and camps, and so on. Parents spend a great deal of time and money for lessons (ballet, piano), training (sending kids to "financial camps" where they learn moneymaking skills), or urging them into competition (forensic, dramatic, athletic). Some parents seem to want "designer children," kids who live up to grandiose expectations of upward mobility and reflected glory for the parents. The child becomes a display thing no less than the trophy wife or the servant, an object that verifies the author's power and parental ability. The effort is to make the child over into a phony something, rather than be accepted as a loved offspring. The potential for resentment and rebellion here is clear enough, but many parents seem willing to accept the risk for the dream of basking in the radiance of the performing thing they have created.

Critics have long ridiculed the upper classes for their pretentiousness, something that many of their children also began to rebel against in the 1960s. Much of this persists, however defensively, especially in the conduct of conspicuous leisure. It is astonishing how much space in upscale mansions and homes resembles a museum, in which no one dares tread and no life goes on. A bourgeois living room often involves no living; it is where expensive things (furniture, paintings, chandeliers, silver, and so on) are displayed. A similar phony effect can be observed in the dinner party, wherein the taste, manners, and fashionability of the host are displayed. Following the rule of attention to detail (as dictated by Martha Stewart and others), the dinner party becomes an exercise in pretentious presentation, restrained eating, and phony conversation, all in the guise of conviviality. Yet there is often no gusto to such occasions; both host and guests are determined to "show off," so appearances become paramount while the joy of eating is ruined by the indigestion of phoniness. The "pecuniary standard of taste" comes to dominate domestic life in the display of elegance. The fun of entertaining is killed by the imperatives of phoniness, of bourgeois display rather than relaxed play. The dinner party or whatever other occasion (a glance through *Southern Living* magazine will give an idea of the range) becomes a pretentious exercise in emulating the standards of the dictators of taste but a crashing bore for those who thought such gatherings were supposed to be fun.

The success of the "entertainment advisement" industry, from books to caterers, suggests the desire to live up to the standards of charm and grace that have persisted in American culture. (In the South, the myth of magnolias and mint juleps persists in the magazines, revealing the desire of the upper-middle class to recapture some kind of antebellum "Twelve Oaks" class.) Yet such conspicuous phoniness may reveal more than that. In the fluid, and in many ways egalitarian, society of today, with great economic shifts, popular uprisings, and critical analysis of social life, people in the upscale classes drawn to such phony behavior and acquisitions may well do so because of great status anxieties, most importantly the "fear of falling." For there is considerable evidence that many "upward-mobile" people have such fears, based in the uncertainty they have been placed in by the new economy and society.[8] One way to shore up a sense of upscale conspicuousness is to buy the artifacts of display and let people see them. A dinner party, a "museum" house, an extravagant foreign car may strain your budget, but it does wonders for your sense of self-worth. Dramatic demonstration that one has "class" (serving squid and champagne) may momentarily at least convince all (including yourself) that you will remain in an upscale class. The fear is real enough, with layoffs of corporate executives, financial ruin in the stock market, looting of pension funds, and the like. There is nothing so pathetic as the "new poor" who have had to abandon the conspicuous displays of their former existence for the mundane ordinariness (serving chicken and cheap white wine) of relative deprivation. Without the ability to show to the world and themselves their adherence to the high standards of pecuniary decency, those who have fallen from conspicuous grace must indeed feel shabby and indecent.

That things are in the saddle has been a common complaint of critics of American life for a very long time. Yet the recurrent theme of these critics does have one resonant chord: if worth is measured in things, the possession of those things affects how you evaluate yourself and others. By attributing value to things, you have adopted an inhuman standard: I am what I own. Such "owning" can become obsessive, so that one lives in what one has. Measuring worth by things is a phony standard, a rule that is easy enough to adopt to oneself. The self thus becomes an object of display, like the host or hostess who presides over a dinner party. You are displayed in the same manner as your things, and are equally as phony. You have become what you value, and in such a state of self-display are, as the saying goes, as phony as a three-dollar bill.

CONCLUSION

When Veblen wrote about the phoniness of the conspicuous classes of rich of his day, he observed that they served as a "radiant body" for the rest of us to envy. The envious vicariously participate in the attribution of worth to personages and their possessions by believing them to have a radiance denied to the rest of us. The rich, the beautiful, the famous, the notorious—they all have a glow, if not a halo. The grave difficulty for a society absorbed with conspicuousness is that we transform them and their places and things into radiant bodies, objects worthy of veneration. This ranges from our worship of celebrities, to our fascination with the palaces and pleasure-domes of the mighty, to the silly attempts by middle-class "wannabes" to put on airs. A society dominated by anxious poseurs will value phony places and things, and do much to gain access to or replicate these valuable environs or objects. As such a desire chains down the social hierarchy, it makes us realize that valuable possessions are for many people the currency of their souls.

There is an essay by the French Enlightenment philosopher Denis Diderot that still holds a lesson for us. The pre-revolutionary period in which he lived was a prior case of a phony culture, with many similar practices and values we associate with American phoniness today. In his essay, Diderot notes that he once lived in a simple room with few possessions, where he could pursue his writing in peace. But an admirer gave him a new dressing gown, and soon he was distracted. His paltry possessions—his room and clothes—seemed inelegant and drab by comparison with his fine new gown. So he felt impelled to acquire new and expensive things that complemented his new gown. Soon his abode was redecorated, and he had a fashionable and elegant wardrobe. Whereas he had once been quite content, he now felt possessed by possessions. Diderot's sense of self had been transformed: he feared that he was now what he had.

Places and things are phony to the extent that they further that inadequate sense of self that impels us to define worth in having, and having more. Places and things are *symbolic property*, valuable to the extent that we attribute worth to them as aggrandizing the conspicuousness of ourselves.[8] Like Diderot, we risk becoming a phony in the process of self-definition through what we surround ourselves with, the property to which we attach symbolic meaning. The opposite is also true: we risk becoming genuine, and free, when we refuse to give meaning to the meaningless, and instead value that which is vital, alive, and humane.

CHAPTER 4

PHONY EVENTS

Our inquiry into the phony has so far led us into the examination of various kinds of people speaking particular types of languages in different sorts of settings wherein they venerate certain varieties of objects. It has been our claim that these people can be best characterized as phonies, that the languages they use are phony, and that the places they occupy and things they play with are phony. It is also our larger claim that phonies set the tone and style of contemporary America, and that they have created a distinctive culture that lacks authenticity and vitality. With that in mind, in the next chapters we want to turn to what phonies do, looking in turn at phony events, phony deals, and phony politics.

In 1962, the distinguished historian Daniel J. Boorstin published a book entitled *The Image*, which introduced a new term into the language of social inquiry: the "pseudo-event." A pseudo-event, said Boorstin, is "a happening," an event that happens but did not have to happen. It is created, designed, staged, and conducted for its dramatic quality and public nature. A pseudo-event is not spontaneous, is conducted for purposes of publicity, and has an ambiguous reality, since its meaning is unclear and pluralistic. Because of the flood of pseudo-events, Americans now live "in a world where fantasy is more real than reality, where the image has more dignity than the original."[1] With the proliferation of the mass media, and such created environments of play as the theme park and the awards ceremony, the occasions for the conduct of pseudo-events have likewise expanded. Pseudo-events are in a sense ritualized and stylized events which present a dramatic structure for audiences, or provide the setting for the audience to enter and participate in the drama itself. The awards ceremony allows the audience to watch a pseudo-event of planned and staged ritual celebration of a media industry's values and personages, the participation of the audience is limited to vicarious experience; more innovative theme parks in a sense allow the individual to enter the setting and become part of the controlled drama (part of the fun of the book and movie *Jurassic Park* is that the control breaks down, making the adventure into a nightmare). A pseudo-event is a phony occurrence, something that happens according to plan rather than occurring naturally. It is imposed on the world through the good offices of publicity, and exists only because of the power of public assertion that convinces people the occurrence is important and real, and deserves our attention and attendance. All the arts of publicity and public event-making pioneered by public relations engineers such as Edward Bernays are brought to bear in order to construct and "bring off" a successful pseudo-event. Pseudo-events—a gala supermarket opening, an interview, a tour of the pleasure-domes of the rich and famous, a beauty contest—are hyped as if they are important. A pseudo-event is neither a social necessity nor a social accident, but it is so represented as the momentary center of the universe. The fact that it requires considerable promotion is a giveaway: if it were a necessity, it would not be necessary to promote it as important, and if it were an accident, it would be thought merely fortuitous.

A pseudo-event is a social ritual conducted by those versed in the arts of manipulatory communication. It succeeds if it is popular, attracting the attention of an audience willing to watch the show. It depends on the cooperation or complicity of the media, since a pseudo-event would not exist without mass communication of the proceedings. A wide variety of "facilitation industries" exist to "cater" such affairs, ranging from those people skilled in arranging the ceremonies for mall openings to those who manage celebrity or rich weddings and funerals. The news media, of course, are an integral part of these occurrences, and giving the correct "spin control" for media reportage is crucial to the successful conduct of a pseudo-event. A celebrity wedding, for instance, is an event in which people actually do get married, at least temporarily; but its actuality is couched in its media function, which for its managers is to translate it into news that promotes the fame of the stars being married, and the celebrities in attendance at the highly public affair.

It is worth noting that the mass media has a long history of not only covering pseudo-events, but also creating them. In the heyday of newspaper competition in American cities (Chicago had fourteen daily papers in 1895), reporters were adept at creating pseudo-events as the subject for sensational news. Media hoaxes often involved hyping a story where there was none, such as reporters converging on the scene of a traffic accident that turned out not to be serious; they would then conspire to concoct a bizarre cause or twist to the story and try to outdo each other in making the story sensational. (It appears that even Mrs. O'Leary's cow that was supposed to have knocked over a lamp and started the great Chicago fire of 1871 was a media hoax, making even that spectacular event more newsworthy.) Ben Hecht, the co-author of *The Front Page*, as a young reporter in Chicago in the 1920s, discovered that there had been a mild earth tremor in Illinois one uneventful day; he hired a work crew and rushed to Lincoln Park, where the crew dug a jagged trench; pictures were taken, which appeared in Hecht's paper with headlines about "Earthquake in Chicago!" and here are pictures of the fault line in Lincoln Park. Similarly, the mass media has been either complicit in or conned by publicity stunts, staged in the spirit of Barnum but requiring media communication of the staged fraudulence under way. Hollywood agents became adept at promoting their starlet clients by getting them "mentioned" or seen in the press through a variety of clever means: picking public fights with someone, diving naked into a public fountain, committing themselves to a political cause, or loudly considering entrance into a Trappist monastery. Fight promoters such as Tex Rickard (and his spiritual descendant, Don King) were adept at hyping an upcoming fight. Media performers such as boxer Muhammad Ali mastered the art of the staged press conference with his opponent in which there would be mock threats and almost-fisticuffs, all of which was designed to heighten interest in the real fight. Publicity stunting evokes the delight of the audience in the silliness of the pseudo-event, but has the effect of making them curious to see more. Legendary film promoters such as "Jungle Sam" Katzman, William Castle, and Joseph E. Levine gained attention to their movies through publicity campaigns (Castle had audiences sign waivers in case they were frightened to death before they could see one of his horror movies), often stirring interest in otherwise wretched films (Levine has been quoted to the effect that you can fool all the people all the time if the advertising is right and the budget is big enough). The "trailer" campaigns, personal appearances at opening by stars, publicity releases for the press timed for the movie's opening, and so forth all were calculated to bring people to the theater. They were in the lineage of circus barkers who convinced people walking down the midway that they were about to see sights and wonders they must not miss. Afterwards, when the inevitable let-down sinks in, people can console themselves with the bemused thought of having been so professionally fleeced.[2]

Since Boorstin called attention to the phony image-making and event-making process, we have witnessed the proliferation of phony events to the extent that they now dominate the news and entertainment media. There is a kind of Gresham's Law in which phony events tend to drive out real ones, since the former is now deemed more dramatically satisfying and therefore more newsworthy than the latter. A pseudo-event is more vivid and contained, less chaotic and messy than a real event. Staging news compresses amorphous and complicated events into the rhetoric and imagery of news artifice. But, as Boorstin understood, the dominance of pseudo-events tends to affect our expectations, and thus our lives. Not only do we expect our news and entertainment to be presented in the formats of pseudo-eventing, eventually we come to see our own lives as being fulfilled to the extent we are able to participate in pseudo-events. This may range from the Society for Creative Anachronisms arranging mock medieval jousts or Renaissance fairs on Sunday afternoons to kids playing violent video games or Dungeons and Dragons. But we seem to feel that we are only alive when we can escape the mundane and quotidian and become part of some sort of reality other than the one we have to live in during everyday existence. Pseudo-events arrange our experience, telling us news that is entertaining, providing us entertainment that is newsworthy, and expanding the opportunities for investing the self in events that are beyond the real—surreal or hyper-real or megareal—but in any case a "higher" reality which beckons us because that's wherein we can "really live." Life only has meaning in the enjoyment of a staged event, in our encounter with the phony. It is as if our actual lives are insufficient and bland, and must be complemented or even escaped by entry into virtual lives that are contrived and vivid. Further, it seems to be the case that we require someone else to "program" our experience. Industries such as computer and TV games, virtual realities, theme parks, and fantasy tours all cater to our desire for heightened experiences above and beyond the routine conduct of our lives. Thus in the last decades of the twentieth century, we have expanded on the pseudo-event, developing a variety of phony experiences we may utilize for self-dramatization. In a sense, these are just variations on the pseudo-event, but we may usefully distinguish them as phony events in their own right.

SPECTACLE

The idea of spectacle is a complement and expansion of Boorstin's prescient concept. A spectacle is a staged show that is contrived for the display of appearances that are supposed to impress us. Appearance is what is important, and the visual sense is manipulated in order to maximize our apprehension of appearances. Thus the arts of dramatization are enhanced by the arts of display, making the visual component of the experience the primary, and primal, experience. So a staged event has not only a pseudo/phony quality in terms of its contrivance, but also is imbued with expanded and colorful aspects that make it more spectacular. In an effort to attract larger audiences, the tendency is to make an event all the more spectacular than previous events, outdoing other events, and upgrading the size and scope of the event. New events become important because media managers and audiences discover their spectacular quality.

This has been a notable trend in the theater. The "block-buster" shows on Broadway and in London have in many cases become more spectacle than play, appealing to people because of the wondrous special effects on the stage, the large cast, and often even the great length of the show. Similarly, American movies made with ambitions for large audiences have tended toward spectacle, with ever more impressive special effects, emphasis on highly paid superstars, and fantastic stories about time travel, biogenetics, and other wonders of the postmodern screen. As an expectation, the desire for spectacle subordinates other more traditional aspects of the theatre and movies—plot, characterization, climax, and denouement. The action rises and falls on the awesomeness of the scenic gigantism—how big and mean are the dinosaurs, the monumentality of the hero, the number of foes slain in ever more ingenious and violent ways, the otherworldly nature of the setting, and so on.

The principle of spectacle may also help explain the extraordinary exposure and admiration accorded fashion models. Fashion models have always been beautiful and admired, to be sure, but now more than ever they are objects of admiration. With the rise of media outlets (CNN and other cable channels) that carry fashion segments, their exposure has helped to display their spectacular bodies and bearing, wearing the equally spectacular (if often bizarre) high fashions designed as colossally expensive clothes. Supermodels such as Cindy Crawford and Claudia Schiffer command large salaries and press attention, becoming in the process "human pseudo-events," celebrities who are known not only for their beauty but also for their participation in the spectacle of fashion. The fashion show is now telecast around the world from the great centers of fashion (New York, Paris, Milan), and is watched because it is a colorful and exciting spectacle of fashionability, a pageant of superhuman-appearing beauties displaying body at the height of its perfection and clothes at the moment of "the latest thing" to be marketed as expensive adornment. The model is an image of feminine allure, adorned for the benefit of the world in clothing fit for goddesses and displayed in glittering settings appropriate for their godly status. Through media exposure, especially display in magazine advertisements, they have become a social icon to be worshiped and emulated by us lesser mortals. We are their auditors, who are called upon to watch, and to learn from and act upon their "model behavior." A model in a fashion show is something exhibited to view as unusual, notable, or entertaining, a standard dictionary definition of spectacle (from *spectus*, to look, to watch), a term closely related to "specter," a visible disembodied spirit or phantasm. The fashion model is a specter, something that can only be looked at as female poetry in motion, a phantasm of olympian proportions. They are spectacular beings who affirm that appearance and beauty are paramount, and in that sense are symbolic figures like any celebrity. But unlike the movie star, they are virtually anonymous (with Crawford, Schiffer, and others, that has changed in some degree, since these have become the love interest of movies stars and royalty), as the lovely personages who adorn the scenery of the fashion show. But in their public personage (their private life is another matter) they are phony beings who are the actors of a phony event, a pseudo-event that envelops in the manna of glamour the marketing of brands of clothing to customers who buy the "fashion design" in the hopeless hope that such adornment will somehow make them look like the models who displayed them.

A related event that uses beautiful young women as the personages displayed in a spectacle of pulchritude is the beauty contest. The "Miss America" or "Miss Universe" pageant is a spectacular collection of women who are recruited and trained for the display of their talents as beauty contestant. Like models, they receive professional training as to how to be a proper adornment for the spectacle, and in this case, triumph in the competition (not all contestants are suitable as "Miss Congeniality"). An entire industry exists that "grooms" young women for the contestant industry, and like athletes, often beauty aspirants move around to "position" themselves for a state or local title. A "Miss River City" or "Miss

State" is often not even from the place, and seeks professional help and funding; like the prep athlete, she is no amateur, seeking titles as a career path. The beauty queen is really a professional, cultivating those skills and attributes that prepare her for competitiveness in the contest industry. The rewards are considerable—scholarships, cash gifts, travel budgets, and most of all, publicity and fame, the keys to subsequent career moves, such as the movies or television. Like the model, the beauty contestant walking gracefully on the platform is a product that is marketed with financial backing and expert coaching and preening, including cosmetic surgery, body shaping, and the arts of self-presentation (such as saying the right thing when asked about world peace or whale hunting). Indeed, there are even professional agencies that recruit potential beauty queens in interviews on college campuses and modeling agencies, and contract to manage the careers of women in search of titles and fame.

The beauty pageant, then, is an elaborate spectacle that displays competitive personages who market themselves as the most beautiful (and to a lesser degree, talented) young woman in the land. As a spectacle, it allows for legitimate exhibitionism, the display of lovely young women for the benefit of admiring audiences (lecherous men refer to such events as "skin shows"). The spectacle features the exhibition of physical ideals by the display of the most perfected specimens. Like the model, the principal actors in the pseudo-event are personages who are exhibited as superhuman and thus beyond the mundane and ordinary looking. The exhibitors of the spectacle construct a "corporate image" of the perfect young woman and show her off as a commodity. The fetishism of this commodity involves the desire to gaze at a beautiful appearance, but also to buy those things which will either gain access to such a beauty or take on the attributes of beauty. The glitter and glamour of the spectacle enhance and encourage those desires. These desires are countered by more recent criticism of such fetishes, since they involve phoniness. The beauty queen is a phony, a marketed pseudo-being whose public personage masks calculated ambitions and often machinations. The spectacle is a phony event, parading a "cattle show" of beautiful women while asserting that they are innocents and the motives of the sponsors of the show (not to mention at least the male audience) are not mercenary or exploitative.

The spectacle, then, is a kind of social drama, a symbolic event that celebrates something deemed valuable. A spectacle can involve deceit, as we suggested with the spectacular display of beautiful women. Since it is a symbolic event, it can be used to associate values that are not evident (such as making money or feasting your eyes on shapely women in swimsuits) with the values that are stated and celebrated. The pomp and circumstance of a political court, be it the kings of old or the modern presidency, always had the "hidden agenda" of shoring up the image of the leader's power and prestige. The values of the State were associated with the personage of the king or president, in the hope that the symbolic celebration of political values would enhance the major celebrant, shoring up his or her reputation. A spectacle may have a "subtext" embedded in its conduct that is not obvious or even consciously intended, but is nonetheless communicated. In all cases, the spectacle is conducted as if it is a necessary and "real" event that has to take place, is important, and demands attention.

The spectacle should be distinguished from ritual celebrations that are meaningful. For religious communicants, for example, a Mass or service is a ritual that has symbolic meaning. But a religious spectacle is different. A spectacle is by definition spectacular, and many people are drawn to the event because of that quality rather than to participate in the sacred. The religious spectacles of television—crusades held in large stadiums, "services" held in superchurches, set in a theme park, or programs conducted on elaborate sets—all lose their aura of sacredness. They are a spectacular show, and people are drawn to them for their vivid and elaborate celebrations of religiosity, as distinguished from religion. Those who attend religious spectacles, either in person or via television, are worshipping at the altar of entertainment, finding not spiritual but sensational nourishment. Gazing at religious shows choreographed on elaborate and colorful sets, admiring the costumed and coiffured evangelical cast brimming with engineered enthusiasm and planned spontaneity, and walking through the antiseptic streets of religious theme parks, one is experiencing a phony heaven on earth, a heaven of the donor's delusions.

A military spectacle is a phony event that communicates false bravado, a "show of force" paraded for public impression and amusement. This can involve simply mobilized forces on parade, exhibitions (such as air shows on Armed Forces Day) or rituals (laying wreaths and honoring the war dead on Memorial Day), or actual armed maneuvers or interventions. In all cases, the aim of the military spectacle is the display of armed power, either potential or real, in symbolic situations. This is clear enough in ceremonial or celebratory situations, but it is also the case in situations where troops are put in harm's way. If there is much public display of controlled images and reports as to their disposition and success, there is also reason to expect that the maneuver is being manipulated for public relations or morale reasons. For instance, the Reagan Administration's invasion of the tiny island of Grenada in 1983 was a military action to secure an unimportant and obscure place of no strategic value, but of great value as a military spectacle. It occurred in the wake of what the Reagan team thought was a legacy of American weakness (as with the Iranian hostage stalemate in the previous administration) that needed to be overcome through the reassertion of American military power. But there was also fear of lengthy and costly military involvement leading to large numbers of casualties and no victory, as in Vietnam. What was needed was a quick and decisive victory with virtually no casualties. The meaningless political upheaval on a small Caribbean island provided the pretext and opportunity for such symbolic reassertion of the legitimate national and virtually unilateral use of military force. Further, it deflected attention away from the disastrous incursion into Lebanon, wherein a Marine barracks had just been destroyed by a bomb, killing nearly 300 Marines. The grim spectacle of the rubble in Beirut was replaced in the news by the heroic spectacle of American troops triumphant, with images of being greeted as liberators by the natives and saviors by American medical students. The press was strictly controlled, so there were no "bad scenes"—no shots of fighting, the wounded and dead, civilian casualties, or accidents. (It turns out in retrospect that in fact the invasion was more of a comic opera mishap than a heroic march to glory, and that many American casualties were caused by "friendly fire," accidentally shooting our own men.) But the televised images added up to a spectacle of a president and his army triumphant over evil (in the shape of Cuban workmen there to work on a runway), and Reagan emerged from it with the claim that "our days of weakness are over. Our military forces are back on their feet and standing tall." The claim was preposterous, in the real sense of not facing an adequate foe; but in terms of public perceptions, in the symbolic sense of a satisfying visual narrative, Grenada was a helpful politico-military spectacle.

The Grenada military spectacle illustrates a key distinction: those events that are analogous to boxing, and those events that are analogous to wrestling. Boxing (when it is not fixed) is truly competitive, a context wherein the outcome is uncertain and real. Wrestling, on the other hand, is always fixed; the outcome is predetermined, and the fun of it is the spectacle that unfolds according to a melodramatic script: the drama is cast as a contest of good and evil, and despite all the machinations of the villainous foe, the hero in the end triumphs. Here the American president and the military could be cast as the good guys coming to the rescue, even though we had every reason to know that the "bout" was no contest. But its satisfactions were great, and the bounty in public opinion enormous. Thus a properly conducted military spectacle such as Grenada leaves nothing to chance, picking for an emblematic contest an enemy that simply provides the pretext for the presentation of the military melodrama. The distinction is one between doing and acting: boxing and war involve doing something that meets real resistance that must be overcome for objectives large enough to seek through force; wrestling and spectacle involve acting out a symbolic drama with an enemy, real or imagined, that is merely a pretext for a media drama that realizes the cathartic pleasures of the theater. The Grenada precedent would lead to the use of military spectacle on other occasions for other purposes. President Bush's incursions into Panama were useful spectacle shoring up the "tough" image of the leader, building on the theatrical instincts of his predecessor (in 1988, there were military maneuvers in Panama that were a show of force, inspiring one American officer there to insist for the news media that "this maneuver is in no way related to real world events"). Indeed, the Grenada model is the prototype of an *exemplary event*, the kind of pseudo-event in which reality is enveloped in a spectacle, serving as an exemplar of the proper conduct of a predictable but highly satisfying public event that communicates heroic power and the triumph of good over evil. An exemplary event is thoroughly phony, in that it is no less a con job than wrestling; but as far as "setting an example," it serves a dramatistic political and military purpose that has nothing to do with its strategic value but a great deal to do with its symbolic value.[3]

The spectacle has become an expected part of American life, transforming every event, whether regularly scheduled or occasional, into a show that must outdo previous shows. Thus every year the Super Bowl championship football show must surpass what had happened in previous years; if the game is dull, as they often are, then the event is enlivened by the congeries of colorful and exciting ancillary happenings—the half-time show, interviews, writhing half-naked cheerleaders, the crowd's diversity and enthusiasm, and so on. Indeed, perhaps the game itself pales besides the spectacle of the humanity gathered to witness it; certainly when it becomes lopsided, the TV network carrying it virtually ignores the game for the more interesting ancillary happenings surrounding the event. The Super

Bowl has become a *megaevent*, hyped through puffery, exaggeration, and other forms of rhetorical expansiveness, and thus elevated in public anticipation as something unsurpassed that must be seen as a once-in-a-lifetime event. But spectacles, like heroes, become a bore at last, so it may be that events televised with the promise of greater and grander magnitude finally begin to evoke an "is that all there is?" response from jaded media audiences. Given the expansion of choices open to media audiences, it may be the case that many people will become "overloaded" on gigantic spectacles, or at least choose between different spectacles (or anti-spectacles, events staged in response to or defiance of larger, more "official" events, such as anti-inaugurals in Washington or anti-Rose Bowl parades that parody or refute the larger event staged by event-makers and the media). One of the great event-makers, promoter David L. Wolper staged one of the more gigantic, and gaudy, spectacles in recent memory in the "Liberty Weekend" celebration of the hundredth anniversary of the Statue of Liberty. What could have been the occasion for sober reflection on the meaning and status of American liberties became instead one of the hallmark events of the Reagan years, a megaevent of such magnitude and sheer tastelessness that the idea of liberty as a value to be practiced was lost in the gigantism of "larger" values, such as popular spectacle as worship of the State and Leader. Further, the message was clear that liberty, or at least access to the official celebration of liberty, was for sale. Liberty Weekend was a megaevent sponsored by commercial firms, televised by the network that bid $10 million for it, and gained access to the best seats in the house by paying big money for them. Thus the megaevent celebrated the power of money rather than the blessings of liberty, since the rich, powerful, and famous were the celebrants who represented America in the dazzling array of events (everything from a dazzling fireworks display to 200 Elvis imitators). Liberty Weekend became a megaevent that celebrated the class and status system of America as it existed in 1986 rather than the ostensible subject of liberty. The structure and conduct of the megaevent gave spectacular support for who was important rather than who was free. It was a celebration of power rather than freedom, the power of political, economic, and cultural elites to dominate the scene while the rest of us are relegated to the role of passive audience destined to watch the powerful act. A social drama of the magnitude of Liberty Weekend is a monumental megaevent of great significance for elites attempting to shore up the image (and self-image) of their own centrality and importance, but in the process it reminds the large audience that they are mere mortals who cannot mingle with the olympian gods who are the actors in the limelight of power, wealth, and fame. In an ironic sense, Liberty Weekend and similar spectacles convey the message that most people are not free, and liberty exists only for those with the power to exercise it at the apex of society with participation in a megaevent. The rest of us are left only with envy and resignation, and a vague feeling that somehow we were left out of the party. This feeling is countered by critical realization that a megaevent like Liberty Weekend is thoroughly phony, and that those who are the vaunted performers in such popular comedy are there because they are phonies. The phony is as dazzled by an elaborate con as the mark, or object of the con; but they want to be part of the bedazzlement, and seek mightily to be included in the best seats, or performances, of the latest megaevent, no matter how lurid and distasteful. Phonies are drawn to megaevents, since such happenings are designed for the shameless display of phony values and personages, and thus offer a chance for the exhibition of surfaces that are the thin extent of their being.

It may be the case, then, that megaevents are inherently displays of social power that feature elites who seek self-exhibition. Phonies are constantly in search of forums for the display of their own wondrous public self for the rest of us to behold, and mega-events—sporting events, awards ceremonies, special events, political galas, and so on—are a chance to be part of a larger and inclusive phoniness. Indeed, one of the curious features of spectacles is their "lightness of being": they have no history, no tradition, no repeatable rituals, no stable set of participants in the same way, say, an established church or university might have. A megaevent happens without context or memory. Each time the Super Bowl occurs, it is an event-in-itself, without interest expressed in its past or future; it is hyped as the big event of the world right now, and that is all that matters. Once it is over, "it's history," meaning that the spectacle, and the participants, are ephemera that disappear without significant memory or social trace. Liberty Weekend resulted in no great rededication to American liberty (or for that matter, freedom of immigration, the great inscription on the Statue of Liberty). The spectacle is a momentary suspension of time, focusing our attention on an artificial megaevent or exemplary event without true or real connection to any predecessors or successors; the enjoyment, or uses, of the event takes precedence over any sense of continuity (the island of Grenada, promised great benefit from the Reagan invasion, was quickly ignored, and has sunk back into obscurity and poverty).

The phony spectacle is an event made larger and often more grotesque by the universalizing power of television, since big staged events can now be seen virtually worldwide. In the last half of the twentieth century, televised spectacles came to a media expectation: something was not important if it was not ritualized in a big show which we could all watch. Some figures, such as Reagan, were more adept at this than others, because of their acting ability. But this also became an institutional expectation, with various organizations dramatizing something in spectacular form. The bravado of military spectacle, the spectacle of summits and signings, the spectacle of popular and political royalty, leisure spectacles such as sporting events, religious spectacles—all were megaevents that were essentially phony rituals conjured up to attribute meaning and purpose to the event under way, whether it was meaningful and purposeful or not. The difficulty was that this resulted in a kind of equality of spectacle, wherein one was accorded the same magnitude and meaning as any other, so it became hard for the mass audience to distinguish what was important and what was not. Too, the ascendancy of spectacle meant for many people that the public ritual was the reality, or at least the culmination of reality, since there was no information on or attention called to hard decisions and organizational effort. For many, the spectacle then becomes by definition what is happening, and indeed preferable to the messiness of ordinary human affairs. Everything leading up to and flowing from the ritualized event is relegated to unimportance. Social focus is therefore not on the process but the spectacle, and the spectacle makes things happen. When Ronald and Nancy Reagan inaugurated their "Just Say No" campaign, this spectacle of a grandparenting couple urging voluntary abstinence from drugs replaced actual governmental expenditures for drug enforcement forces (Reagan was cutting the budget for the Drug Enforcement Administration). The spectacle was sufficient, superseding the daily grind of interdicting drugs, and reassuring the audience that the government, in the guise of the domestic theater of the Reagan presidency, cares about the social impact of drugs. The spectacle is here utilized in the spirit of King Canute, who gave orders to the waves to stop; they didn't, but it was an impressive spectacle. Drug enforcement on the streets and at sea was hurt by the budget cuts, but what mattered was the spectacle of a Canutean president giving orders to the drugs to stop. Domestic spectacle thus becomes the focus of official policy, acquiring the moral authority of symbolic action but ignoring the less satisfying uses of instrumental action.

In the future, we may well see the spectacle recurrently vested with authority. If doing things becomes less effective, then acting out things in an authoritative manner as if something were being done may become a symbolic substitute. The phony event substitutes for and supersedes the real event. If historical and social processes are out of control, the only way to exercise authority is to claim control over ritual actions which offer ceremonial power over the world. The spectacle becomes a form of sympathetic magic, exorcising devils from the realm and commanding helpful spirits to watch over us. Then it is more than a diversion and an amusement; the spectacle takes on the authority of higher ritual, as if vicarious participation in sporting, religious, or political pseudo-events provides personal and social deliverance. Our deliverance from evil becomes a matter of believing in the magical properties of the spectacle, preferring to believe in the symbolic comforts of faith rather than the instrumental efficacy of good works.

DESIGNED EXPERIENCES

The ascendancy of the spectacle as a phony event with very real consequences is part of a larger process: the preference given to the dramatic event staged for social audiences. In the contemporary world, the "visual culture" seems to give impetus to the conviction that we must believe what we see. Thus what we wish to see becomes a choice that tends people toward the "improved upon" great realities designed to capture our seeking and anxious imaginations. In a sense, the encompassing myth of the age is that the camera is an eye through which we can see the world we prefer. Since actor and audience find each other, we are brought together by the desire to enact dramas which depict what we wish to see. The "post-modern" view is that the world is as we conceive it, and that we have a choice in seeing the world of our conception. Freedom consists of imagining the world as we wish. Given such a choice, we often wish for a world that is "more so"—more beautiful, more orderly, more delightful, more interesting, more exciting, more sentimental, more moral, or whatever, as we like it. Thus what is real is what we choose; what is chosen is designed to satisfy our choice. When we choose something else, what was previously chosen evaporates; what we now choose takes on the magical aura of the experiential real. For reality is now experience, or rather what we choose to be experience.

For those who have the resources, in the emergent "post-consumptive" world, experience is the thing. People seek out those experiences which are vivid. People go to places, involve themselves in relationships, acquire hobbies, live in houses, even seek careers that are for them an experience. We buy those material possessions which have for us an experiential quality. Advertisers appeal to the experience of ownership ("O what a feeling!" in a car ad) or the experiences that flow from the use of a product or service (the sexual experiences promised by perfume ads). Indeed, an entire industry has developed to cater to our desire for vivid experiences, since we now choose those preferences which let us encounter realities we wish to add to our inventory of experiences. Entrepreneurs now create realities which we may pay to enter for the experience. People seek and demand an increasing range and depth of new experiences, much of which is driven by fantasies entertained in their mundane existence but ordinarily unrealizable. These fantasies are "realized" in places created to cater to them, through the staging of fantastic events for the seeker to enter and "live through." (This development was anticipated by the movie *Westworld* and the TV series *Fantasy Island*.)

Such leisure pseudo-events are termed "designed experiences." A designed experience is a ludenic exercise staged in a world apart from quotidian reality, where one enters and experiences an event that is designed to satisfy such a long-held desire. Thus there is a market for purchased dream-states, a temporary movement into a ludenic pseudo-world of extraordinary properties. There are, for example, fantasy resorts that provide vacationers with a wide variety of "things they had always wanted to do"—riding in a hot air balloon, golfing with star professionals, starring in a video movie, playing battleship in rubber boats on a man-made pond. One large hotel chain has invested heavily in fantasy resorts, since now harassed two-career couples will want to amuse themselves by escaping their hectic lives for a quick but diverting excursion into some fantasy experience, such as meandering through a simulated tropical rain forest or driving a race car. "Experience brokers" arrange for fantasy vacations in numerous exotic and even dangerous locations around the world, for those who have entertained the fantasy of climbing the world's most famous mountains (one broker remarked that you could just about open a thriving singles bar at the foot of Everest), taking part in primitive rituals in remote jungles, learning bullfighting in Spain, or even observing the fighting in Beirut or Belfast. "Experience design firms" arrange trips for amateurs to take part in archaeological digs, scientific expeditions, life in a strange culture, or other "academic" pursuits. But many of them are more self-indulgent and downright lurid. Many designed experiences involve such things as spending the night in a haunted house, a day in a "Westworld" town, or on a case with private detectives (recall Captain Picard's "private eye" fantasy on *Star Trek*'s holodeck). People who are willing to pay can sing in a nightclub, direct a symphony orchestra, direct a play, or appear in a movie. They can also become a sultan with their own harem for a weekend, or play the sadistic warden ruling a women's prison farm. Or they can become a monk under monastic discipline for a spell. In all cases, they have escaped into a fantasy world wherein events of their dreams are in some way acted out for them, or allow them to act them out in some contrived manner, ranging from some quite "normal" desires to more marginal and pathological yearnings.

One remarkable role-playing leisure excursion is the adult and amateur baseball fantasy camp. For those willing to pay, non-athletes who have always yearned to be a major league baseball player can go to a week of contrived spring training where retired major leaguers serve as camp counselors and fellow trainees. The ersatz jocks become engrossed in their new athletic status, as if some of the athletic prowess of their new "teammates" might rub off on them. (Trainees get a variety of gifts if they successfully "complete" the spring training, including a replica of a major league contract.) Thus frustrated athletes who are neurosurgeons or accountants can engage in the male bonding of a team with identifiable celebrities who validate their claim to their new, if fantastic, status. To be "accepted" as bogus athletes by greats such as Mickey Mantle is to live at a boundary, as if one could have stepped over into the world of the major leagues given a few breaks. The baseball fantasy camp lets middle-aged men relive the childhood fantasy that "someday I'll make the majors." The designed experience of the baseball camp allows men to indulge in a pretense, and the hired major leaguers who are part of the pseudo-team let them pretend. For them, to be a phony big league ballplayer for only a moment is apparently enough.

There are now also a variety of such camp experiences other than baseball. A rock'n'roll fantasy camp was established, which allowed paying customers to join a band, make a recording, learn from "coaches" such as lead guitarists and drummers, and associate with rock figures such as Mick Fleetwood. At the conclusion of the camp, they get to perform for a live audience, and entertain dreams of a career as a rocker. At the Sportcasters Camp of America, real sportscasters teach campers the rudiments of TV anchoring, interviewing, voice modulation, and play-by-play technique over a week; the aim is not to train sportscasters, but to give frustrated play-callers a chance to get on the air for a brief time and vent their latent abilities. At the U.S. Space Camp in Huntsville, Alabama, campers can play astronaut on shuttle mission simulations, go on moonwalks, and live in a space habitat. At a Los Angeles Muscle and Fitness Camp, one can work out and pump iron with bodybuilding superstars, eat training table meals with the muscled, then compete at week's end in a competition. At the Authentic 1870s Cattle Drive in Colorado, various "city slickers" can drive cattle for a week, eating sourdough biscuits and beans, sleep under the stars, and wear chaps and spurs. And a soap opera fantasy experience is run in a Washington suburb; for a fee, people get rudimentary training in soap acting, and then play roles in a taped soap opera (entitled "Fantasy"), then are given a copy of the half-hour show to take home as a memento of their brief Warholian moment as a soap star.

Access to designed experiences is not confined to the wealthy who trek off to vacation spas, fantasy camps, and the like. Rather the designed experience is becoming a widespread feature of American leisure life. Restaurateurs use a variety of motifs to "frame" the dining experience, everything from elegant to contemporary to nostalgic. The good old days of, say, the 1950s, has become a concept: one dines in a recreated imitation of a 1950s teenage hangout, complete with neon, bubble gum colors, juke box selectors in the booths, waitresses in cheerleader outfits (and who perform dance routines), bartenders in fountain aprons, and so on. Such restaurants surround the patron with a phony world that is supposed to conjure up warm memories of the 1950s, an allegedly simpler and better time; but we may wonder if those charming surroundings make the food any better. When eating becomes a "dining experience," it has acquired surroundings that are supposed to augment, but may be better than, the food. There are now many dinner-theaters around the country that "intermingle" the dinner with the play, to the extent that the diner-patrons are a part of the theatrical experience. One can become part of a medieval festival, complete with singing buxom wenches, a tournament and joust, contrived feudal intrigue, courtly ladies and jesters and knights, all performed in indoor arenas with tiered seats surrounding a sand-filled jousting pit. Experience brokers offer "murder weekends," where paying customers go to a mansion or on a chartered train, becoming part of a mystery, since a "murder" occurs among the actors who intermingle with the patrons, who are then supposed to collaborate in solving the "case," all interspersed with parties and buffets, "action sequences" by actors, provided "clues," with an "inspector" or some such letting the patrons question the "suspects," and even letting the customers take on new names, intrigue in the plot, and have different outcomes. Such designed experiences also can be staged at one's home: at wealthy parties, not only might the host stage an elaborate game such as a contrived murder, but he or she might also hire guests who are to "make a scene" for the amusement of the guests. There is a touring theatrical "wedding," entitled "Tony 'n' Tina's Wedding," which satirizes working-class urban Italian weddings and allows intermingling of cast and guests at the reception: you can witness the whole ghastly and tasteless satire, including the gum-chewing bridesmaids, the pregnant maid of honor, the groom's divorced mom and dad fighting with each other, his blond bimbo girl friend, the drunken and lewd ushers, and so on, in broad stereo-typical strokes, but broken into subplots for the enjoyment of the overhearing audience. Other variations include a theater wherein guests observe the intrigue unfolding during dinner at the official home of Cyprus's British governor prior to World War I. Another "participation play" occurs at a high school prom in 1963, wherein the patrons, in the midst of dining and dancing at the prom to vintage music, elect a prom queen and then try to figure out who murdered her. All of these examples illustrate the desire to experience theatrical excitement closer to oneself than before; the separation of play and audience by the proscenium is abandoned in favor of becoming a part of the pseudo-action. The experience is designed for the patron to become a participant-observer of the play, finding in this new designation a momentary thrill gained from entry into a created world of adventure, mystery, and romance.

Phony events are increasingly available to ordinary people to enter right at home. The development of fantasy games has made it possible to use the TV screen to spend many hours (one estimate has schoolchildren spending more time daily playing video games than studying) in the presence of an entertaining and absorbing fantasy, often violent. Much controversy developed among parents and educators about the graphic nature of these games, since kids seemed to enjoy the blood and gore of such games as "Mortal Combat," complete with decapitations and other carnage. Then there were the many (often bootleg) pornographic games, such as "General Custer," with Custer's soldiers bent on raping as many "native American" squaws as possible. In many games, TV or otherwise, there is now the possibility of assuming the role of an imaginary character in a designed environment. The most famous of these is "Dungeons and Dragons," in which "player characters" can become part of the intricate structure and intrigues of the game. Devotees play these games for long periods of times, so engrossed in some cases that the rest of the world is "tuned out." Even though participation is vicarious, some players have become so involved that parents or friends have thought them pathological. Now with computer nets and the like, it is possible to keep playing the many games that create an entire world apart to which we may escape. Rotisserie baseball creates entire leagues of players, statistics, seasons, histories, franchise moves, player drafts, and so on. People who play it become preoccupied, sometimes again to the point of obsession, with an all-absorbing game that becomes a primary part of their lives to the exclusion of other activities, such as work and parenting. The many games available are designed worlds of escape, creating empires or baseball leagues or winning military conflicts. They allow those who seek escape to spend an inordinate amount of time in gaming, to the exclusion and perhaps detriment of real-world responsibilities. Escapist fare is often sought because one's own existence is deemed unexciting and dull, so perhaps the popularity of these games is a commentary on the state of interest in marital and work life in contemporary America.[4]

The potential for "personal" designed experiences that involve no travel has been further enhanced by the advances in what is called "virtual reality." Through the use of computers, sensory equipment has been invented which allows the participant to go to places and do things that involve no movement. These "artificial realities" or "virtual environments" come to you, surrounding the participant with a designed experience increasingly of his or her own choosing. We may now enter worlds that appear to be present but in fact aren't, but that line is blurring. Virtual reality makes imagination real, at least in the sense of creating structures we can literally surround ourselves with. The technology is developing to let us structure our imaginations, exercising our capacity for make-believe that overcomes recalcitrant physical reality. As it develops, this newfound capacity may become the ultimate expression of solipsism, since the individual can spend time in universes of her or his own creation, relating to creatures and things of her or his own choosing, and willing the outcome of stories in that universe ruled by one person. But it doesn't have to be: in the future, people will be able to share a virtual reality of their joint making. It is not clear how "real" virtual reality can be made, but it does seem to expand the possibility of creating, and living in, phony worlds to the exclusion of the mundane existence of "normal life."

What is of note in all these developments is that for many people designed experiences are preferable to real ones. Phony events are sought since they are to be preferred to real ones. If we assume that the "real world" is one in which the individual has imperfect control, then it may be the case that designed experiences provide delightful moments of controlled pleasure, or in the case of games, controlled chance. The effort to flee to imaginary social worlds may well belie some kind of crisis of boredom with mundane existence, since designed experiences have now become a vast growth industry. American students, as any teacher can tell you, are bored with school; adults are bored with marriage, work, and orthodox leisures such as television; the wealthy are bored with the round of the usual pleasure domes of conspicuous consumption. Widespread boredom is a clear signal that a culture is in trouble, the trouble that results from stagnation. It may well be that the search for experience in designed settings, be they fantasy resorts or virtual realities, is not unlike the otherworldliness that beset the Roman world of the early centuries A.D. The "retreat" of many people into the ecstasies and mysteries of otherworldly religions and philosophies in search of alternative and superior realities to the boring humdrum of the *Pax Romana* augured the inability of the Roman world to cope with the pressing problems of internal corruption and external threat. It may well be that we have become the victims of our own success, creating a world of comfort and relative peace to the extent that many people feel so trapped in it that they want to escape. Social roles may be so unsatisfying that alternative "game roles" are sought for excitement and elevation.

The social consequences of such a shift of focus and interest can be considerable if it becomes a persistent widespread pattern. If people spend considerable amounts of time pursuing the pleasures of phony events, then real events—events that are supposed to matter, since they occur in the hard-edged bumpy world of political, economic, and cultural conflict—become marginal. (Cable TV alone gives us a clue, since with the many choices we have, events such as a State of the Union address gather a smaller share of the whole audience; in large urban media markets, reruns of old movies will gain a larger audience than a presidential debate occurring at the same time.) It becomes a social matter of "where we live": we can find life in the subjective reality of phony events conjured up for our ludenic pleasure, rather than the objective reality of actual events which intrude on our palpable existence. Phony events are created by artistry, whereas the material conditions of life are matters of process; but artistry cannot change process. The world through the looking glass of awards ceremonies, beauty contests, virtual realities or whatever is make-believe, but it is only that. If such events are taken as "more real" or prettier than the more boring or frightening world of mean existence, then we are drawn to such "places" for preferable events to watch and enjoy. But the world we left behind does not evaporate, and events with material consequences do happen there; if we begin to mistake the phony event encountered in "virtual" worlds for the "truly real and beautiful," then neglect of the common realm of human activity becomes easy. But the world as traditionally known is no daydream on the other side of the looking glass; it is not designed for the delight of our personal play-experience. That world is not the sum total of our impressions of it, nor is it the product of design staged for our benefit.

It has been said that virtual reality is a technology that makes imagination real. In some measure, that is the case with all phony events. The technique of design is utilized in order to structure an experience that appeals to us. The event is phony because it is either social or personal theater that makes the imaginary seem real. But the phony event has become so pervasive and available that now we think the imaginary real, and even for some, the real imaginary. If we continue to confuse the two realms—the fantastic and the factual—then we are indeed in for some interesting social consequences. Make-believe may make belief, but belief in the imaginary as a superior and higher realm of truth and reality is a conviction that is sustained only by the most ardent effort to ignore the inferior and lower realm of grinding social process. Phony events are ceremonies of innocence, no matter how lurid, for they commit us to the gaiety of play, reverting us to the imaginative gardens of childhood.

CONCLUSION

It has been opined that the great myth of our media age is that the camera is a human eye. We watch as social voyeurs the proliferation of phony events as if they had some grounds, when in truth they are ephemeral figures that vanish like ghosts at dawn. There now exists a vast "unreality industry" that has mastered the artistry of staging phony events for our voyeuristic pleasure.[5] Yet once the show is over, the stage is dismantled and the troupe moves on, and we follow the camera eye to the next extravaganza. Phony events occupy our vision of the world, often several at once as we graze across the cable. Certainly we look forward to and structure our schedule so that we can enjoy the next big phony event. Since we find phony events so appealing, it must stem from our desire to see a qualitatively better happening than we can see in everyday life. If our lives are so dreary, then we must sense that the illusions that are projected onto the social stage for our enjoyment stem from a fundamental self-delusion, the idea that those illusory chimeras are somehow better than we. Boorstin concluded his classic work noting that "we must discover our illusions before we can even realize that we have been sleepwalking."[6] But the difficulty is that the sleepwalker proceeds on the self-delusions of dreams, discovering in the illusions before him verification of the deep delusions on which he or she acts. Illusions are images projected onto our social or personal cave walls, inspired by the dream of desire that makes us wish for a world of perfected events with the proper dramatic logic and choreography. The development of games or visual technology that lets us enter illusionary worlds only enhances and enlarges our capacity for creating the phony. To paraphrase Pogo Possum, we have met the phony, and he is us.

CHAPTER 5

PHONY DEALS

"Let's make a deal" is perhaps the primal scenic statement in American life, expressing the essence of our desire to get along with each other through contracting agreements. The country was founded on a Constitution which was the product of an intricate set of political deals designed to hold the country together. American politics, as Madison envisioned in *Federalist* No. 10, was to be one of conciliation and compromise between potentially warring factions through practicing the art of the possible. American culture would be pluralistic, with toleration among religions, ideologies, and groups; diversity and cultural choice would become one of our great strengths. American business would be capitalist, with the "free marketplace" governing the exchange of goods and services, making for economic good deals that profited everyone. These three areas of American life would all be enriched by the free and rational exercise of different kinds of marketplaces—the political marketplace would involve the open clash of ideas and interests in the competition for power through electoral success; the cultural "marketplace of ideas" would operate through the freedom of expression, with good ideas and habits driving bad ones out; and the economic marketplace would be made fair through the "level playing field" of competition. These ideals of the deal seem hopelessly quaint in retrospect, but they still form a major part of American popular thought. Various institutions—the government, the popular media, the stock exchanges—would serve as "honest brokers" in a freely competing democratic society.

What this conception of society did not take into account was the practice of the art of the deal. Not everyone in American society was, or is, an honest broker. The injunction for us to make a deal often means that at least one party to the deal is dishonest. Human transactions involving the exchange of something of value mean that someone can manipulate the situation for advantage. When people are negotiating over the outcome of a relationship, who "wins" is often the result of the winning party's artistry in dealing, in successfully defining the situation. The definition of the situation is then in many cases a matter of gaining the upper hand. Simply put, the confidence man or woman can "work the con" in the transaction, making a raw deal seem to be a good deal. The exchange becomes a matter of winning, using the guise of trustworthiness to pull off the scam. Thus the art of the deal becomes the art of the con, since the "dishonest broker" in the exchange has engineered a phony deal.

Phony deals permeate every area of American life, from the most intimate to the most inclusive transactions, including sex and sales, relationships and contracts, piety and promotion. We are conned into phony deals with friends and lovers, preachers and salespersons, politicians and promoters. America originated in the promise of bogus land deals, and we have been falling for con jobs ever since. It is one contemporary measure of the extent of the con that it is a common warning to trust no one. We do not trust the motives of those we suspect are making a pitch, and fear being so gullible that we "get burned" by the art of the con that we don't tell family and friends when we are for fear of ridicule ("how could you have been so stupid?"). Our latent admiration for the artistry of the confidence man is counterbalanced by our often manifest disgust at the manipulations of the con artist. Programs such as *60 Minutes* rely heavily on that latter emotion, since many "investigative" TV programs rely on exposing outrageous cons by a variety of social undesirables. Indeed, we cannot make up our mind about the confidence man, vacillating back and forth from time to time in either admiration and envy, or repulsion and rejection.

Let us look at one common manifestation of a con man who makes a phony pitch: the male who pursues females with prurient interest and ulterior intent, in an effort at sexual conquest. At various junctures, both men and women have expressed, or at least attended popular expressions of, the male sexual adventurer, those popular figures in the Casanova tradition. Casanova was famous (or infamous) for his sexual exploits, which often included the "conquest" of women whom he deluded into "dangerous liaisons" through the adroit use of flattery and false promises. In all cases, the woman (often quite married) was treated as a sexual object in the sense of yet another objective to be overwhelmed into surrender. More recently, Hugh Hefner's "playboy" was a mythical but successfully marketed role model, someone who regarded sexual liaisons as a game involving the chase of a female prey until she was successfully bedded. The sexual pursuit of a beautiful young woman for its own sake was deemed a legitimate social enterprise, requiring the use of male guile to overcome her moral or personal restraints to casual and uncommitted sex. Teenagers of a previous generation had a more telling phrase for males who were successful at such a pursuit: "the make-out artist." A male was "on the make" and a girl was subject to "being made," connoting the use of male advances that involved subtle forms of persuasion and even coercion in "making" her have sex. Ian Fleming's "James Bond" was perhaps the most sophisticated version of the modern Casanova, the handsome virile man whose skill at social stealth as a secret agent is complemented by his skill at sexual stealth. In the 1950s and 1960s, such figures drew wide admiration for their sexual exploits, as a manifestation of their power and freedom: women were a form of social conquest that complemented their success in other areas of life, such as politics, business, and espionage. The difficulty was that the idealized relationship—the momentary conquest of the unattached woman by a conquering male—was made possible through the art of the con, a deal made by a phony pitch wherein consent is sought and gained for selfish and physical reasons, the realization of orgasmic pleasure without involvement. Thus in more recent years, the ideal of the male sexual con has been under attack by feminist leaders, and also ordinary women who have come to recognize and resent a phony deal when they see one. The sexual con is seen by many women as a form of salesmanship, an exercise in persuasion that has little to do with the ardent expression of affection but a great deal to do with the satisfaction of the male ego through totemic power. He may promise love and devotion, but what he wants is sex.

Sexual double-dealing is just one obvious and widespread example of our penchant for the phony deal, an exchange of goods or services wherein one party takes advantage of, and "wins" over, another. Phony deals tend to be "zero-sum games," in which one "side" to the relationship wins and the other side loses. Sexual gaming truly is a double-deal: the dealer has dealt an expressive "hand" that, if accepted, leads to exploitation and a sure loss. The poker metaphor is apt: the dealer has stacked the deck so that the other player is "not playing with a full deck" and courts losing in the game of wits. The male exploiter of women is cheating, "dealing from the bottom of the deck," in an effort to defeat and use the female player. The double-dealer is thus dealing two hands: his own, a winning hand, which gives him expressive power, and hers, a losing hand, which puts her at an disadvantage. She has been double-crossed by a phony deal, action contrary to a professed promise.

The collapse of trust between the sexes stems from this duplicitous use of the promise. Americans have always been beings who lived on the promise of American life, seeking the promised land and the American dream of fulfillment. But a promise is believed because of hope, that something done now—a present deal—will lead to the fulfillment of those hopes. Put your trust in me, we are constantly told, and I promise you that you will realize your dreams. But this appeal to confidence can be, and often is, phony. Keeping promises is a moral injunction that is part of our popular social code, both as an ethical concept (the Golden Rule) and as a folkway (Abe Lincoln's "honesty is the best policy"). The female who trusts the "honorable intentions" of a male because he has promised her his love and devotion may discover to her regret that she has been "had," both relationally and sexually. The consequence of such experiences is the learning of distrust, sometimes generalized to include all eligible males. Generalized suspicion of the motives of men makes true intimacy and passion more difficult, since "surrender" may mean another bitter aftermath of felt betrayal and loneliness. The woman has fallen victim to a phony, someone adept at sexual deals which benefit himself at the expense of the female "mark." (We may here note that women are equally capable of such sexual double-deals, "loving and leaving" men with the same cynical skill and faked intentions; no one sex or sexual orientation has a monopoly on phony dealings.)

This fear of being used badly by a confidence-building sexual partner has led to a variety of "formalized" relationships, in which the parties make legal agreements that are designed to avoid or thwart betrayals, both sexual and financial. It has become common for couples to sign "marriage contracts," spelling out the obligations and duties of each partner, and designating what can and cannot be gained from breaking off the relationship. The wealthy often arrange for "pre-nuptial agreements," which avoid a nasty legal battle if the spouse turns out to be goldigger or gigolo who faked love in order to get married for the sole purpose of bilking great amounts of money out of their rich mark. Even live-in unmarried lovers will sign "palimony" agreements wherein they agree to a variety of arrangements—not suing for money allegedly agreed to, consenting to have regular AIDs tests, and so on. All these trends in sexual relations are the result of our fear of sexual phonies, people who might use our capacity for affection or lust for their own ulterior purposes. The prevalence of phonies poisons the sexual well for many people, making them incapable of trusting even those people they live with or are married to. Legal constraints on exploitation of one kind or another reveal the extent we wish to go to not fall prey to sexual predators or deceivers. As in many other areas of life, when we meet a potential sexual partner, many of us initially assume or suspect that he or she cannot be trusted, only changing our mind after they have gained our confidence, and even then attempting to insure against being "had" through legal documents. When "matters of the heart" must be hedged by the formalities of legalism, it is clear that the "holiness of the heart's affection" has been tempered by our basic distrust of even those close to us. We want the promise of fidelity so much that we are willing to consult our lawyer to guarantee it. Despite our pessimistic fear of sexual betrayal and victimization, we cling desperately to the older optimistic promise of sexual happiness, in a state of gloomy optimism where we "hedge our bets" about our dear ones to protect ourselves from overconfidence.

The difficulty is that such legally defined relationships are phony, an attempt to enforce love by signing a piece of paper. Phony relationships such as these are sustained through written guarantees, not the bonds of affection or requited love. But we so fear that our affections are misplaced that we transform them into a phony deal in a pathetic effort to be loved alone.

A similar process is at work at colleges and universities which adopt sexual codes of conduct. Passions run high among students of that age group, so sex on campus is a reality, and sometimes a problem, especially since the sexual revolution of the 1960s. But in recent years, there have been concerted efforts by the administrative bureaucracies of higher education to regulate sexual behavior among students. Highly conservative schools, such as Bob Jones University or Liberty University, try to ban sexual activity, writing elaborate rules about kissing (Roman Catholic schools became famous for attempts to ban French kissing and girl's patent leather shoes that reflect up), prohibiting holding hands in public, regulating skirt length below the knees (Brigham Young University had conflicts with female students who insisted thigh exposure was their own business), and enforcing strict dormitory hours (with no "visitation" privileges). But public schools, and private schools with "liberal" traditions, have tried to regulate the more open sexual activity on campus, often stemming from feminist ideology and concerns. Fraternities, for example, were often the host institution to male attempts at sexual seduction, through the atmosphere of partying, the use of alcohol and drugs, and the availability of private bed space. But concerns about "date rape" and the sexual exploitation of women led to the articulation of elaborate rules of sexual conduct, not so much in an effort to ban it as to ensure "proper" sexual sensitivities and conduct. Some schools (Antioch College was one) wrote rules about obtaining verbal consent before one moved from one "level" of sexual activity to another, of insisting that people ask questions about HIV status, condom availability, and expressed consent before proceeding with intercourse. There was no effort to actually enforce such rules of passionate exchange, but there was an institutional expectation that these rules should obtain in sexual intimacy. Such rules are designed to "protect" the parties to the transaction so that no one (especially the female) is exploited, used, or taken advantage of. In the process, they introduce a regulatory framework to youthful romance and sexual encounter that gives legal equity to the relationship. The institutional fear that motivates such elaborate legalisms is the suspicion that one party to student sex is a phony, willing to seduce or even force sex upon the other without regard to the expressed wishes of the other. But again this is the attempt to guard against the threat of phoniness by "rationalizing" a relationship or encounter that is by nature irrational. And to expect that each "level" of activity can be so regulated by administrative edict as to ensure against the exercise of selfish lust is preposterous. Schools that introduce such rules are expressing a wish that promises made in the clinches of student passion are sincere, honest, and honored; but to expect that the power of persuasion will not be introduced by someone who wants to exercise his or her will on the other is wishful thinking. There is something patently ingenuous, even Canutean, about attempting to regulate out disingenuous behavior in an area of life notable for false appearances and lack of candor. Both liberal and conservative college rule-makers are not willing to let alone an area of life that is notoriously ungovernable; even though the approach of the former may be therapeutic (sex should be mutually consensual and not hurtful) and the latter punitive (sex is forbidden and punished if caught sinning), they both fear exploitation (largely of women) by phonies (in the guise of lecherous fraternity boys or professors who— for the liberals—traumatize women students who then need therapy, or—for the conservatives—"ruin" the "girls" who are then fallen and shamed).

This bureaucratic and legalistic approach to the putative regulation of sex suggests that we are unwilling to take risks with the most fundamental kinds of human relationships. At this juncture of history, with our "sense of an ending" at century's close, we fear that we live in a world of "sexual anarchy."[1] Like people at the end of the nineteenth century, we have many similar fears: the fantasy of sexual chaos, the threat of the "new woman," the fear of the exercise, and the loss, of male power, and the presence of a epidemic sexual disease. Both individuals and organizations respond to these threats with efforts to thwart exploitation and wrongdoing by sexual phonies who take advantage of the rapid changes in sexual mores and practices. Instituting new rules, both draconian prohibitions and hopeful guidelines, are designed to reduce the element of risk in sexual relations. But this demand for regularity also reduces the element of excitement and even danger, with sexual relations taking on predictable patterns that make it "correct" but boring. Sexual daring disappears in favor of forming relationships with undaring people who agree to restrictive or "sensitive" rules and practices that make the relationship safe. People want desperately to be safe from phonies, to the extent that they insist on the codification of sexual promises.

In recent years, college administrators have also codified rules governing sexual relations between professors and students. Among some academic circles, the mythic figure of the "lecherous professor" has become a demonic presence. Legends abound about professors who use their position of authority and power to seduce students. Male professors are accused of a wide litany of outrages and abuses, taking advantage of naive and admiring female undergraduates who find them intellectually impressive and mature males who are not their fathers. Academic culture has an array of prototypical stories about legendary professorial lechers. Feminists and moralists have used the tales about male professors to accuse large numbers of them of seduction and even a form of date rape, using the power of classroom domination and even the lure of grades to "snow" girl students. There are also many legends about the female students who offer their bodies to professors in exchange for grades. Too, since many people outside the academy think professors are largely homosexuals, stories circulate about faculty-student gay affairs, or more ominously, homosexual faculty members forcing their attentions on attractive male students. And to complete the picture, there are a cluster of "academic legends" about lecherous female faculty members. One of the most widespread and persistent is the apparently fictional story of the woman professor (always beautiful) who would pick out handsome young male students in her classes for a semester's dalliance; at the end, she would grade them on their classroom and bedroom performance (in one version, the male student is incensed because she gives him a B, averaging an A for his classroom work and a C for his bedroom performance; in another version, she is a lesbian and the student is a girl, referring us again to the fear of homosexual rape). These mythic tales have contributed to the proliferation of sexual codes governing faculty-student relations. On some campuses, the definition of "harassment" has been expanded to include a faculty member putting his hand on a girl student's shoulder during a counseling session in his office, another telling a joke to a couple of female students they deemed "sexist," and another paying women students what he deemed a compliment on their looks—which they deemed an insult and turned him in. On other campuses, earnest committees have developed elaborate codes of conduct governing faculty sexual behavior towards students, on the assumption faculty are the aggressive party that initiates and insists upon sex and the students are the aggrieved and wronged party. Accordingly, codes take on the solemn air of bureaucratic language and preplacement of blame (Indiana University: "All amorous or sexual relationships between faculty members and students are unacceptable when the faculty member has professional responsibility for the student...Voluntary consent by the student in such a relationship is suspect, given the fundamental nature of the relationship"; William and Mary: if a professor becomes involved with a student, "the faculty member shall report the situation promptly and seek advice and counsel from an appropriate administrative superior"; and so on[2]). Such codes reflect the popular mythology that there is a cadre of lecherous professors bent on seducing and thus in some way traumatizing the victim. In the dramatistic logic of such codes, the perpetrator is always guilty and the victim is always innocent. The threat of faculty lechery is deemed to be so imminent in its instigation and brutal in its consequences that formal rules must be written to forbid fates worse than death for tender undergraduates. Formerly mild-mannered Professor Pinko Q. Bedwetter is transformed into a glandular Mr. Hyde with raging hormones, a barbarian lusting at the dormitory gates eager to rape at will. On the other hand, students have been restored to virginal innocence, as if the sexual revolution had never happened, and they know not the vagaries of sex and affairs to the extent of being easily conned by cunning professors bent on their exploitation. These are all astounding assumptions, leading us back to the core image of the professor as a phony and students as sincere and gullible children. In some measure, the administrative teams that wrote such rules were complicit in the popular belief in professorial dishonesty. It is widely believed that professors are slackers, with an easy high-paying job that requires little or no work from them; that they are incompetent at anything but their tiny area of academic specialization, and often not even at that; and that they are immoral or amoral, somehow "overeducated" to the point of easy moral turpitude. These popular beliefs are not true, but they add up to the suspicion that professors are phonies in what they profess, so therefore it is also easy to believe that they would use their academic status and power to use students sexually. Professors have traditionally been thought to be B.S. artists, propounding ideas that are silly and impractical but which are taken seriously by gullible and impressionable young students; since such ideas are "un-American" and "subversive," the populace should be on its guard against the expressed nonsense of academic "eggheads." The fear of sexual subversion by professors is a newer development, occurring after the passage of the Cold War: now professors are not so much a political threat as they are a sexual threat, now not so much interested in subverting the minds of their students as they are interested in subverting their bodies. Their phoniness is not thought to be political, but rather carnal. What they deal in is not an alien ideology, but rather an alien doctrine of sensuality.

These new campus sexual rules posit a phony deal between cunning professors and victimized students. We may suspect that sexual reality is more complicated, and that human passion in the erotic setting of higher education more difficult to predict, codify, and regulate. The rules themselves are phony, preplacing blame and culpability on the part of faculty members and inviting the destruction of reputations and careers on the flimsiest of evidence and silliest of reasons by an accusing student. The prudery of this new academic puritanism includes assuming guilt until proof of innocence, that students are not capable of either passion or ulterior actions, and that the teacher-student relationship is a business deal: school is a factory and the teachers merely functionaries whose relationship with students is confined to bureaucratic management—processing knowledge to paying consumers who wish to acquire the product of knowledge. Students are paying customers who want a warranty guaranteed by the organization that they are "educated" without anything vital or risky happening to them.[3] The rules attempt to restore sexual virginity but actually help perpetuate academic virginity, eliminating the vital element of education.

SCHOOL AS A PHONY DEAL

We have consistently argued that phony cultures eliminate vitality from their institutions and behavior, making organizational life artificial and jejune. The codification of elaborate rules governing actions, thoughts, and passions indicates the trend toward bureaucratic controls and domination, eliminating surprises, innovations, and risks. The growing malady is one of substituting the phony for the vital and energetic. The new mandarins of education bureaucracies exercise control over organizational actions, passions, and thought. Rules governing the conduct of faculty members and students in their relations with each other codify proper behavior to the extent that such relations are formalized and killed: school is a business deal, and should be conducted in the deadly spirit of a legal transaction, with each party carefully observing the letter of the educational law. Classroom and counseling session become matters of organizational procedure, not unlike any other job. But the idea that school relations are something special or unique is lost. The regulation of passion into proper categories of interaction takes the phoniness of school one step further, since such rules are imposed to "regularize" within acceptable legal boundaries the conduct of sex, as defined by school administrators who see the need for the indirect supervision of private and intimate behavior. This impulse to regulate, or at least to state idealized codes of conduct, transforms behavior (for those who take it seriously) into something done according to the rule book, encouraging phony attempts to live up to the rules or to circumvent them. Finally, such rule-making spills over into free thought. We have already touched on "political correctness," which is a form of educational bureaucratic language designed to preclude or suppress "bad" thoughts and force students into officially approved "good" thoughts. The regulatory impulse is of a piece, but since schools, especially in higher education, are supposed to be bastions of free thought, the attempt to force students to use phony language and profess phony attitudes is especially ironic. The "idea of a university" becomes lost in the shuffle of rules and regulations that govern relations, and even give formal definition to official knowledge. An ideological or merely bureaucratic regimen becomes an invisible organizational superego, governing action, passion, and thought, encouraging phony relations from sex to examination answers. School becomes an instrumentality of control rather than freedom, codifying expected behavior into rules rather than providing the context and encouragement for the free exercise of thought, action, and emotion.

     This astonishing development in the conduct of school has prompted many critics to question the worthiness of the vast system of both public and private education. It is urged that schools don't educate, since students graduate from even the most prestigious schools with spotty knowledge; that professors make too much and teach too little (since apparently they spend too much time either doing research or pursuing sex with students); that schools have become too expensive, bureaucratic, and routinized; and that curricula have become overloaded with ideological or academic interests; and that perhaps most of all, students don't take school seriously enough to attend to their organizational responsibilities. If the clientele of school—the student body—doesn't believe that attendance at school is important enough to put a great deal of sustained effort into, then the institutional structure has no underpinnings in the class it is supposed to serve.

     Veterans of the classroom in higher education can tell you that all this has been developing over recent decades, concomitant with the enormous amounts of money, reform, and studies aimed at improving education. The difficulty is that many students have intuitively come to understand that school is a phony deal. School is built on assumptions and conducted with procedures that turn them into objects to be processed. School assumes that they learn at the same rates; those that don't are stigmatized as slow or uneducable. School teaches competition, ignoring the social need and individual desire for cooperation. School is designed to humiliate publicly those who don't come up with the right answer, when what people need is the development of self-confidence and respect. Students learn that school is not for them, but for the organizational complex that commands school. They learn that much of what is communicated to them in school is propaganda, designed to make them into what the organization thinks they should be. They understand that battles over curricula involve interest groups arguing over whose propaganda should prevail in being presented to them as truth. They know that now there is less connection between success in school and a successful career, since they can expect to change jobs often, move in search of work, have fewer fringe and retirement benefits, and often become locked into lower-paying and less fulfilling work than previous generations. For many of them, school is a bore and an irrelevance, a painful duty occasionally attended to but something that interferes with their true education, at play with the mass media and their peers. Students suspect that school is deliberately boring, something designed to break their spirits so that the drones who conduct class will have a docile audience, that the functionaries who write textbooks will have buyers, and that the administration that processes them can continue to grow through the ever-increasing amounts it charges them.

Contemporary students learn that even though the costs of higher education keep going up, they get less institutional attention and time, and it takes longer to graduate. If there are prestigious faculty members, they never see them (at elite schools such as Yale, Harvard, and Stanford, graduate students teach a significant fraction of undergraduate classes; consequently, on any day, fully one-third of undergraduates at such schools don't attend class—in a sense, a strike-by-absence against an institution they disdain). They know that money goes for university presidents' travel, for degree programs few people take, for prestigious professors who never teach, for athletics, band and cheerleaders, and sports promotion, but that classrooms are overcrowded, good teachers don't get tenure, and the bureaucracy ("assistants to the dean") keeps growing, that getting something approved or signed becomes a monumental task. It now takes five to six years to graduate at some schools because of budget cuts, faculty unavailability, and administrative indifference. Students "blow off" school because they realize that it is not designed for their needs or wants. After minimal encounter with the way school works, students learn very quickly the extent of the hypocrisy: despite all of the official rhetoric about their commitment to quality education that focuses on individual development, and how much each student is considered a valuable member of the "Siwash family," the student doesn't count, so why bother? The most important message students learn in school is about school, their first formal institution: school is a phony deal, a hypocritical transaction that ingrains in them suspicion of and cynicism about all adult institutional operations.

This student attitude is especially prevalent in the 1990s, wherein many young people in school sense that no matter how hard they try, or how much they learn, it will make little difference in their lives, given the economic and social conditions that prevail. School for them is not only out of touch, it is also out of date: it has little relevance to "where they live" their cultural "fun" lives, and decreasing relevance to their economic lives, since many of them believe that they have no prospects. Among the student class, we may be witnessing a "revolution of falling expectations," with the onset of falling or stagnant living standards, poor dead-end jobs with low wages and no benefits, intractable social dislocations and problems which political elites either ignore or can't solve, American-based corporations "disinvesting" in the United States, and the general decline of the American empire. In such a climate, the phoniness of deals crucial to the quality of life of ordinary people becomes all the more obvious and pointed. Schools are run by an entrenched meritocracy that attempts to perpetuate the myth that school makes a big difference in people's lives, observable emerging conditions to the contrary. But if the clientele of school come to disbelieve the myth of the institution, and see the bureaucracy as hypocrites and often enough incompetents, then the stance they adopt in reaction can be described as cynicism.

Cynicism emerges in conditions wherein people have been consistently and repeatedly "burned" or "stung" by a phony deal. By the time students reach their junior and senior years in college, they have been in school for perhaps fifteen years. By that time, the accumulation of experience has taught many of them that after all that exposure to education they still aren't educated. They have suffered through the educationist-inspired lesson plans, curriculum changes, innovative teaching methods, audio-visual aids, television courses, group discussions, field trips, examinations and tests, textbooks and assigned readings, problems and laboratory assignments, homework and out-of-class projects, and lectures. But for all that, something crucial is missing: a sense of completion, of having achieved an integrated and larger view of self and the world. One leaves the bureaucracy of school having been constantly told of the worth of the deal, but discovering very quickly that in many crucial ways, school didn't prepare one for the world. Thus the promise of school was bogus, sustaining public and private investment in school that feeds the bureaucratic order, but doesn't improve the quality of education rendered. Students may remember the "good times" at school—friends, parties, sports, road trips, sex— with nostalgic fondness, but few remember a memorable course or professor, and many leave with a sense of incompletion and frustration: the work, the business, the purpose of school was not memorable.

It is no wonder, then, that reformers who wish to improve school, and anti-intellectual right-wingers who want to destroy school, find it easy to attack school as phony. The "education is the answer" rhetoric of the educational establishment has set it up for easy attack, since education has not turned out to be the answer. The promoters of school got into the habit of overpromising the benefits of school, which became difficult to sustain when the democratization of school—giving access to previously excluded groups—made it all the more impossible to demonstrate that school was making for better citizens. The phoniness of school has become embarrassingly obvious in the wake of the "cultural pessimism" of the 1990s, with the attendant economic insecurities and political changes that feed popular cynicism. For school sold itself as a deal that was part of the general myth of progress, that individuals, and society, could constantly improve through rational effort that led to self-improvement, and thus greater wealth and happiness. But when school was democratized, cultural conservatives and educational establishmentarians concluded that education for the masses couldn't guarantee progress, and urged abandonment of public schools in favor of elite private education (or religious-based education) in enclaves that guarded the "educable" few from the "uneducable" many. The uneducable many learned quickly from school that their education didn't matter to power elites, so many of them didn't take school seriously. The evidence of underfunding, violence, over-worked teachers, decaying buildings, "deferred maintenance," and so on teaches them that the system has abandoned them, so therefore they will abandon the system. Yet too, "privileged" students who attend better schools are well aware of the gap between what an elite school, or state university, promises and what it delivers. Students at high-class private colleges know that these schools have often pulled the "Veblen ploy," selling the school as a high-class education because it charges extremely high tuition, a kind of academic pitch based on "conspicuous consumption." But if both middle-to-upper-class students, as well as lower-class students, are pessimistic about their prospects, as well as their country's, then it is no wonder that school is regarded with considerable cynicism. If the sense that school is a phony deal continues to be widespread, then support for school in its present form will decline further.

Any superior high school senior in the market for higher education knows something about the pitch. For the "education market" is highly competitive, given the limited number of potential students available for recruitment. So the available student is beset by school propaganda, including fancy brochures with lots of color pictures of students in dialogue with dynamic teachers, green-treed sylvan campuses, handsome male students and beautiful female students, colorful fall afternoon football spectacles, solemn but joyous academic rituals, and successful and confident graduates in gowns. But that's not all: the student can expect to receive repeated mailouts, videotapes that dramatize the "educational experience at Siwash," phone calls from recruitment personnel at the school, visits from recruiters, and even sponsored trips to tour the school. If sought by several schools, the beleaguered student is likely overwhelmed by the attention. He or she may well pick the school that was presented as most attractive in a variety of ways, but in any case they have bought the pitch. But when they attend the school, and see that image and reality don't equate, there is likely to be a considerable measure of disappointment, a sense that the school was oversold, and over the years of the "educational experience" a vague sense of having been conned into a phony deal that has less payoff than was promised.

On the other hand, schools desperate for students often compound the phoniness of the transaction by permitting students a wide degree of academic and personal latitude. Many schools tolerate a great amount of student disinterest, apathy, inattention to work, deadlines, and other academic disciplines, habitual non-attendance and displays of open contempt when in class, and outrageous antisocial behavior at parties, games, and other public gatherings. Students often adopt the attitude that faculty and administrators exist to cater to student whims since, after all, students pay faculty salaries. And since they have nothing but contempt for the academic system, students tend to adopt a stance of militant anti-intellectualism, bragging about how they went through school without reading books, entering the library, or attending lectures (not to mention campus theater, art films, visiting lecturers, and similar "highbrow" fare). Here cynicism about school translates into self-destructive behavior, wherein blatantly displayed stupidity and bestiality are deemed virtues. Such learned immaturity is acquired in school, but often not abandoned in the world beyond school, with disastrous consequences for the individual. Contempt for the phony deal of school can translate into self-loathing wherein one confuses trashy behavior with "unphoniness." Too, school may well teach others to be a "smooth operator," a social *courtier* who believes in none of it but is decidedly on the make in social systems and relationships: since institutions like school are phony, phoniness is what works; to succeed in like institutions (or in school itself), I must cultivate the arts of personal phoniness, tihsllubing my way to where I want to go and for what I want to get. Veterans of higher education are familiar with the on-the-make professor, who masks his or her desire for institutional advancement and power in the rhetoric of institutional and academic ideology ("the Siwash family," "curriculum reform") and personal sophistry in public relations with academic colleagues and students. The academic smooth operator understands that the phoniness of school can be taken advantage of for purposes of personal advancement. By exploiting the very phoniness that sustains the enterprise—the illusion that the institution is the sole dispenser of knowledge and wisdom—the academic make-out artist can rise to the top simply by saying and behaving as if she or he believes in the official bunkum of school. If Machiavelli were alive to revise his great treatise to observe the uses of intrigue in school, he would write not of the lion nor of the fox but rather of the weasel.

The attacks on school are often motivated by people with phony purposes. Cultural conservatives, for instance, may well attack public school not to improve it but to destroy it, replacing or superseding it with religious-based or patriotic-based indoctrination that makes for obedient and subservient subjects and service workers. They have no interest in the plight of poor or middle-income students, nor wish to enhance their lives through learning; such ideologues simply wish to preserve the prerogatives of capitalism and prevent social change. But they mouth the ideological slogans of conservatism ("privatization," "school choice," "deinstitutionalization"), while not saying what they really want, which is to do away with public support for education. What they don't understand is that American society is already so atomized and fragmented that the destruction of school is by now so well advanced as to likely be irreversible. Students have figured out that ideological agendas for school are phony, and seek their education elsewhere, in popular culture. The icons and narratives of popular culture have, for instance, taught the young more about sexuality than gender theorists of both the academic Left and Right. Popular culture has become their school. School cannot compete with the compelling and vivid messages of popular play, which seems to American youth to possess an authenticity and relevance denied to the dreary routines of school. School traditionally required a clientele who thought the investment in time and effort over a long period of years was worth it; the payoff would come through delayed gratification and suffering through the pains of schoolwork which would lead to wealth, success, career, and financial security. School was a pragmatic rather than scholarly bargain: if you got a "good education," there lay ahead social rewards rather than intellectual ones. Programs such as the G.I. Bill, Pell Grants, and the National Defense Education Act were enhanced by popular images of social success—a professional career, a suburban home, a lovely wife, children, a comfortable retirement.

Thus the wave of personal cynicism and antisocial behavior among students is likely a reaction to a deal gone sour. Education in an era of cultural pessimism may be virtually impossible, given the abandonment of the institutions and promise of school by its clientele. Students at virtually all levels have figured out that school is a bum deal because what is taught is propaganda, stories and lessons that the larger society does not believe in or practice, so why should they pay attention to messages that will do them no good in "the real world"? In an ironic sense, students of recent years have demonstrated remarkable "adaptive intelligence," learning their lessons well: they understand that a hypocritical society cannot be mastered unless one is as clever as the phonies who run it, so school is something to be circumvented, used, or even "trashed." Certainly it is not something to take seriously, since society does not either: students learn early that school is a marginal institution, underfunded and run by often underqualified and even incompetent people who are badly underpaid, that serves other social functions than education—as a conduit of propaganda, as a host organization for children whose parents work or simply don't want them around, as a disciplinary instrument for problem children, as a psychiatric and health clinic for students otherwise neglected, as a virtual prison for the difficult and troubled. They also understand that they are not only the "captive audience" for official propaganda, as they witness dreary battles over the curriculum and thus whose propaganda will prevail; they are also the audience for commercial propaganda, as they see communications companies con school boards into allowing "news" channels into the classroom for "free," with the proviso that the students not only watch the packaged news programs to better "inform" them but also the commercials for products that sponsor the news. Students, however, are smarter than their "teachers" know, and are learning valuable lessons, not the least of which is that school is a phony deal. Having learned that, in one way or another they "drop out": they may still be in school, but their energies and interests are elsewhere, in the popular culture and peer groups which will not lie to them.[4]

In a larger sense, what we may be witnessing is the eclipse of the belief in progress, both personal and social. If the journey leads students nowhere, they are most likely to not care to go on a trip to nowhere. Further, they will seek sources and modes of learning from elsewhere that teach them what they can do. Popular culture provides people who see no hope in school with alternative ways of social behavior, many of which do not involve delayed gratification nor a commitment to progress. In such a milieu, the promise of school is superseded by the promise of popular culture. School was predicated on a sense of purpose, that the future was assured for those who worked to achieve; popular culture, and merely "hanging out" with peers, is predicated on the immediate experience, to be enjoyed now since there is no progressive permanence beyond the present. Much of popular culture may be as phony as school, but at least it is fun phoniness that satisfies the desire to learn socially relevant messages. One may learn a variety of potential behaviors and roles—violence, sex, bad manners, insults, lewd jokes, and the like on the one hand, but also peacemaking, abstinence, good manners, and so forth on the other. In any case, popular culture may supersede school in importance for a variety of reasons, not the least of which is the relevance of popular experience for the "life lessons" one needs to learn in order to cope with the world beyond the self-enclosed world of school. Young people wish to believe they can find the real, the honest, the sincere, the authentic either in peer relations or in chosen items of popular culture—a novel, a movie, a song. Their friends and the popular experience they sought may be just as phony, but at least they are not the sustained institutional hypocrisy of school. A rock group may be openly contemptuous of their audience, but at least they are selling a bill of popular goods devoid of pedagogic artifice. The belief in progress, as exemplified by school and the virtue of "getting a good education," is superseded by amusement and the virtue of having a good time.

SELLING

It has often been remarked that perhaps the fundamental transaction in American culture is the sale. As a nation of dealers, we have studied, celebrated, and transformed into a sacral act the "art of the deal." We say only half-cynically that every man has his price and that everything is for sale. We have sold everything from land to livestock to human beings, with a view towards a good deal and realizing the main chance. Americans early on acquired the ethic that someone could gain the whole world but not lose his or her own soul. Indeed, there were second chances everywhere: whores with golden hearts, ex-cons with a record, reformed drunks, wastrels who misspent their youth or family inheritance, all were redeemable if they had something to sell, including their own story. We are all prodigals, able to return to the fold if we can instill enough confidence. Indeed, one of the major American products for sale is confidence itself.

Americans created a society governed by the myth of the pursuit of individual happiness through the exercise of rational self-interest. Figures like Jefferson might dream of a realm of civic virtue peopled by political men imbued with *civitas* who would make a moral democratic State through democratic discussion and decision. But the popular reality was that of the exercise of self-interest rather than civic virtue, the activities of economic man competing and conniving in a marketplace rather than political man discussing good government in public forums. The successful exercise of self-interest would lead to the acquisition of worldly goods, property, and wealth that produces human happiness. This was the origin of the "gospel of wealth," and the rise of the ethic of dealing. The measure of one's success was in the ability to make and profit from deals, ranging from horse-trading to land speculating to loaning money at interest. We have traditionally praised the wealthiest amongst us as the happiest of men, since they have realized the American dream of perfect happiness produced by their successful exercise of self-interest. Virtue then came to be equated with interest, with the reward in the attainment of happiness. The political realm was thus deemed inferior to the economic realm, or more positively, government was supposed to create the conditions for the successful interplay of interests. In its extreme, this limited government to the social Darwinist "policeman and night watchman" functions; but even today, government is enjoined to provide a "level playing field," to promote competition, to facilitate enterprise, to be the servant of private interests. (Economic successes would often go into politics, since their success allegedly "qualified" them for public office as men of private attainment who would bring "sound business sense" to government.) In any case, there is always much concern that the government provide a "good business climate" and promote "consumer confidence." Government is thus in the business of making belief, promoting confidence in the economy, and extolling the virtues of initiative, risk, and growth. Government is a salesman for business, attempting to sell us the proposition that what's good for business is good for the country.

Political salesmanship and business self-promotion hide the fact that much of what is being sold is bunkum. Businesses customarily seek rigged deals, such as government contracts, special exemptions, privileged status, and virtually anything they can arrange to escape the rigors of the "level playing field." Nor do businesses often like to deal fairly with their employees, since they regularly escape to places that will protect them from the horrors of unions, regulations, employee rights, and the like. Niceties such as high wages, permanent employment and careers, and health and retirement benefits are fast becoming as archaic as the forty-hour week (businesses routinely work their employees for thirty-nine hours a week to avoid paying benefits). By some estimates, fully one-half of the American work force will be temporary workers ("temps") by century's end. But despite the deterioration of the lives of ordinary people in a shrinking and less well-off work force, we are constantly told that the capitalist deal is good for us. The rich may get richer, companies may abandon communities and loyal work forces, pension funds can be raided, executives may write themselves fabulous salaries and "golden parachutes" while the companies they run fail, real income may continue to fall, yet "free enterprise" is extolled as the best economic deal around. The dreary maxims of business school and editorial page propaganda about the joys of capitalist endeavor may increasingly fall on suspicious ears of those many who are regularly bought and sold in a marketplace that benefits them less and less. As the "creative destructiveness" of international capitalism becomes all the more destructive of individual lives and the global environment, it remains to be seen how much propaganda will be necessary to sustain what many people now suspect is a phony deal.

Selling capitalism itself, then, may become a major task of salesmanship for the agencies of business propaganda. This task will be complicated by the continued fall in the standard of living, the disappearance of retirement and health care, and other "personal" rewards of the system become obvious. If the United States experiences "Argentinization"—becoming more like countries like Argentina, with the few living in fabulous wealth and the many struggling—then capitalism may well be seen as a phony deal that benefits the many not at all. The symptoms of such a development will be clear enough: huge permanent debt, structurally high unemployment, a stagnant economy with falling real income and living standards, "disinvestment" in the country with capital fleeing abroad, and intractable and violent social problems.[5] The capitalist deal always was the bargain that if people let enterprise flourish, regardless of the social and environmental costs, they would share in the wealth. But if capitalism is no longer producing general prosperity, then its future becomes uncertain. In a world of scarcity and deprivation, the "revolution of falling expectations" means that the victims of the system will direct their ire towards those few who still benefit handsomely. Capitalism always survived not through the gold medals awarded the few, but the consolation prizes awarded the many; if the consolations given the many who are employees no longer "trickle down," then people can be expected to regard a system that no longer rewards them as a phony deal.

If these economic conditions are what is prevailing in our time, then we can expect much rhetoric in defense of the system, in effect selling, or rather reselling, capitalism itself. We may well be asked to engage in a massive act of denial, wherein we are urged to "not see" the many social and individual dysfunctions produced by the failure of the economic system to sustain and spread prosperity. It may be the case that televangelists will be enlisted in the "conservative" cause to give renewed energy to the "gospel of wealth," that capitalism is godly, those who enjoy fabulous wealth are being rewarded for their piety and tithe, and that all of us can bribe God to let us too share in the financial manna from Heaven. The propagation of the "prosperity theology" common to televangelists would likely include a condemnation of reformers who urge the redistribution of wealth, tax burdens falling on the rich, and social programs that benefit the poor. The faithful who cling to the dream of wealth acquired as a godly reward for belief will be complemented by the demonization of those who disbelieve and thus fall from grace. The "positive thinkers" will re-emerge in new guises, making another and more desperate effort to salvage the capitalist ideology from historical ruin. "The popular psychology of positive thinking," notes one observer, "had flourished among people able, for reasons of culture and politics, to imagine that the only thing wrong with their lives was within themselves."[6] Both political and theological apologists for capitalism—talk show hosts, conservative politicians, eminent evangelical divines, and similar shills—will be increasingly called upon by systemic powers to invoke the "spirit of capitalism" as our savior, if we only believe in the "mind cures" that will reinvigorate our will to acquire and thus the economy as a whole. But we may rightly suspect that ideological line is a phony pitch: responsibility for success or failure is placed with the individual, absolving the political and economic system of any flaws or failings: the capitalist system is deemed perfect, but individual entrepreneurs or employees are imperfect, and the economic sin of failure or penury is placeable at their doorstep. Rather than the system failing people, people fail the system. Capitalism becomes all the more perfect as it excludes or exploits ever more people dependent upon its good graces.

The desire for revitalized personal entrepreneurship has been exploited by the burgeoning industry of self-improvement, especially those who billed themselves as "motivational experts" or "self-enrichment consultants" and the like. These dynamic individuals exploit the urgent hope of riches gained through the development of individual skills, ranging from vague methods of improving one's attitude to learning how to make money in some specific area, such as purchasing real estate or doing direct mailings. In the former case, one can watch TV on weekend morning hours to see the pitch made for tapes, books, seminars, and so forth featuring some motivational guru who will teach people how to become positively motivated, mentally alerted, emotionally oriented to make money. Capital appreciation becomes a matter of psychological training, as if the right attitude and good intentions guaranteed mastery of the marketplace. The guru is usually a glib and upbeat dynamo, exemplifying in his or her personage the virtues that lead to success (usually displayed in the fabulous and ostentatious homes, cars, and other paraphernalia of philistine wealth they have acquired through conning people into investing in their self-improvement schemes). In the latter case, the guru serves as an exemplar of success through a particular gimmick, such as buying and selling real estate, and can now generously offer others the secret of his or her success, for a price. It is touching to watch the faces of the people who attend these motivational presentations, at weekend seminars in airport motel meeting rooms: they seem ardently to want success as measured by money, and sense that the normal avenues of opportunity and upward mobility are denied to them. This is a chance, however fantastic or unlikely it may be to a skeptical observer, to escape the fate of so many other people, trapped in dead-end service jobs or betrayed by their employer. The motivational industry captures the fear, especially among the *petit bourgeoisie*, of falling, or going nowhere, of not realizing any significant monetary, and therefore, prestige gain. But what those who buy into these self-improvement or get-rich-quick schemes do not wish to understand is that the deal is phony: acquiring a positive mental attitude doesn't alter the constricted job market, and learning how to buy real estate doesn't mean you can sell it at a profit. What is being sold in such self-help deals is confidence, the hope against hope that by acquiring some new attitude or skill one can now magically acquire the Midas touch. The "goods" of self-confidence and hustle sold are bogus, since they do not affect objective economic conditions or the odds of failure. But one can market and sell the intangible of hope, the entrepreneurial dream of quick and easy riches within the reach of those who wish desperately to believe that wealth is a matter of subjective reorientation. The con game is to inspire confidence enough to entertain such hopes, which enriches the confidence-builder, but who is not around when the hopes of many are inevitably dashed on the rocks and shoals of economic misfortune. The popular injunction "every person a big winner" is logically and socially impossible, but as a sales pitch it caters to the financial and emotional insecurity of those caught in an economy and culture of pessimism and loss. The selling of the success ethic on television signals the extent of the quiet desperation among those many Americans who define their self-worth by their power to accumulate and acquire. Those attending the self-help seminars or listening to the tapes are buying the winner's attitude, with only the vague hope and promise that they will wind up in the winner's circle. The fear of being a loser in a society that does not reward or recognize losers is deep, especially in the new emerging economy of the late twentieth century, which deliberately creates more and more people who lose. "Positive thinking" becomes a heroic stance more than an agenda, giving people the "mind-power" to believe at this late date in the individualistic American Dream, despite the odds. In an economy which is disinvesting in the work force, the enterprising individual compensates by attempting to invest in herself and himself. In a world of economic emptiness, the ambitious person attempts to fill the soul with mercenary energy and skill. Perhaps for many, the con of the self-help scheme is enough, and they really do not expect instant, or even eventual, success; for others more naive or hopeful, it may come as a bitter disappointment when the rewards of riches do not quickly and easily follow.

The self-help con game does remind us that the cultural heroism of selling is still as much ingrained in American life as buying. Yet as cultural critics have long noted, selling forces the seller into phony relationships which define role relations. Plays such as Miller's *The Death of a Salesman* to Mamet's *Glengarry Glen Ross* touch on the life of the salesman, wherein the acid of the con had seared their souls. The ubiquity of selling is most evident, and effective, in the practice of advertising, one of the great cultural imperatives of American life. We assume as a people that everything can be legitimately sold, and thusly, everything can be bought. An education can be bought: the student contracts with a school and a faculty in order to get an education. What they get is a credential, which is a phony substitute for an education. But they believed the advertising: the school promised an education, usually without undue pain or duress. Like any product, school was sold as something that would deliver. (This is why students, and parents, become irate when a student makes low grades or is denied admission to advanced programs: they were sold on the idea that academic success was guaranteed and "given," not earned.) A religion can be sold: televangelists desacrilize religion into a matter of electronic affiliation and programmatic tithing rather than metaphysical reflection and prayerful search for the holy. God and Mammon coexist easily in the gaudy theological mansions of TV, with the praise of the deity intermingled with the ever renewed pitch for more money. It pays for those who bill themselves as the vicars of God to advertise.

The social ethic of selling has become codified in the articulation of advertising as a way of life, what anthropologist Jules Henry has called "the pecuniary philosophy."[7] Truth, he notes, is what sells, what the communicator wants people to believe, and what you can get away with. Thus the very principle of social communication in the economic realm is based on phoniness: one must cut deals in order to survive, and the "best" deals are those which achieve the pecuniary purposes of the seller through verbal and imagistic obfuscations and associations which seduce the buyer. The pecuniary philosophy becomes central to the cultural practices of a civilization, defining what one can legitimately do to another. The practices of advertising thus become a standard of public communication, with the phony pitch or pep talk at the core of transactions. The apparent success of advertising inspires all those who practice sophisticated cons, on behalf of not only products such as cars and body aids but also universities, charities, interest groups, and so on. The difficulty is that for the wary, aware of the phony pitches common to advertising for traditional products, the entry of advertising into newer areas of persuasion makes them suspicious of the motives, and the quality, of the new product being advertised. For if a university or charity or whatnot has to spend a great deal advertising, is it not possible that their "product" lacks the same kind of distinctive qualities one found lacking in buying mass-produced cars or aspirin? The claim establishes the lure, but doesn't deliver the promised qualitative change in one's life. An advertised education then becomes just another commodity given the glitter of the pitchman to lure the suckers. It is likely that the fierce competition for students has contributed to colleges and universities becoming the host institution for youthful play, providing a place for students to party and have sex, for alumni and students to watch sports, all in the context of lax behavioral and academic rules wherein serious intellectual work is impossible. Schools have sold not only their new "resort" status as a place to come to have fun, they have also sold their souls by selling out. The acid of the con has affected the integrity of academic institutions (and for that matter, departments and majors within schools, which shamelessly and sometimes desperately compete for new students and majors through pitching their program as more fun, easy, exciting, and money-making than the others). The pecuniary philosophy makes social transactions such as selecting a school, a charity, or a religion one of selling and buying, as if one can buy education, philanthropy, and grace; with the same mercenary tokens, it is also assumed that one can legitimately sell learning, generosity, and piety.

We may expect that phony deals involving selling will continue into the future. Professions that formerly included constraints on open selling are becoming receptive to maximizing profit through marketing. Lawyers, for instance, advertise on TV for clients; insurance firms make media pitches for various kinds of suspiciously cheap and generous life, health, and accident insurance; and doctors are not far behind, in many places selling the benefits of their medical talents. Yet many critics argue that these pitches are cons: lawyers take a large percentage of any settlement they make after luring people into litigation; insurance firms have often become notorious for avoiding paying off claims; and doctors, in the estimation of much of the American public, have simply become ripoff artists, charging outrageous fees and doing needless tests to maximize profits. It is interesting to note that in public opinion polls, such professions have plummeted in public esteem; confidence in their profession falls as they try more ardently to sell us their services. Lawyers and insurance salespersons always had a modicum of suspicion attached to them ("shysters"), but doctors were cultural heroes in popular stories (Dr. Kildare, Dr. Gillespie, Marcus Welby, and so on), a role depiction that has largely disappeared: doctors are not heroes to a public that finds it difficult, if not impossible, to pay their medical bills. In all cases, expanding the effort to sell their talents has made these professions seem anxious to gain wealth rather than serve society.

The ethic of selling becomes a moral imperative, an activity that becomes legitimate in every area of social endeavor. The myth of competition is invoked everywhere, even though the deal may be rigged (professions, for instance, are often guilty of setting prices—for medical services, for instance—at an exorbitantly high level below which no doctor or hospital is supposed to go). A society in which everything is for sale also means that everyone is for sale. "Every man has his price" becomes a cynical but universal truth that reduces human beings to items to be bought and sold. But the acid of the con affects those many who have their price, both those who buy people and those who sell themselves. One has to become a phony to play the selling game, exploiting the market in people; one's motives in using people are couched in the phony language of capitalist necessity ("what the market will bear") and self-interest ("the firings were dictated by our restructuring plan"). And one has to become a phony to be bought at the going price, "selling out" for a price laid down by the highest bidder. The model of "economic man" in practice becomes a cynical and phony exercise of exploitation in which everyone evaluates himself or herself in terms of price and profit, how I can buy others and how I can sell myself.

CONCLUSION

A society based on the art of the deal transforms many human relations into phony deals. The socio-logic of a dealing society affects the logic of relations: if people see each other as someone who has to be, or can be, dealt with, the potential exists to deal with the other as object, not subject. If social success is equated with winning, then the other becomes someone who can be bested. The ethic of competition is introduced even into primary relations, making every transaction a matter of negotiation in which trust is problematical. In a sense, distrust of each other, even in sexual and friendship matters, increases the utility of phoniness, since one feels the necessity of "protecting" oneself from the potential con of others. A lover or spouse, a friend or acquaintance, certainly a business or professional relation, becomes a transaction in which it is deemed wise to assume the other is a double-dealer. In a society where everyone is that untrustworthy, then everyone becomes a phony who masks himself or herself in the guise of social role-playing that does not reveal too much of one's motives or intentions. The only sensible relationship is game-playing, the art of the deal as practiced by a society of double-dealers. "Games people play" excludes the truly intimate, charitable, or sincere, in a fluid and transparent society of ever-renegotiated contracts between bargaining players without the elevating moral of trust.

CHAPTER 6

PHONY POLITICS

It is arguable as to whether American politics is cause or consequence of the rise and pervasion of phony culture. In the former argument, we might urge that American politics became a major forum for the activities of the confidence man, the political phony who appeared in the guise of the republican idealist, and even the charismatic adventurer, but who was a masquerader. In the latter position, it can be argued that American politics and politicians are derivative: the phony culture—con artistry, the languages of promotion and selling, the valuation of double-dealing, and so on—made politics into an enterprise in which the phony practices of the larger culture overwhelmed the republican norms of *civitas* and *gravitas* we inherited from the classical tradition. In the former case, we have a political theory of culture: the practices of politics set the norms and standards for society. If politics is corrupt, venal, and phony, so too will be the larger society which emulates the political order. In the latter, we have a cultural theory of politics: the culture "drives" the political order, since it is the political system and its denizens who emulate the cultural order. Both arguments have been made, but perhaps it is a false dichotomy; we may here be Solomonic and declare both meritorious and useful.

The point, however, is that there is a powerful relationship between the values and practices of a phony culture and politics. Politics in a phony culture tends itself to be phony: one cannot succeed in a political culture that is phony without utilizing the resources of phoniness. Whatever the sources, we now expect politics to be phony, politicians to be phonies, and the political process to resemble the other and related cultural processes—celebrity, phony language, promotion, and so forth—with which we are familiar. As American culture has become more phony, so too has American politics, to the extent that we see politics and politicians as part of a seamless, if badly rent and torn, cultural web that covers a corrupt and cynical world. The cultural practice of phoniness has perhaps had its most devastating impact in politics, since the exercise of power has such great consequences for the rest of us. The more phony politics and governing become, the less we trust the process.

Here we must make a distinction. Since Machiavelli, we have gotten used to the idea that politics is a pragmatic art fraught with expediency: powerful people do expedient things in order to accomplish goals. Machiavelli wrote that in the actions of men, we must always look to the end. The realistic pragmatist has to weigh what means are *adequate* to realize a desired end. A Machiavellian politician is goal-oriented, attempting to use power—sometimes roughly and ruthlessly, as in wartime—in order to achieve an end that has political benefit and results in social good. But phony politicians seize upon the mistranslation of Machiavelli where he is supposed to have said that the end *justifies* the means, which he never did. Phonies in whatever area of life are always trying to get off the hook by attempting to justify what they are doing: they are not so much interested in accomplishing anything as looking good. Phonies are trying to get away with something, to con people through means that have to be justified to cover them up. Great politicians— Bismarck, Talleyrand, Richelieu, Lincoln, Franklin D. Roosevelt— seek adequate means to realize very substantial goals. Phony politicians seek justifiable means to realize very insubstantial goals, mostly creating smoke and mirrors which obfuscate their true objective, which is largely self-aggrandizement through image management. The great politicians produce great results: a united Germany, the Congress of Vienna, French national power, a preserved American union, the New Deal. The phony politicians only produce phony results: a momentarily enhanced ranking in public opinion polls, the sweet cheats of a staged and choreographed public pseudo-event, a cream puff interview on a TV news program, the false cheer of greeting crowds at airport stops. The "light" politician is a political man without qualities, the stuff that political dreams are made of, an apparition who suffers from the unbearable lightness of being. His political means are wholly narcissistic, in need of justification by faith because they accomplish nothing substantial or lasting; all his or her activities are directed at using political means to try to display the political self as a legitimate exhibition on display. The phony politician is no Machiavellian; he or she is absorbed with self-justification so he or she is regarded as great, rather than concerned with the adequate manipulation of means that produces great results. The phony politician sees himself or herself as the great result that is to be produced, a daunting ego who wishes the world to

"Look at me!" as justifiably great. The phony politician, motivated by megalomania and exhibitionism, seeks to justify his or her lofty position and self-estimation through the manipulation of others' faith; the Machiavellian pragmatic politician, motivated by realistic and goal-oriented considerations, seeks to use the necessary political means adequate to realize politically desirable and consequential goals.

We are familiar with both kinds of politicians, but in the media age, where the potential for self-exaltation is all the greater, the phony politician has become more prevalent. The "media politician" seeks the representation of his or her image in the camera's eye, as an act that enlarges the public self to gigantic and universal size (stemming, one suspects, from an inadequate conception of self that drives the individual to overcome through media projection that creates the power of fame). The will to power has been superseded by the will to fame: the phony seeks power over self-image, not over the instruments of power that would lead to objective change towards some future good. Political action is no longer instrumental, but rather representational. The phony wants to be a political celebrity whose personage is admired and worshiped and whose media *persona* is known far and wide; she or he has little interest in managing and achieving measurable and consequential outcomes of lasting impact. The phony believes the political world is transitory and illusory, and so directs effort toward the manipulation of images rather than objects, affecting subjective opinion and not objective political or economic forces. The phony politician is self-seeking, uninterested in the traditional political goals of instilling virtue or appeasing interests, but much interested in popular happiness in terms of satisfaction with his or her popular image. Since the phony is the center of the universe, all the political planets and asteroids are supposed to revolve around the sun. People are supposed to derive their happiness through the enjoyment of themselves.

The phony politician is a manifestation of the political culture of narcissism.[1] The narcissist not only is the center of his or her own universe, she or he wants to be it for other people too. The narcissist is interested in other people only to the extent that they validate and justify the greatness and centrality of the one, as seen by them in the representation of the popular self. The popular self—the public *persona* that wishes to be popular—is "performance-directed" (rather than inner-directed or other-directed), attempting to orient people towards the contrived image. Like the actor, the image politician wants his or her audience to "Look at me!" and manufactures a series of performances to attract attention and admiration. The phony politician is known only through chosen performances, those "designed experiences" selected to convey his or her majesty of political being. Such personages possess no integrity of being, nor moral structure of self: rather they are "protean," human chameleons who can change shape like the god Proteus in order to effect the desired responses as situations and opinions change. The phony politician is "on," self-conscious about her or his role performance so carefully designed and enacted. If she or he gains acclaim and approval, the self is validated, and the narcissistic desire for self-display temporarily satisfied.

The phony politician is a creature of a media culture that can project images that are artificially enlarged and enhanced. The popular self that is displayed is a phony product marketed by the same people and skills that have informed advertising and promotion for a long time. A prominent and ambitious politician surrounds herself or himself with a collection of "flacks" and "shills," to use the vernacular. These are people skilled in the creation of phony words and pictures, artifices designed to convince people that the politician, like any other thing sold, is an exemplary figure who is both majestic and ordinary, kingly and a regular fellow, above us but one of us. Politicians with substantial political selves and equally substantial political goals used to surround themselves with men and women skilled in the formulation and implementation of policy innovations—powerful industrialists, interest group leaders, bureaucrats, and politicians like themselves, all of whom knew what was required to get things done. Now the phony politician surrounds himself with media manipulators, people who are skilled in formulating and implementing image innovations. The phony politician's policy orientation is image projection.

Like so much of phony culture, this suggests an historical and cultural shift from work to play. Machiavellian politicians used to do political work, based on the idea that the real world of power could be manipulated in order to achieve substantial results. The contemporary phony politician is committed to political play, based on the idea that the symbolic world of media communication can be manipulated to achieve insubstantial non-results. In the age of media politics, so much of what is "done" is political flim-flam designed to make the political leader look good. In a visual culture, that is literally true: much effort goes into the cosmetological appearance of the politician, both in the sense of his or her physical appearance (any experienced hairdresser can point out to you which senators dye their hair), and in the sense of "political cosmetics," using that physical appearance in political appearances that provide visible non-actions that substitute for results (appearing at a media pseudo-event with police heroes rather than increasing budgets for crime fighting or setting goals for crime reduction). Politics becomes an enterprise that accomplishes little but communicates much of the wondrous and mighty acts of accomplishment of the politician. Never before have people known so much of the acts of political princes that did so little for so few.

Some of the phoniness stems from the fact that the politician has to operate in a phony media environment, in which the symbiotic relationship of press, pundits, and politicians conspires to create an artificial culture of political theatrics on which they all feed and survive. The players in this ongoing popular drama comprise the Washington branch of the larger media culture, now indistinguishable from other centers such as Hollywood. Like Hollywood, they form a local community wherein everyone uses everyone else to create large-scale, mass-mediated, widely communicated fictions. Hollywood became famous as a media community noted for its mutual exploitation within and the remarkable ability to project fictive but deeply satisfying moving images without. The "movie colony" was mean, driven, and often downright savage in its creation of the great "dreams for sale," but its internal phoniness did not diminish the popularity of its creations. Similarly, the media culture of Washington now consists of phony communicators creating fictive but satisfying political images. The "political colony" of Washington may be equally ghastly in its contemptibility, but the communicators do succeed in "phonying things up" for our consumption. Like Hollywood, they are in the business of selling dreams, only here it is political fictions. The image-makers of Washington are singularly concerned with the popularity of their political creation, the phony message that gets through and impresses people. Press, pundits, and politicians relate to one another in their attempt to control "spin," what messages do get through and what impressions people are supposed to be left with. Like Hollywood, the media-driven Washington is a place of immediacy and temporariness: what is important is the constant renewal of interest and approval among media audiences lured back once again to the theater. Political theater differs from the movies only in that it has a claim on a resemblance of factuality: rather than a feature film, the Washington media culture produces a "never-ending and infinitely revisable docudrama." Like Hollywood, the D.C. popular drama aims at appealing to the shared subjective reality "out there" in the larger society of media consumers. Political reality in such a world is defined as the reality of perceptions, those complex images and stories which are communicated and received; there is much concern with the structure of perceptions and the fidelity of their reception. The media culture of Washington competes, conflicts, and cooperates in the making of the American political docudrama, with new episodes, actors, and plot twists, but with old stages, story lines, and messages all in revised dramatic formulas and conventions. Politics for most people has become something that is a metareality, a function of television and the news business and the ubiquitous corp of semi-official interpreters who collaborate on keeping the docudrama going. "Politics is not about objective reality, but virtual reality," a reality that is a virtual world with its own internal logic, rules, and language. Yet such a virtual world is deeply reflective of our common absorption in virtual realities. Contemporary media politics "portrays a society where to be knowing is to admit the fraud of one's functions in the act of performing them."[2] Phony politics is perhaps the ultimate virtual reality, wherein the condition and fate of the nation and the world is dependent upon the process of constructing (and deconstructing) that dynamic and protean reality, which in itself is a phantasmagoria, a fraudulent creation designed to inspire confidence at the moment. The confidence-game of media politics supersedes substantial questions; indeed, the "insubstantial pageant" that unfolds in Washington must be mastered before substantive questions can be addressed. But there is also a kind of Gresham's Law of media politics: insubstantial pageantry tends to drive substantial deliberation and resolution out, directing our attention at symbolic actions that dramatize the process and the players, but subordinating or hiding the fact that nothing of pragmatic utility gets done.

The confidence men and women of Washington are our new rulers. They are articulate, well-informed, and engaged. But their orientation is towards the making and unmaking of political confidence, and their expertise is largely in the promulgation of messages that confirm or deny the conventions of the virtual docudrama unfolding at the moment. The political communicators of the District of Columbia are essentially creatures of the dramatic arts: they are actors and actresses, playwrights and rhetoricians, critics and commentators, as if they were part of the communications environs of Hollywood or Broadway. (Washington columnists are in the tradition of Waldo Lydeker of the movie *Laura* and Addison DeWitt of *All About Eve*; media stardom and production in Altman's film about Hollywood, *The Player*, differs little from what goes on in Washington.) The world of the political con is self-contained and self-referential: those established in the political media games of the moment feel strongly that they belong there, are an important part of the process, and utilize media forums to express their views. In some measure, the drama of mass-mediated Washington is a *Rashomon* game, a warp and woof of communicators attempting to define the situation in a world where no version of events is authoritative, and "what is happening" is a matter of perspectives as to what the drama unfolding means and augurs. Narrators and commentators are trapped inside the confines of their referential and virtual world, so the internal drama is observed and interpreted from the limited perspective of being an "insider," and also from the limits of the ideological, partisan, editorial, or political viewpoint that competes for power over the ephemeral reality under discussion. The discussion reveals that those engaged in the political discussion rarely are able to transcend their roles, so the discussions—such as those that occur on TV news talks shows—have the quality of "windowless monads" talking past one another, each competing for the power over the situation's definition, or sometimes even as an expression of a "position," proclaiming the self-importance of the actor's perspective regardless of its relevance.   But as in the ancient Japanese story *Rashomon*, no single version of events and processes is authoritative; no one, even the presidential "spin" team, has the power to overawe or overwhelm the discussion to the point of a single definition. Indeed, as viewpoints and spokespersons proliferate, the definition of situations becomes increasingly multiple and diverse. Without a common and definitive agreement on the facts, values, and conditions extant in a situation, the media culture becomes for outsiders a quarrelsome and tedious group of public chatterers who confuse more than enlighten.

The difficulty is that Media Washington is a phony culture. It is committed to talk, not action. The participants in the docudrama concentrate on the internal dynamics of the ever-renewed story, forgetting that the world beyond the notorious Beltway lives in real time and quotidian existence. The media culture lives in media time and electronic existence. Success in that rarified world consists in making messages that command attention and respect. Those who make them assume the roles of political authorities, competing for a place in the spotlight in order to illuminate not only the political situation but also themselves, since they are an integral and dominating part of the process. We expect politicians to wish to see themselves at the center of things, including media attention. In a media world, those who would rule want to be seen, listened to, and heeded. We are all aware of the extent to which politicians cultivate the histrionic and cosmetic arts that help them project an appropriate and attractive *persona* through the media. Politicians are "in role" as they enact their dramatic part in the political play, and they may be quite phony in what they profess and how they act. They are quite capable of "bad faith," saying and seeming what they in fact are not. The elaborate organizational and rhetorical structures of political "image management" means that the role enactment is separate from the person, and that the politician is thus a poseur, putting on a political front. One of the reasons we are so suspicious of politicians is that we fear their public image is a "put-on," a contrived public self presented to us to curry favor. Distrust of politicians in the media age stems from doubt more about their sincerity than their sanity. We suspect they are phonies rather than madmen. If they do harm, it is because they are lying to us about themselves; they are not what they represent themselves to be. Their game is confidence and not control; they rule through talk and not tanks. They have little need for punitive powers if they can convince us of their right to rule through persuasion.

The difficulty with media politicians is that their orientation, often their preoccupation, is with media results rather than public benefits. Their occupation is supposed to be that of a public servant who presides over the execution of beneficial policies; but now their concern is with media self-presentation that affects popular perceptions. The formulation and implementation of policy becomes secondary to the media representation of a phony personage. Indeed, media image-making can serve as a dodge for costly or controversial policies which hurt one's popularity. Thus insubstantial actions that dramatize the politician make for media results, substituting for public benefits. The politician becomes the show, orienting the people away from ideas about being a public and toward becoming an audience. People then come less to expect public benefits but do expect political entertainment. In lieu of pragmatic action, politicians take dramatic action.

Media dramatics phony things up: the politician then avoids the hard choices of policy and highlights the phony actions of the political actor dramatizing his or her "concern" or whatever emotion to a problem or event. In an important sense, focusing attention on media results—augmenting one's popular reputation and standing—relieves the politician of political responsibility, measured in terms of benefiting the real lives of citizens. But if citizen has disappeared in favor of audience member, then the opportunity arises for phony politics that accomplishes nothing but dramatizes everything.

As media politics becomes more substantial, the recognition of its phoniness is resulting in several popular responses. There are recurrent popular revolts when many people realize that phony politics produces few public benefits (e.g., health care, job security). Many others "see through" the political scam and "turn off" politics, often literally by switching to another channel. Among such people, their cynicism and disillusionment have made them apathetic or alienated, often willing to vote for "movement" candidates who promise either a return to substance or a radical shakeup of the system. Media politics, like any other phony enterprise, depends upon popular gullibility, the ability of political actors to con audiences into believing in the authenticity, and efficacy, of their act. The political will to believe is a strong force, but the existence of a gap between the quality of people's lives and the political showmanship they witness that is designed to substitute for or draw attention away from that lack of quality may dash popular credulity. Nothing destroys political phoniness like incredulity, the discovery that much of what you see or hear from media politicians is tihsllub.

PHONY PUNDITRY

It is not only politicians who make for a phony politics. In a sense, the media, and more specifically the Washington press corps, collaborate in making politics phony. They do so in a variety of ways, not the least of which their acquiescence in media politics as we have described it. Since they are creatures of the media, they have a stake in the maintenance of the system of communication that obtains now. In that sense, they are all conservatives: media reporters and commentators cooperate with politicians, political operatives, and other political actors to keep the docudramatic miasma of popular stories going. Reporting and commenting are a symbiotic corollary of the politician's effort at dramatic self-presentation, the running narration and interpretation of the purported story. The tension arises in the insistence of the media to tell the story differently than the politician may have intended it, and for the commentators to give a different slant to the story than was hoped. They practice in their storytelling the "ironic model": everything that a politician says or does is phony, because his or her dramatic strokes are "a metaphor for something he is hiding."[3] Political action is deemed metaphorical, since it is designed to project a commitment to action rather than action itself. A media stance against crime taken with a "photo-opportunity" with a gathering of police officials is seen by the press as a metaphorical action rather than a real one (e.g., calling out the National Guard), because, they assume, the politician thinks the media event to be the primary focus of action. The double irony is that the media focuses on the media event staged for the media, but also reports and comments that the media event is phony, and that no real action is forthcoming. This is precisely the source of the "adversarial" conflict between politicians and independent media organizations: they need each other to perpetuate the docudrama, but the media insist that they should report the "inside dope" about what the politician is really up to. Their attitude toward the phony politics they helped create is profoundly cynical. But they equally insist on using their own metaphors, couched in their own cynical perspective, and expressed in the ironic language of hidden political motives that inform the activities of politicians. In large measure, the ironic tone of news stories that purport to "get behind" the real motives of a political operation (such as the White House) uses the metaphor of "the news day," describing how what is being said or done by the politician and his or her team is an effort to use the press and media outlets for their propaganda. The politician is presumed to be preoccupied with media politics; pseudo-events are staged for media effect; the press is solicited for support of some presidential initiative; their symbiotic adversaries in the press office aim at "spin control" and "damage control," which the press is duty-bound to report; they must point out that the thematic message or "line" of the moment is a calculated media strategy. In a sense, the metaphor of the national media is basically "media politics": the politicians are attempting to use the media to propagate their messages, but we, the press, know what they are up to and will point this out to you. The Washington media reveal the fraudulence of the other party to the transaction, but do not offer to withdraw or refuse to focus on the fraudulence in which they gladly, and lucratively, participate. The irony compounds because the media use of the media metaphor to explain Washington politics calls attention not only to the phoniness of politicians but also to the media complicity in the fraudulence. Such a self-referential to the docudrama thus often tends to undermine not only confidence in the presidential (or congressional, or bureaucratic) message but also in the press itself, who come to be seen as either the destroyer of presidential reputations for the public, or even more strangely, as the destroyer of their own reputation by reporting their complicity in phony media politics. The D.C. media circle is unbroken, but in the process those in the audience observing the dizzying turn of the news wheel discover that it goes nowhere and tells them nothing they didn't know, namely that the phony politics of the capital has little to do with them.

The people outside the capital do know that news is a growth industry, especially in the area of commentary. The old ideal of "objective reporting"—reporting empirical factualities—has been superseded. (In a sense, all aspects of the national press—liberal, conservative, or whatever—have accepted the canons of the "New Journalism.") Since the media are part of the process of reporting "media actualities" (media events created for press coverage, or governmental responses to real events) rather than empirical factualities (an event that occurs without media help), they feel the need to interpret the action. Such "media actualities" are in a sense factless: what occurs is a metaphorical docudrama, with "factoids" (facts used for propaganda purposes) placed in a metaphor that gives the presentation context ("This bill means jobs," "This measure means law and order"). Thus a presidential pseudo-event, an interview, a congressional group making a media-event proposal, a "fact-finding" trip by a congressional delegation, a forum on the late election, and so forth, all share the characteristic of media actuality, which press commentators feel comfortable interpreting.

Such interpretation is phony, since nothing happens in such constructed events. But the importance accorded them has provided the large corp of press commentators with a whole new area to interpret, since they belong to organizations that collaborate in the design of political media events. Too, they interpret such media events in media forums which are in themselves media events (talk shows, forums of reporters, round table discussions, interviews by other reporters, "sound bites" on the news). It was the habit for empirical events (e.g., a war, a coup d'etat, an election) to be interpreted by "experts" recruited from academic or professional groups (e.g., the foreign policy elite, economists, political scientists). But press personnel, often with dubious qualifications, became instant experts on an ever-expanding range of topics and events. Experts on one thing became experts on everything, and non-experts (reporters, usually) became experts simply by virtue of having a media forum and being reasonably articulate (if not particularly smart or knowledgeable). Thus empirical events in the real world become subject to interpretation by media figures whose grasp of them is suspect, but who are undaunted in their willingness to comment on the action out there without hesitation. Such interpretation is often phony, since the reporter-turned-expert has little idea of what she or he is talking about. Too, interpretation of media events is also phony, since the celebrity media expert may have a firmer grasp of media ephemerality, but since nothing consequential happens in such non-events, the interpreters spend a great deal of time and effort belaboring the importance of nothingness.

This media enterprise is called punditry, and the practitioners of this rhetorical art are deemed pundits. They are largely celebrity figures who have access to some media forum which allows them to expound their view of things, usually topical occurrences in the news. The media pundits tend to lack depth or breadth of perspective, but they do not want for bloviation. The only effective qualification to become a media pundit is B.S. artistry, the ability to appear to speak as with authority on virtually any matter. The proliferation of commentary in the many media forums has been a perfect opportunity for the emergence of phony expertise, coming from people who acquire the reputation for wisdom or knowledgeability merely by being there. But now one becomes a pundit by being there, and taken seriously by other pundits. Once given access to a forum to speak authoritatively on anything, the self-made pundit must then impress audiences by performing the popular role of pundit. He or she must appear to be wise by being impressive, expressing wisdom through media opining, the rhetoric of punditry.

Contemporary media pundits, then, are neither knowledgeable or wise. They are simply good at the rhetorical artistry expected of a popular news activity, commenting on news. Since much of the empirical news (a war abroad, a complex treaty) is beyond the experience or expertise of most people, they watch or listen to media pundits expound on that news. Punditic rhetoric is in the authoritative manner, but it is still phony talk by someone who is merely glib and always self-promoting. Indeed, their talk is often dishonest, in the sense that they are not always free agents exercising their commanding and soaring intellect to explain unfolding processes. Many of them are ideological or partisan mouthpieces, shilling for a right- or left-wing agenda, a party, or a candidate. In our indulgent media culture, they move back and forth from pundit to White House advisor to candidate (in Pat Buchanan's case) without anyone noticing the conflict of interest. Their colleagues do so because their prime common interest is their own career, which is enhanced by moving from one media role to another.

The contemporary media pundit is an exemplar of the political culture of narcissism. The journalist as hero has always been around: Stanley finding Livingstone, Hearst's reporters promoting war with Spain, Edward R. Murrow reporting live from London during the Blitz, Woodward and Bernstein uncovering the Watergate story. But these heroes were doing journalistic adventuring or investigating; by contrast, punditic heroes sit in a studio and pontificate about what they think is happening. In their hermetic world, they conjure up metaphors and arguments which purport to make sense of what's happening, be it empirical event or media event. As you might expect from participants in a media event, the pundits are adept at the analysis of pseudo-events that appear in the political media. But their major concern in these forums is the conveying of punditic authority, displaying their "media self" for all to admire. Their interest in punditry revolves around their consuming interest, the display of self as a dazzling hero of commentary.

In contemporary news-making, there is an expansionary principle at work for punditry. Everybody in journalism, to paraphrase Jimmy Durante, wants to get into the act. Reporting is not enough; everybody wants to be a pundit. Punditics offers a journalistic step up, allowing the reporter the prestigious status of commentator, thus enhancing reputation and fame. There are more pundit programs on TV, more talk radio hosts commenting on things far beyond their disc jockey capacity, more columnists in newspapers and magazines. Indeed, journalistic "beats" now seemed to include not only reportage but also commentary and analysis beyond the usual confines of journalism. Reporters talked less of the sources, and more of their own personal "take" or "sense" of what's happening. Rather than reporting objective facts, they frame events in their own subjective insight into the unfolding dynamic of subtle relationships and rhetorical stances. The task of the reporter-turned-pundit is to analyze his or her own take on things and share it with the rest of us, revealing the quality of the reporter's perception of political perceptions. With over 17,000 journalists in D.C., such take talk proliferates as journalists compete for power over what the most up-to-date take is at the moment, which of course must be abandoned when new takes begin to acquire plausibility. The conventional wisdom is quickly superseded by yet another conventional wisdom, and so on endlessly, as takes on what's happening are adopted and abandoned. There seems to be a move from "straight" news reporting to news analysis, with the professional reporter becoming a professional interpreter and even entertainer. The competition among this expanding corps of news analysts is fierce, since they are in the business of opinion mongering, attempting to make their take on things the credible one at the moment. There is, notes one observer, "competition among pundits to see whose view prevails [which] depends less on the inherent validity of the position than the rhetorical skill with which it is put forward."[4] The shelf life of opinions and metaphors is short: as soon as a pundit establishes a position that commands attention, it becomes the conventional wisdom that must be refuted and transcended for a new clever perception. What is at stake in such a "take race" is the elevated status of being an opinion leader, at least until the next take cycle, which begins anew immediately.

Punditic talk, then, is cheap, proliferating as more "analysts" get into the act. A kind of media Parkinson's Law prevails: news analysis expands to fill up the time available for its expression. But that expression has become all the more implausible and unheeded simply because it is so prolific and the soothsayers who bespeak punditry are such media creatures that much of what is opined is worthless. There seems to be an inexhaustible supply of people willing to express themselves in the media as a qualified pundit able to say important things about virtually anything. But the lure of self-expression stems from a desire for fame rather than shedding light on the world. The typical contemporary media pundit wants more than anything to illuminate herself or himself. Opinions are expressed not out of conviction but rather of expediency: what would be the best thing for me to say right now to further my punditic career? A line is taken because it is the line to take at the moment; the moment it is no longer fashionable or plausible, it is abandoned. The contemporary pundit is concerned in the main with her or his staying power. Opinions are adopted and abandoned on the sole basis of whether they further one's access to media expression and celebrity. Contemporary pundits are not intellectuals, for whom ideas applied to the study of current affairs was important. There are no Walter Lippmanns or Arthur Krocks among them (even George F. Will is merely a collection of pungent quotations and pithy sentences arrogated within the frame of an ideological contraption that is less than generous or magisterial: one study of Will's dissertation found that at age twenty-six he was "fully formed as the opinion-maker that he would become," in the middle-journalistic and sniffily arrogant manner of the pseudo-aristocratic Tory with an "inexperiencing nature"[5]). Indeed, since an intellectual air isn't popular, and since the media are moving increasingly toward "tabloid news," anti-intellectualism is the media manner to affect. Thus TV "news mud wrestling" shows such as "The McLaughlin Group" and "The Capital

Gang" involve displays of staged incivility by ideological shills and party hacks masquerading as knowledgeable analysts. The reasoned dialogue is replaced by the shouting match, as ambitious pundits compete to shove their take onto the group and the larger audience. Intelligence and insight on such shows are measured by shouted interruptions, snarled insults, and outrageous statements that "outtop" everyone else. The pundits seem determined to display their childishness, with instances of pique, narrow-mindedness, prejudice, ignorance, arrogance and snobbery, blind allegiance to partisan or ideological cliches, stubborn refusal to discuss, cynicism about politicians they hate, inflexible positions, and so on, *ad nauseum*. They have abandoned any semblance of media etiquette to assert their macho (the women do this too) image as "tougher-than-thou." Their rhetorical stances are so drearily predictable that they can only be labeled Orwellian "doubleplusgood duckspeakers," mouthing their self-assertive reactions to things from points of view that please rather than enlighten. They are incapable of transcending their own narrow political and temporal viewpoint, and they badly need new cliches. (Similarly, the radio talk show hosts are incapable of intellectual empathy or enlargement; all they can display on the air is their shallowness and incivility.)

The pundits have deteriorated into a collection of self-promoting phonies. Political opinion leadership has become a narcissistic enterprise of puerile opinionaters, using the opportunity to put themselves on display like willful and spoiled brats. The political culture is the lesser for their abrogation of responsibility. They give new meaning to advocacy journalism, because what they are advocating is their own indispensible fame; the opinions expressed serve that end, and are as disposable as yesterday's newspapers or last week's program. (It is always amusing to look at tapes of old programs, which reveal that punditic predictions are as often as not quite wrong.) Worse, their narrow and immediate focus on gossipy events and individuals makes all stories equal. A sensational "tabloid" trial is dealt with in the same flippant and sneering vein as a major treaty or law. Rather than in historically rooted or conceptually grounded analysis, they engage in debates over who "wins" or "loses," who looks good and who doesn't, who's hot and who's not, as if they were doing a gossip column (they are less in the tradition of Lippmann and more akin to Walter Winchell). Their judgment is exercised in the political "stirrings" of the moment, fixing credit and blame for the latest outcomes or situation. Since their concern is with their own famous reputation and power over opinion, they assume that is what motivates politicians, moves politics, and makes the world go round. So much of what they talk about is much ado about nothing, belaboring the obvious and elevating the trivial to glean what miniscule advantage or disadvantage exists at the moment for someone of importance. Their "overanalysis" often vastly exceeds the true significance of the person or event under discussion; since they vastly overstate their own significance, they cannot resist the temptation to elevate nonentities to the status of entities, since that is what they are about in promoting their own media image. They finesse responsibility for dealing with tabloid trivialities by "lateral attribution," noting that "a story is circulating." Since a rumor or gossip is their standard fare, such trivia is deemed newsworthy, since "people" (meaning the important personages whose names they like to drop on the air) are talking about (at dinner parties in Georgetown) the latest take on people and things in the capital, including (most importantly) the media celebrities. They live in an enclosed universe of virtual news, wherein even the most scurrilous rumor (of sexual deviance among the powers that be, of unhappiness in the First Family, of money scandal in the Congress) is given weight and consideration. A story that makes it onto the news agenda may be totally phony, but in the virtual world of casual and ethic-free newsworthiness, since it is circulating it makes the news. A tale about sexual misconduct, for instance, may be wholly false, either a rumor making the rounds or disinformation put out by the politician's enemies' (a Washington gossip columnist used to put out rumors deliberately, just to see how long it would take for the rumors to get back to her: a day was the usual time). The truth or falsity of a story is an irrelevance in the virtual world of news-mongering and -commenting. We have always known that news is not truth; but now we know truth has only an arbitrary and temporary relationship to news. News has become a function of punditics, an enclosed world of endless commentary in which the drama of pundit heroics in the act of opinionating assumes an importance far above and beyond the mere mortal world which is the putative subject of punditry.

Not only have the pundits transcended in attributed importance the political world they are supposed to explain to the rest of us, they have also abandoned any sense of time. They exist in a "virtual present," a mediated now on which they comment.[6] It is a dream world supported by the great myth of our media age, that the camera is an eye. The eye directs us toward talk of the present moment, defined by the punditic take on its virtual composition. No history, no causality, no recurrent patterns lead up to the current political situation; since what is important is the virtual kaleidoscope of current relations as they see and name them, past and future disappear as relating to the present. The virtual present is a media world, a world of communicators whose communications themselves are the primary data. The punditic hero sees through the present, and can be counted on to see through the next present, as gleaner of immediacy, even though the two times have no discernible relation to each other. The pundits are the Greek chorus of the American political drama, only in that their discordant songs dominate the play.

The punditic class treat their subject, politics and politicians, with a large measure of contempt. The heroism accorded the pundits (particularly by their own numbers) allows them to altercast politicians as villains or fools, and politics as a cynical and poorly played game. The pundits are giants who study pygmies, drama critics who judge the plays, intellectuals who dissect the stupid. They see politics as a phony charade, without mentioning that punditics is equally a charade, a ritual of media power centered on the heroic analysis of the immediate situation taken out of time and thus out of context. The punditic art is set in the context of no context, the place of no place, the time of no time. Given the assumptions on which that media art proceeds, and the system of which it is an integral and indispensable part, the pundits could be nothing else but phonies, since they help sustain a phony political culture. Since now many of the familiar celebrity "career pundits" are perennial powers of talk who chatter on endlessly, the only hope seems to be to set a term limit on pundits.

THE PHONY SYSTEM

It is common for pundits and "real people" to decry the gridlocks, stalemates, and practices of the Washington political system. As the twentieth century neared end, many people began to wonder if the inherent phoniness of the system was such that it could no longer sustain itself. There were questions: "Caught in the middle of a long sleep, the American mind began to ask itself: Were we taken? Had there been, for a long time, something phony about the Cold War?"[7] There was the sense that the American system was collapsing of its own emptiness: "Political decadence occurs when the forms that a State pretends to observe are known to be empty of all meaning."[8] There was the common observation that words and images didn't mean anything, since they were used to convey immediate mass-mediated impressions and not matters of political conviction or even policy, since no one was committed to such inconveniences (we may recall that Secretary of Defense Caspar Weinbarger, defending the faking of "Star Wars" test results to fool not only the Soviet Union but also the Congress, maintained that "a deception did not take place, although a program to practice deception existed"; in the same honest spirit, Eliot Abrams, testifying before the Iran-contra committee in 1987, made the key distinction between "lying" and "leaving a false impression"). Words were used, and images staged, by the many actors who represented interests in the wired world of Washington, but they emanated from programs to practice deception and were designed to leave false impressions. Everyone in the system sought to "cover" themselves through the general use of "plausible deniability": what was said or imaged was part of the process, but no one was responsible for the veracity or consistency of political communications. People were separate from what they said or projected, as if they had no moral connection to words or images that they used. They were what you used, but even if you used them, you could still deny you really meant them. After all, the words and images were phony. Since we expect politics to be phony, we shouldn't be upset if people use phony words and images. The "truth that matters" is in the control of perceptions in the cyberspace of political messaging, a constantly tentative and mercurial undertaking over which mastery is always uncertain.

As politics becomes more and more an insubstantial pageant, it may be the case that fewer and fewer people outside of the system itself believe it to have any substantive value for their lives. A phony political system may not be able to fool all the people all the time. Indeed, even when the system does respond with measures that increase the public weal and well-being, the people may have been so corrupted by so much phony talk and imagery that they no longer trust the system to respond benevolently and adequately. It can be argued that the initiatives in health care, gun and crime control, and free trade in the 1990s make for a better country; but they do not seem to affect much public distrust of government and cynicism about politicians. Political figures such as Bill Clinton and Jack Kemp are likely as sincere and well-meaning as one can be in the world of politics, but both inspire more contempt and disfavor than they probably deserve. Similarly, American government at all levels struggles mightily to deal with difficult problems and rapid change, but apparently never to the satisfaction of the mass public, which seems entrenched in their alienated and downright uncivil mood.

In some measure, the blame for this public mood can be traced to the phony system. Now government was getting the people it deserved. For many people thought the system, as defined by what they saw and heard about it, was above all self-sustaining. In the popular mind, politicians have come to be seen as narcissists motivated by megalomania and exhibitionism. Politics has become a dishonorable enterprise, and "career politicians" much condemned. Thus those politicians who are honest and realistic public servants become as much an object of popular scorn as those who are "media politicians." Indeed, the former are infected by the success of the latter. But there is a popular paradox here: the more that people seem to "fall" for media pitches (the success of Reagan and other politicians relied on mediated politics), the more many of the same people seem to express great displeasure with the state of the very politics they help to create. It is as if they cannot get enough of media bamboozlement (campaign advertising, photo-ops, pseudo-events such as "town meetings," presidential theater), but then feel guilty about being taken in yet again, girls and boys who can't say no. They seem to want both the romanticism of the world of political appearances manipulated for them, but also the realism of the world of political action that produces results, the media cake that can be eaten too.

The major historical danger of the triumph of phony politics is that people at all levels of society will no longer be able to take government and politics seriously. A "civic culture" is sustained by *gravitas* and *civitas*, the ability to take public matters seriously and the willingness to participate in citizen rule of the republic. Political obligation is supposed to reside in the role of citizen, which ultimately guides and controls democratic government. But American culture has become increasingly frivolous, committed to play rather than work, to artifice rather than action, to the media actuality rather than the policy factuality, to the phony rather than the authentic. The youth revolt of the 1960s was symptomatic of the search for "authenticity," since many of the activists of that age did sense that the world was becoming phonier. Despite the protests of social critics, much of American life has become phonier as the ethos of the confidence game has pervaded every area of society. But this pervasion has made it difficult for many people to take things seriously or to participate in social and political groups and events. Made into consumers of everything, Americans have become more frivolous, regarding important matters like government and politics as one more phony activity to watch as a show. Rather than the exercise of the rights and interests of the citizen, there is now the passive amusement of the audience consuming political media events, ephemeral talk and images, the phony pageant of insubstance. Politics and politics have no gravity, and are thus lighter than air, elevated by their electronic status as shadows on the television cave wall; neither have they civility, since the relationship between politician and public is a dramatic rather than political one, a transaction of actor and audience rather than civil authority and citizenry. The citizen has been superseded by consumers of images, who evaluate the political show on the basis of dramatic rather than political criteria. The show is seen as a show, without meaningful relevance for the conduct of our lives. We simply cannot take it seriously. The political show is part of our "carnival culture," a state of tastelessness in which all shows are equal, equally entertaining and equally unreal.[9] If political life is a theatric carnival, then we may be excused for thinking that we are loosened from any political responsibility or even seriousness in our own lives.

The terminal phoniness of our politics may account in some sense for the breakdown of civility in American society. Devoid of any sense of moral gravity, we feel no obligation to respect the phony or obey the rules made by the phonies. If the "show of society" is a carnival, then we are freed from not only political but also moral obligation. The savage and cynical economic wildcatting of the 1980s was conducted by capitalist buccaneers with no moral restraints, setting an example for the rest of us: if capitalism at that level is a form of robbery, then why can't I find ways to take the loot and run also? We witness through "festive viewing" the carnival life of celebrities, with their affairs, parties, suits, pleasure domes, and so on. Since they conceive the essence of life to be sensate play, then why are we not justified in doing the same, devoting our lives to fun rather than toil, no matter how much it puts us in debt or to crime? If the goods of the world are gotten by the phonies, then why shouldn't I be a phony too, exploiting other people for money, sex, or power? If life is a confidence game, why can't I play it as well as important people, conning my way through life in order to get what I want at other people's expense? Our observation of the passing show of culture, economics, and politics convinces us that we are as expendable as the ephemeral figures of medialand, so we abandon any sense of permanent values and moral grounds. In our relations with others, then, we have no stake in civility; if incivility works in hostile takeovers, "downsizing" loyal employees, union busting, and "golden parachutes" for executives who write themselves generous payoffs as their company fails, then the same tactics can work at the street level. If incivility works for celebrities in their treatment of spouses, lovers, and friends, then the same kind of mistreatment also can work for people who live in slums and trailer parks. If incivility works for politicians who take campaign money from big interests, stalemate essential legislation for the interests that pay them off, destroy the environment and local communities at the behest of corporate "development," then we may conclude that bribery, selling out, and destruction are equally justified for us. Our cultural heroes serve as negative exemplars: entrepreneurs become greedy megalomanics, celebrities become shameless exhibitionists, and politicians servants of special interests. Since such figures provide us with norms of leadership, we emulate them in their greed, vanity, and cynicism, and pride ourselves in being as phony as our betters. Since they represent the pinnacle of moral behavior in the system, those of us in the middle and on the bottom deem them worthy of emulation, in lesser degrees of greed, vanity, and cynicism.

The political system in particular takes on a kind of remoteness that separates the citizen from any sense that participation matters. The passing show of political affairs comes to be seen as something that occurs "up there" in the phony world. To use a metaphor, government is exemplified by the motorcades one sees in Washington or New York: the sleek and elegant parade of limousines, accompanied by police escort and press buses and Secret Service agents, moves noisily through the streets bearing important personages, sweeping normal traffic and commerce out of its path as it speeds to large events and other great personages. The motorcade swiftly passes, protected by armed escorts and bulletproof defenses, perhaps acknowledging the presence of the crowd but rarely stopping to commingle with the ordinary folks on the streets, especially if they are mean. The motorcade goes to protected and richly appointed places for speeches and meetings and ceremonies, therein often invoking the popular will that is supposed to emerge from the people on the streets just passed through. The passing presence of the motorcade conveys power to the people on the street who pause momentarily to watch, but not participation. The motorcade is "them," the phony presences we see on television but who have no interest in or effect on the conduct of our lives.

Indeed, many people conclude that participation of any kind is either fruitless or precluded. In the former instance, the citizen habit of voting has fallen on hard times, with low turnouts in even the most important elections. Many political scientists and pundits wishfully attribute non-voting to widespread satisfaction which lowers any urgency to vote, equating apathy and contentment. But we may suspect that many people are not so much apathetic as alienated, actively "turned off" by the phoniness of the system. When people follow a campaign for office, they are struck by how phony it all is: the smiling vacuity of a candidate, his or her "image" along with the loving family and the "personal" story of the climb to success; the pseudo-events and phony issues, the lack of genuine debate and straight answers, the "sound bites" and slogans; the use of campaign consultants and technocrats who make the ads and coin the slogans and groom the candidate into a non-person without human qualities or contacts. Voters are not fools: when they conclude that the primary effort of the campaign for office is to con them into believing nonsense, they rightly take the correct action, which is to stay away from phonies. Phony politics is more likely the major source of non-voting. The non-voter is not apathetic nor content: he or she actively concludes that they cannot reasonably register either content or discontent in a phony event—the election—that has nothing to do with their lives, so why bother?

Similarly, participation is often not taken because it is precluded by large organizations who wish to control the agenda of interest expression. One of the ideals of democracy has been the "grassroots" movement, the spontaneous rising of the people to further or protest something to the political system, pushing an issue onto the agenda of government and "petitioning the government for a redress of grievances." But the authentic grassroots movement has now been precluded by organized interests who conduct phony "astroturf" movements. These interests may hire, or ally themselves with, professional firms and spokespersons who propagandize their view. The idea is not to join a true movement that bubbles up from the bottom, but to agitate for the creation of phony discontent through carefully designed media messages that appeal to the popular mind. Many write-in and call-in campaigns are orchestrated by interest groups and professional agitation firms that create the illusion of spontaneity over issues ranging from congressional pay increases to health reform. Interest groups will create phony "front organizations," mobilize sympathetic radio talk show hosts and newspaper editors, hold "town meetings" stacked with their own agitators, and so on, all contributing to the false sense that a great groundswell of public outrage or sentiment has emerged from the grassroots of the hinterland. In reality, the astroturf movement is phony, giving the false sense of widespread public participation for or against something. The health insurance industry, threatened with meaningful health reform in 1994, attempted a campaign that would instill fear in people that change would result in disaster for the health care system. The ploy was to attempt to convey the impression of widespread public opposition to the president's proposal emerging from the grassroots, when in fact the campaign was financed and engineered by the lobbying organization and propaganda firm hired by the health insurance industry. Sometimes the "ordinary citizens" deluging the capitol with phone calls are calling from phone banks set up by the lobby, and the letters of outrage are solicited (even paid for) by the lobbying organization. All this makes the process of expressing an interest in what the government is doing suspect, since every emergent wave of expression may well be phony. Separating what is authentic from what is phony then becomes difficult to ascertain. A popular expression of opinion on some matter of public importance may well be orchestrated by big interests conducting an astroturf campaign for their own purposes. (Or big politicians with big ambitions: some wags thought that H. Ross Perot's "United We Stand" groups around the country could form the basis for a movement-party designed to benefit their founder's presidential bid not dissimilar from the "John Doe Clubs" that the rich magnate wished to use in Frank Capra's film *Meet John Doe*.)

A political system that runs on artifice cannot be expected to forever enjoy the confidence of the many who come to distrust its operation. A phony political system is light on bread and heavy on circuses; systemic "outputs" are symbolic gestures that emanate from the propaganda machines of the State. Especially since the presidency of Ronald Reagan, politicians and their "handlers" have learned the high art of imaginative fraudulence. The system has become very good at producing electronic messages which "frame" people's view of what government does, who the leading icons are, what phrases and images will play with mass audiences. Political calculation focuses on command of the latest virtual present, with outputs defined in terms of dramatic success rather than more mundane political goods—high-wage and permanent jobs, rising living standards, fair treatment by the law and corporations.

It may be the case that in the "post-modern" world, the large State systems that developed over the last two centuries will become increasingly unable to guarantee the kind of permanent prosperity and national ascendancy that characterized previous eras. In such a situation, we may see much more of what has been called "ceremonial politics," in which large dramatic events and everyday political communications from leaders are essential ritualistic. Ceremonial politics supersedes "parliamentary politics," the effort to manage and satisfy competing interests.[10] Parliamentary politics continues, to be sure; but it is less interesting and certainly more painful, in an era of "the endangered American dream," wherein intractable economic and social problems make a "shrinking pie" difficult to administrate without considerable sacrifice and discontent.[11] Ceremonial politics maintains the facade of governmental omnipotence through control of the sovereignty of images.

The difficulty is that most people do not live in the realm of political virtuality, but rather live in the existential dynamics of quotidian coping. They are outside the "virtual Beltway," in the popular matrix of everyday life. At crucial moments in their lives, they are faced with realities that no amount of official artifice can quell— serious illness without health insurance, permanent unemployment, the threat of bankruptcy, the inadequacy of retirement income, the threat of crime. At such times, the inadequacy of political artifice is clear enough. The consumer of images becomes aware of the fact that the political virtuality consumed as entertainment is phantasms, ghosts whose main characteristic is their phoniness. The underlying malaise of the political system, then, stems from the practice of phony politics. A political system sapped of vitality has social consequences, for people themselves lose confidence in not only government but also social institutions and eventually themselves. The system becomes suffused with artifice, and the widespread practice of artificiality destroys both mutual and self-confidence. Mutual confidence is destroyed by the practice of exploitation, and self-confidence is damaged by the ethical soullessness of endless win-loss calculations. Lives of "quiet desperation" become common, wherein people can trust no one, including themselves.

At some point in time, it becomes a question as to how much longer a phony politics can sustain itself. A political system based on artifice lacks the vitality for renewal, and thus threatens to deteriorate further in inefficiency, corruption, and decadence. Political systems, like any other organization, are prone to entropy, with things running down over time. We need only point to historical precedents such as Rome and Great Britain to note how highly sophisticated and successful systems of power lost their ability to adjust, innovate, and prosper. Similarly, the ancien regime in France before the revolution of 1789 was sustained by a politics of artifice. In all cases, the rulers proceeded as if the citizenry shared their somnambulistic assurances as they conducted the ceremonies of rule, unaware of the processes of change outside the confines of the Roman Palatine, Whitehall in

London, and Versailles. At some point in such cases, politics ceases to be substantial and becomes phony, with effort directed at sustaining the illusion of "same as it ever was" rather than solving problems. Political systems in decline turn to phony politics in self-defense, substituting veneration of leaders and values for contemporary solutions. The Roman magistrate becomes an emperor, and the values of the ancient republic are extolled (the daughters of Augustus learned to spin cloth in the old manner); the American chief magistrate becomes an "imperial presidency," and "family values" are celebrated. At such junctures, phony politics is reactionary, simply because the world has changed beyond the recognition of rulers and those many who do not wish to deal with change. Mythic efficacy takes precedence over pragmatic efficacy. The long-term consequence of phony politics in such situations is disastrous. King Canute could make a point about the helplessness of a ruler before the waves of the sea he ordered to cease; but in states imbued with phony politics, the waves of the historical sea, including the barbarians and competitors at the gate, are ordered to cease without admitting the helplessness of rulers before the deluge.

CONCLUSION

THE CONSEQUENCES
OF A PHONY CULTURE

It has been the continuing thesis of this book that American culture is becoming increasingly phony. In some measure, our inquiry has been taxonomic, in that we have outlined the ways in which social phoniness are manifest. We should note that even though there are historical and characterological features peculiar to the United States that have given impetus to phony people and phony culture, the potential for phoniness is a human trait that can manifest itself in other times and at other places. (The dedication of this book should remind us that only humans can be phonies: the charm of pets, or "animal companions," is their natural and unaffected directness; the dog or cat genuinely loves you.) Nor should we leave the impression that phoniness and conning are totally bad things always to be avoided. Social circumstances may be such that the exercise of con artistry has its uses. Oskar Schindler, the antihero of *Schindler's List*, managed to save Jews from the Nazi Holocaust simply because he was a smooth operator who conned the Nazi bureaucrats into sparing his Jewish workers. But it is our task here to inquire into the consequences of phoniness for American culture now and in the future, and to speculate as to the potential for American and other cultures in the future.

What are the consequences of a phony culture? Phoniness is a social condition that inhibits trust, legitimates the artful con, and encourages cynical role-playing. If the philosophical ground for the republican idealist is a kind of populist romanticism, and for the charismatic adventurer a version of achieving realism, then for the confidence man it is pretentious cynicism. The confidence man and woman, Lindberg concluded, is our hero, perhaps the ultimate consequence of individualism in American life, a feature that lets the adept skilled at "making and packaging a self do so." In a sense, American phonies play themselves, transforming relations into maneuvers: "It is the experience of turning social manners, habituated gestures, and badges of appearance back into *self-conscious gambits*, so that one's very capacity to play roles proves one's detachment."[1] Even those with "sincere" or "genuine" motives and morally commendable goals are drawn into the artifices of confidence (charities are increasingly committed to fund-raising through propaganda and image-making through public relations, raising suspicions that United Way, Girl Scouts, or whatever is run by phonies, a charge that must be addressed through more propaganda and PR, and so on in an endless cycle of phony relations). Presidential candidates are made and packaged by their media consultants, raising the suspicion that the candidate is not what he or she represents, that what we see is a phony self, that she or he is in the race as a self-conscious gambit, a political con act, politics as performance art. Potential lovers distrust each other because they fear exploitation, that their partner might be a phony using their relation to conduct maneuvers of momentary advantage but the relation will be abandoned when she or he is not usable any longer. The fact that we are afraid of being conned—"had"—suggests that a residual part of ourselves resists abandoning ourselves totally to phoniness, that we still long for something authentic. We realize that we are far separated from the natural and genuine by devices of our own making, and wonder if there is some way to simplify things to recapture a lost innocence or "simple gifts" of straightforwardness.

Yet for all our yearnings, the advance of phony culture is unrelenting. Every day we build more theme parks, casinos, retirement or rich enclaves, fantasy resorts, and simulated replicas of real places. The economy of work is slowly being superseded by the economy of play—service industries such as restaurants, tourism and travel, entertainment, sports, and so on. Disney history replaces authentic history in northern Virginia; the Civil War, World War II, even the Holocaust become remote to us through recreative simulation, making them seem somehow unreal, as if they didn't actually happen but were invented to amuse and frighten us. Politics occurs in a virtual reality of constructed images and phony messages, devoid of relevance to the world of ordinary human struggle and problems. Problems are "resolved" through phony symbolism; a fair tax system is replaced by state-promoted gambling, with governments complicit into turning their citizens into gambling addicts. The media culture of Washington, New York, and Los Angeles exists in a precious and frivolous celebrity world of self-important demigods—actors, reporters, writers, talkers, singers, and so on—who live apart and above the quotidian world. The elite celebrity subculture is (to paraphrase Michael Kelly) a phony social strata wherein complicit knowledge functions to sustain the self-important acts of fraudulence one performs as a member of the elite culture.[2] In such self-conscious communities, those "in the know" are aware of the fraudulent gambits they perpetuate with each other and with their mass auditors; but as communicators their concern is with perpetuating their status and selling their message through the projected artifices of performance art. They create the self-image of celebrity, the simulated image of television programs, the superficial melodramas of the daily news, the latest best-selling novel. Our architecture—cities, malls, developments—appear generic, interchangeable and soul-deadening, monuments to our lack of imagination and daring. Many people sense that American culture has reached dead ends: the ritual structure of the television day hasn't changed for decades and movie formulas repeat over and over again the same stories; religious worship and church attendance fall off as organized religion becomes either dreary repetition or politicized forums for celebrity divines; school has become a deadly routine that drives students at all levels to boredom and distraction, seeking learning elsewhere; the much-vaunted family continues to disintegrate or alter out of all recognition. The common culture seems to atrophy from a lack of interest: as turnout in elections falls, we may soon give an election and nobody will come.

Too, we may speculate as to the extent to which the pervasion of phoniness has affected our selves. Psychologists write of the "fictive personality" or the "protean self" or "role flexibility," the extent to which we are willing and able to become a phony *persona* enacting self-conscious gambits in the world of shifting appearances and affected pretension.[3] In such a world, we are never ourselves; there is no stable center to personality, and thus the center of culture cannot hold. Yeat's mere anarchy is loosed upon the world in the ephemeral forms of social chameleons who continually renew self and role in ever-changing adaptations and pretensions. We may, with Holden Caulfield in Salinger's *The Catcher in the Rye*, decry the hypocrisies of the phonies who are everywhere, but we would first have to free ourselves of our own penchant for phoniness, and the disquieting possibility that we *like* being phony, or conversely, that we like being conned by phonies. Phoniness has the comfort of detachment: we can hide behind the mask of Melville's masquerade, and delude ourselves with our own presentation of confidence for the world. In such a phony world, we become what we masquerade ourselves as, until such time as we can mask ourselves as something else for some new purpose. In a dissociative universe, appearance is the only reality, and the drama of human relations our ongoing social play in which we play ourselves. We have become, at least for the moment, our artifices. In such a condition, we so fear facing our natural condition or knowing our true selves that we become the prisoner of our own carefully constructed facades and affectations. At that point, we have become so phony that we don't know who we are apart from our self-conscious gambits, and have lost touch with whatever truths we might have wished to know about ourselves. We have made the structure of artifices that contain ourselves, and now we must live there in the phony life.

The difficulty is that if carried to its culturological conclusion, such a society of phonies is unstable. It lacks tradition, depth, humane values, a sense of continuity and meaning, historical placement, social purpose—a center that can hold against the opportunistic agendas of the phonies. The consequences of the phony culture in America are now becoming obvious by what it lacks. American culture lacks *veracity*, a habitual adherence to truth and a respect for knowledge. For in a phony culture, honesty is not a virtue, and in many quarters—politics or the media, for instance— would evoke only a condescending sneer. The notion (from Czech philosopher-politicians Vaclav Havel and Vaclav Maly) of "life in truth" seems hopelessly naive to the habitual con artist or the successful political or media star who made it by opportunistic self-presentation. Secondly, a phony culture lacks *fidelity*. Faithfulness, loyalty, bonding, your "word," and so forth, become resources to be manipulated rather than ties to be honored in a world without trust. Like veracity, fidelity has severe limits for a phony, who is convinced that every relationship can and should be betrayed if the right opportunity for something better comes along. Bonds cannot be respected in such a world, since they are a fetter on the art of the con. Finally, a phony culture lacks *quality*. In a world of manipulated appearances, people have no core of being and no respect for character or excellence. People do not feel enjoined to do the right thing or make a quality thing because it has intrinsic merit. Rather something is done because it is the opportune thing to do. The quality of an act is reduced to histrionic persuasion; the quality of a thing is in making it attractive as an object of desire. In a phony culture, veracity, fidelity, and quality tend to be driven out, replaced by the arts of B.S., the exploitation of relations, and the pretense to, but disregard of, qualitative merit or worth. Lacking respect for *logos*, *pathos, and ethos,* a phony culture is dishonest, disloyal, and cheap. In such a world, democratic and civilized values are thought to be hopelessly without relevance or intrinsic merit; since phonies assume everyone acts out of calculated self-interest, the idea of doing something for the common good or because it is the right thing to do seems ludicrous.

We may lay much of the blame for our present malaise, then, on the ongoing process of transforming Americans into living a synthetic and demoralized life. We now lack contact with nature, with respect for value other than the art of the con, with an ability to regard life and society as serious matters. The synthetic life of a phony culture lacks *civitas,* regard for the civil order beyond one's own opportunism, and *gravitas,* the ability to take things seriously. A phony culture dominated by the confidence man exhibits a kind of popular sophistry, a cynical disrespect for enduring values or the gravity of good and evil. Such considerations interfere with the conduct of the latest con. Yet it is this regard that imbues us with such a widespread sense of cultural pessimism and historical disjunction, making it impossible for us to cultivate respect for public agendas that renew and perpetuate civilization and to take seriously people who recommend public deliberation. A phony culture regards anyone who professes such ideas as altruistic fools or phonies like ourselves. Lacking any desire for permanence, the phonies who work the important social cons in America regard everything as impermanent, exploitable, and up for grabs. If nothing lasts or means anything, do what you can get away with and grab what you can without getting caught.

A phony culture is unstable because it is not on the level. It does not confront and wish to know reality; rather it arranges reality to remove the existential challenge and rough edges. It does not pursue happiness; rather it makes happiness into a commodity. All relations are negotiable because everyone comes to assume that the other parties to the transaction are not on the level. Every ideological or political assertion, every economic proposal, every cultural artifact, is regarded as the tihsllub of some vested interest. Everyone who speaks or writes or makes images is a phony trying to work a con. Every social relation, even of the most intimate nature, cannot be trusted, since the person you are married to, a friend with, or a business partner with may be a phony who will shaft you in a heartbeat. At the outer edges of such a culture of mistrust is a Hobbesian state of nature, a jungle of untrustworthy relations that can deteriorate into betrayal and savagery. The ultimate consequence of a phony culture would be to loose mere anarchy on the world, an anarchy of fraud if social peace can be maintained, but failing that, an anarchy of force.

If a phony culture is unstable, it can then be superseded by a political society that people find more satisfying or secure. If people are unsatisfied with a situation of phony talk at the top and exploitation and disorder at the bottom, they could hope for some reformed democratic order that would build on trust earned by civil authorities who exemplify and honor genuine values such as veracity, fidelity, and quality, and who try to instill civil habits such as respect for the facts, honest dealings, and the instinct of workmanship. Such a reformed social democracy would be different from a phony culture in that it would be on the level. The consequence of restoring the value of leveling with each other would instill a sense of mutual respect and even trust that would lessen the value we now place on the successful con. Confidence could be exchanged through mutual consent rather than gained through the persuasive con game. This would require modification in our basic practices of individualistic self-interest and self-assertion, but it would have large benefit in the pervasion of trust and the condemnation of phoniness. Such a change would introduce the potential for stability in both self and society, based in the astonishingly simple idea of leveling with one's self and everyone else. But to bring such a desirable future about, we would have to level with ourselves and be willing for social authorities to level with us. Leveling with each other would go a long way in dispelling phoniness. Trustworthiness is enhanced by treating other people on the level, and democratic spirit is strengthened by the "leveling" impulse: equals deal with each other on the level.

There is another, more demonic, possibility. A phony culture is a network of artifice, a miasma of large and small pretenses in order to gain some advantage. Throughout most of society, such pretension is merely the ordinary cons of people "on the make," "on the take," or "on the run." They have something to hide and something to gain, so the resources of artifice are put to work in not leveling with people. But pretension as a principle of civilization may convince people that the social order is a swindle, and make them yearn for something more ardent and exalted in which they invest their beliefs, their wills, and their energies. They may will to believe in a movement and leader that establish a coherent and simple world of monocular belief, unified wills, and coordinated energies. The dissociation of consciousness and fragmentation of social relations is overcome by a new order that promises to end pretension and exploitation. But it does not do so by reinstituting the habit of being on the level. Rather it does so by instituting a new and more coherent form of domination, one that pretends to end pretension and end exploitation through a new mode of pretension and exploitation. In the past, the most spectacular forms of such rule were Nazism and Communism, the ultimate nature of which George Orwell understood so well. Twentieth-century totalitarianism was a new kind of phony culture, one that instituted phoniness as a policy through spectacle, surveillance, and secrecy. Totalitarianism was not on the level, and eventually it collapsed through the weight of its own self-delusion of benevolence even as it expanded its demonic power. Totalitarian states were led by a phony personage (e.g., Hitler), utilized phony language (Goebbels's propaganda), exalted phony places and things (the Nuremberg rallies, Horst Wessel), practiced phony politics (the "final solution" that scapegoated Germany's "enemies"), and so on, all with disastrous results stemming from the basic delusionary state of a mesmerized political culture, one that finally was destroyed in the *Götterdämmerung* of Berlin in 1945.

Yet if Americans are soon to be tempted by some form of "reform fascism," it may resemble less the vision of Orwell and resemble more the vision of Aldous Huxley's *Brave New World*. Huxley saw a future totalitarianism that is equally phony, but this time will be more scientific and "friendly." Huxley's world would be based in scientific management and behavior modification, using organizational technique in order to engineer human compliance. Everyone would be taught to respond to life through slogans ("Everyone works for everyone else"; "Everybody's happy now"), to live in puerile dependence on organizational management of our work and play lives, and to love our planned servitude. Yet this world of "total administration" is an artificial universe, one dominated by technocrats and run by technique. A Huxleyian world is just as unfree and phony as an Orwellian one, only full of smiley faces having a nice, if thoughtless, day.[4]

There is another sinister potentiality we must consider, what Jewett and Lawrence call "Pop Fascism." In an appendix to their classic book, *The American Monomyth*, they contemplate popular phenomena such as *Star Wars*, Rambo, Reagan's movie fantasies projected onto the political world, and Oliver North, asking the question, "Can any republic, including our own, sustain a democratic ethos while celebrating the pleasures of Pop Fascism in its living rooms and theaters?"[5] We may speculate whether an American Caesar would come in the guise of a populist democrat who gains absolute power as the people's choice. Pop Fascism would include many Orwellian and Huxleyian features, in the former case including restrictions on freedom, the expansion of the police state, scape-goating of enemies, the expansion of prisons into concentration camps, and the worship of leader and state, and in the latter case including the expanded use of suggestive propaganda and conditioning, multimedia spectacles that glorify the state, the use of controlled pleasure to convince people they are happy, and so on. The great addition would be the use of popular culture to augment leader and state control. Spectacles of power that associate political and popular celebrities as legitimate authorities, popular language and image that convey popular identification, and the enactment of popular rituals that have mythic resonance for populaces, all have potential uses for an American benevolent despot. For example, religious celebrities could be recruited to support a pious Caesar in televised spectacles that accord him or her godly authority; the popular language of televangelism and popular piety could be adapted to political rhetoric; and the rituals of state could become an occasion for the celebration of popular myths, such as zealous nationalism and righteous empire. Given the right circumstances and leader, the vast resources of popular experience, everything from popular music (e.g., country-and-western's reactionary populism, rock 'n' roll's barbaric rebellion) to popular radio and TV (e.g., talk radio's savaging of "pushy" groups such as blacks and women, TV's guest shows that are essentially degradation ceremonies designed to "get the guest" by a kind of electronic Jacobin assembly), could be mobilized by a new electronic order. Such a "revitalization move-ment" could utilize aspects of popular culture (and suppress others) to underscore a new authoritarian order led by a popular Caesar (figures like Ross Perot or Oliver North are symptomatic of this temptation). Pop Fascism would be no less phony than previous despotisms, only it would seem to accord with and validate popular experience. Pop Fascism would recreate the American world as a puerile and idiotic place, with both sinister and preposterous dimensions, built upon the habits of phonies that preceded and helped shape it.

We may wonder, then, if the unstable conditions of our millennial time will continue to create a revulsion against phony culture, or by some kind of perverse historical logic, we are being transformed into something that is at once phony and demonic. In terms of culturologic, it seems that cultures have three distinct choices as to their "way of life": cultures can be either vital, artificial, or deadly. A *vital* culture is on the level. It faces reality, deals with empirical knowledge, attempts to adapt to changing environments, and has energetic and functioning institutions and individuals. A vital culture has popular vitality, is able to learn and create, and values the human bonds which perpetuate the culture but do not preclude change and innovation. The orientation of such a society is towards improving the quality of this life, and renewing for each generation the promise of the future. At its best, it is committed to life in truth. By contrast, a *death* culture is committed to the instrumentation and realization of death. This can be the "normal" living death of overconformity and "dead-end" overwork or overplay. If a society is characterized by the great majority leading lives of "quiet desperation," the excessive repression makes life an agony. Those who work themselves to death have overvalued acquisition or advancement; those who play themselves to death have overvalued indulgence and intoxication. In both cases, people are driven to self-destruction. At their worst, death cultures celebrate and maximize death. Nazi death camps and the Gulag archipelago, the development of the nuclear war machine, the wanton destruction of life in warfare, all exhibit the "genocidal mentality." Yet more normal life features deadly qualities—the pollution and destruction of the environment, the exhaustion of natural resources and the exploitation of natural beauty, the expansion of death subcultures in slums, reservations, prisons, and schools, the retreat of the rich into spiritless enclaves or towers, and so on.

The third choice, or strain, in cultures is artifice, the conventions of an *artificial* culture. The forces of vitality and destructiveness are perhaps always there in the "life against death" struggle, but so too are the forces of phoniness. We may hypothesize that a culture of artifice tends to occur in a period of stagnation or decline, when a culture has reached a point of ritualized stagnation at the apex of its power, or is in slow decline where vitality and initiative have moved elsewhere. The post-Augustan age of Roman political culture was a period of institutional artifice, as the "decline and fall" slowly came upon them. The artifices of Roman ascendancy and normalcy celebrated a power and authority that steadily disappeared, no matter how much they wished to believe in its continuation. The *ancien regime* in France had reached a state of political and cultural stagnation by the eighteenth century. The courtier spirit pervaded society, emulating the phony political subculture of Versailles. In both cases, the artifices of "high society" and court life gave ritual reassurance that things were the same as they ever were, when in fact they could not stop the "dry rot" of a stagnant or dying political culture, nor inhibit the shift of power elsewhere or outbursts of vital revolt. An artificial society in a sense denies both life and death, substituting the rituals of artifice for vitalistic action and contemplation of social entropy towards decay and demise. All the reassurances of the confidence man turn out to be measures of benevolent deception, which only hasten the process of stagnation and decline. Such social and political orders are at that moment in a state of *decadence*, wherein the moral and civic center of the culture has been eroded to the point that cynical and corrupt exploitation dominate in an atmosphere of "deluge mentality": get all you can while you can.

For Americans in the late twentieth century, a probable consequence of a phony culture, then, is that it will continue to contribute to the social drift towards decadence. The artifices of phoniness give great impetus to the cynical use of human beings for one's own purposes. Such an exploitative culture destroys the human capacity for altruism and transcendence. In doing so, nothing comes to matter except self-aggrandizement gained by any means necessary. In such a popular philosophy are the seeds of widespread corruption, both of action and of spirit. The social consequence is the spread of individual and institutional decadence, which slowly saps the vitality from the body politic and the social order. Phonies become ascendant in periods of decadence, and the cynical sophistry that makes them important and successful becomes the source of stylistic emulation for the entire society. On observing the narcissistic decadence of the celebrity culture, the sophistry of the courtier culture of Washington, the lavish and arrogant self-indulgence of the corporate elite, American youths grow up inheriting the same cynicism, expressed either as a desire to become as decadent as they (one makes lots of money to indulge oneself) or to become resigned to the petty decadence of lifelong penury and no upward mobility in "McJobs." When "Generation X," the young people coming of age in the contemporary world, use as mottos such terms as "Whatever," "Why bother?" and so on, they express no confidence in the integrity of their elders. Moral reformers and eminent divines may call for spiritual and national revitalization and remoralization, but they are not taken seriously in the circles of power which set the standards of action through their use of the con, phony doubletalk, lifestyles of flaunted fame and riches, and conspicuous and ostentatious display of glittering public self. Decadence is most harmful at the top of society: the Roman orgies of the late empire were on Palatine Hill;

the foppish and expensive excesses of eighteenth-century society were most apparent at Versailles. Phoniness becomes for many something to admire and emulate; for others, it becomes something to rebel against. The early Christians thought the Roman elite decadent and doomed to perdition, and themselves the humble vessels of new virtue; the Parisian masses thought the aristocracy and court as self-absorbed and uncaring, and themselves the carriers of the new revolutionary order. In the long run, decadence has the consequence of destroying a corrupt order through the excesses of its own vices. Like any other con artist, once the phonies at the top are found out and exposed, emperors and all others who are in the limelight because of phonying themselves up suddenly have no clothes. At that point, phony culture is in large historical trouble.

If the United States is to avoid such a fate, it will have to recognize these dreadful consequences of a phony culture. Rather than the doubletalk of the confidence man, Americans would have to embrace straight talk, following the clear injunction of noted university press editor Ernest Callenbach in his valedictory essay: "No bullshit!"[6] A culture of artifice is pervaded by a popular philosophy of cynicism that has pragmatic use for gaining people's confidence but which limits social perspective. We would have to give up our belief in the con artist's sympathetic magic, which promises us wonderful things if only we believe. In many ways, the confidence man is an American mythic descendant of the magician.[7] The con artist conjures up for us through magical language mysteries and wonders; through the magical powers of his or her artistry, we are promised a better life; magic can circumvent or alter recalcitrant reality for our wishes and desires. But if we recall Callenbach's injunction, we will remind ourselves that incantations and spells do not change the hard edges of our lives, and that no amount of phonying things up can alter the necessity of dealing with the world beyond our ardent dreams and wishful idylls. Suspending belief in magic is as difficult as suspending our wish for kings and desire for immortality, but is certainly as bracing. The will to disbelieve in the phony is a hard choice, but by doing so we might discover the merits and functions of living life in truth, both for ourselves and for the reform of our society.

NOTES

INTRODUCTION

[1]Robert Hughes, *Culture of Complaint: The Fraying of America* (New York: Oxford UP, 1993).

[2]Gary Lindberg, *The Confidence Man in American Literature* (New York: Oxford UP, 1982) 7.

[3]Daniel J. Boorstin, *The Image: A Guide to Pseudo-events in America* (New York: Harper Colophon, 1964) 209.

[4]See Jacques Ellul, *The Technological Society* (New York: Vintage, 1964); Lewis Mumford, *Technics and Civilization* (New York: Harcourt, Brace, and World, 1963); Marshall McLuhan, *Understanding Media: The Extensions of Man* (New York: McGraw, 1964).

[5]"Phoney, Phony," *Oxford English Dictionary*, Vol. XI, 2nd. ed. (Oxford: Clarendon, 1989) 700.

[6]Erving Goffman, "The Interaction Order," *American Sociological Review* 48 (1983): 1-17.

[7]Jean Baudrillard, "After Utopia: The Primitive Society of the Future," *New Perspectives Quarterly* 6 (Summer 1989): 2, 52-54; *Simuations* (New York: Semiotext(e), 1983).

[8]Christopher Lasch, "'Traditional Values': Left, Right, and Wrong," *Harper's* (Sept. 1986): 13-16.

[9]Lindberg, *op.cit.* 45.

CHAPTER ONE

[1]Bronislaw Malinowski, "The Language of Magic," *The Importance of Language,* ed. Max Black (Englewood Cliffs, NJ: Prentice-Hall Spectrum, 1962) 72.

[2]This inverted term was suggested by Professor Ned Hockman, emeritus professor of communication at the University of Oklahoma.

[3]Harry Frankfurt, "On Bullshit," *The Raritan* VI (Fall 1986): 81-100, quotes from 81, 95-96.

[4]*Ibid.* 97.

[5]Advertising is discussed in James E. Combs and Dan Nimmo, *The New Propaganda: The Dictatorship of Palaver in Contemporary Politics* (New York: Longman, 1993).

[6]T.C. Frank, "Buy Hip," *Utne Reader* July/Aug. 1992: 102.

[7]Gary Lindberg, *The Confidence Man in American Literature* (New York: Oxford UP, 1982) 120-24.

[8]Candice Jacobson Fuhrman, *Publicity Stunt! Great Staged Events That Made the News* (San Francisco: Chronicle, 1989).

[9]R.D. Rosen, *Psychobabble* (New York: Atheneum, 1978) 25.

[10]Donald Meyer, *The Positive Thinkers* (Middletown, CT: Wesleyan UP, 1988) 382.

[11]See William Lutz, *Doublespeak* (New York: Harper, 1989).

[12]Frankfurt, *op. cit.* 99.

[13]John Taylor, "Take Journalism," *New York* 28 Apr. 1993: 10-12.

[14]Thomas E. Patterson, *Out of Order* (New York: Knopf, 1993).

[15]David Remnick, "Radio Free Limbaugh," Washington *Post National Weekly Edition* 28 Feb.-6 Mar. 1994: 23-24.

CHAPTER TWO

[1]Christopher Lasch, *The Culture of Narcissism* (New York: Norton, 1979).

[2]Erving Goffmann, *The Presentation of Self in Everyday Life* (Garden City, NY: Doubleday, 1959).

[3]Robert Jay Lifton, "Protean Man," *History and Human Survival* (New York: Random, 1968).

[4]David Riesman, *et.al., The Lonely Crowd* (New Haven: Yale UP, 1961); Jay Martin, *Who Am I This Time?: Uncovering the Fictive Personality* (New York: Norton, 1988).

[5]Leo Lowenthal, "Biographies in Popular Magazines," *Reader in Public Opinion and Propaganda,* eds. Bernard Berelson and Morris Janowitz (New York: Free, 1953) 289-98.

[6]Nelson W. Aldrich, Jr., *Old Money: The Mythology of America's Upper Class* (New York: Vintage, 1988); Lewis H. Lapham, *Money and Class in America* (New York: Ballantine, 1988); Thorstein Veblen, *The Theory of the Leisure Class* (many editions, first published in 1899).

[7]Walter Bagehot, *The English Constitution* (many editions).

[8]Daniel J. Boorstin, *The Image: A Guide to Pseudo-events in America* (New York: Harper Colophon, 1961) 57.

[9]David Lehman, *Signs of the Times: Deconstruction and the Fall of Paul de Man* (New York: Poseidon, 1991); Michele Lamont, "How to Become a Dominant French Philosopher: The Case of Jacques Derrida," *American Sociological Review* 93 (Nov. 1987): 3, 584-622.

CHAPTER THREE
        [1]Randy-Michael Testa, *After the Fire: The Destruction of the Lancaster County Amish* (Boston: UP of New England, 1992).
        [2]David Guterson, "No Place Like Home," *Harper's Magazine* Nov. 1992: 64.
        [3]Mark Leyner, "Great Pretenders," *The New Yorker* 8 Nov. 1993: 140.
        [4]Philip Gourevitch, "Behold Now Behemoth," *Harper's Magazine* July 1993: 55-62.
        [5]David Guterson, "Enclosed. Encyclopedic. Endured," *Harper's Magazine* Aug. 1993: 49-56.
        [6]See such works as Michael Sorkin (ed.), *Variations on a Theme Park: The New American City and the End of Public Space* (Noonday, 1992); David Rusk, *Cities without Suburbs* (New York: Vintage, 1992); Ron Robin, *Enclaves of America* (Princeton: Princeton, 1992); Mike Davis, *City of Quartz: Excavating the Future in Los Angeles* (New York: Vintage, 1991).
        [7]Barbara Ehrenreich, *Fear of Falling: The Inner Life of the Middle Class* (New York: Pantheon, 1989).
        [8]Diderot and symbolic property are discussed in Grant McCracken, *Culture and Consumption* (Bloomington: Indiana UP, 1988).

CHAPTER FOUR
        [1]Daniel J. Boorstin, *The Image: A Guide to Pseudo-events in America* (New York: Harper Colophon, 1961) 37.
        [2]Candice Jacobson Fuhrman, *Publicity Stunt: Great Staged Events that Made the News* (San Francisco: Chronicle, 1989); Fred Fedler, *Media Hoaxes* (Ames: Iowa State UP, 1988).
        [3]Bruce Miroff, "The Presidency and the Public: Leadership as Spectacle," *The Presidency and the Political System*, ed. Michael Nelson (Washington: Congressional Quarterly, 1988) 271-92; Roland Barthes, *Mythologies* (New York: Hill & Wang, 1972) 15-25.
        [4]Gary Alan Fine, "Fantasy Games and Social Worlds: Simulation as Leisure," *Simulation and Games* 12.3 (Sept. 1981): 251-79; Phillip Kotler, "'Dream Vacations': The Booming Market for Designed Experiences," *Futurist* 18.5 (Oct. 1984): 7-13; Gerald A. Brandmeyer and Luella K. Alexander, "'I Caught the Dream': The Adult Baseball Camp as Fantasy Leisure," *Journal of Leisure Research* 18.1 (1986): 26-39.
        [5]Ian I. Mitroff and Warren Bennis, *The Unreality Industry: The Deliberate Manufacturing of Falsehood and What It Is Doing to Our Lives* (Birch Lane, 1989).
        [6]Boorstin, *op. cit.* 261.

CHAPTER FIVE

¹Elaine Showalter, *Sexual Anarchy: Gender and Culture at the Fin de Siecle* (New York: Viking Penguin, 1990).

²"Who Wrote the (Rule) Book of Love?" *Harper's Magazine* Sept. 1993: 36.

³"New Rules about Sex on Campus," *Harper's Magazine* Sept. 1993: 34-42.

⁴Louis Menand, "What Are Universities For?" *Harper's Magazine* Dec. 1991: 47-56.

⁵Edward Luttwak, *The Endangered American Dream* (New York: Simon, 1994).

⁶Donald Meyer, *The Positive Thinkers* (Middletown, CT: Wesleyan UP, 1988) 382.

⁷Jules Henry, *Culture Against Man* (New York: Random, 1963) 45.

CHAPTER SIX

¹Christopher Lasch, *The Culture of Narcissism* (New York: Norton, 1979).

²Michael Kelly, "David Gergen, Master of the Game," *New York Times Magazine* 31 Oct. 1993: 64.

³*Ibid.*

⁴John Taylor, "Take Journalism," *New York Magazine* 28 Apr. 1993: 10.

⁵David Bromwich, *Politics by Other Means: Higher Education and Group Thinking* (New Haven: Yale UP, 1992) 147.

⁶Susanne Langer, *Feeling and Form* (New York: Scribner's, 1953) 412.

⁷Norman Mailer, "By Heaven Inspired," *The New Republic* 12 Oct. 1992: 27.

⁸Gore Vidal, qtd. in *The Nation* 27 Jan. 1992: 88.

⁹See James B. Twitchell, *Carnival Culture: The Trashing of Taste in America* (New York: Columbia UP, 1992); Norman Corwin, *Trivializing America: The Triumph of Mediocrity* (Secacus, NJ: Lyle Stuart, 1986); Paul Fussell, *BAD, or the Dumbing of America* (Summit, 1991).

¹⁰Daniel Dayan and Elihu Katz, *Media Events: The Live Broadcasting of History* (Cambridge: Harvard UP, 1992).

¹¹Edward Luttwak, *The Endangered American Dream* (New York: Simon, 1994); Kevin Phillips, *The Politics of Rich and Poor* (New York: Random, 1990).

CONCLUSION

[1]Gary Lindberg, *The Confidence Man in American Literature* (New York: Oxford UP, 1982).

[2]Michael Kelly, "David Gergen, Master of the Game," New York *Times Magazine* 31 Oct. 1993: 64.

[3]Jay Martin, *Who Am I This Time? Uncovering the Fictive Personality* (New York: Norton, 1988).

[4]See the essays in Aldous Huxley, *Brave New World Revisited* (New York: Harper, 1958).

[5]Robert Jewett and John Shelton Lawrence, *The American Monomyth*, 2nd ed. (Lanham, MD: UP of America, 1988): 277.

[6]Ernest Callenbach, "The Unbearable Lightness of Leaving," *Film Quarterly* 45.1 (Fall 1991): 3.

[7]Carol S. Pearson, *The Hero Within* (New York: Harper, 1989) 116-50.